FOOD TRUCKS

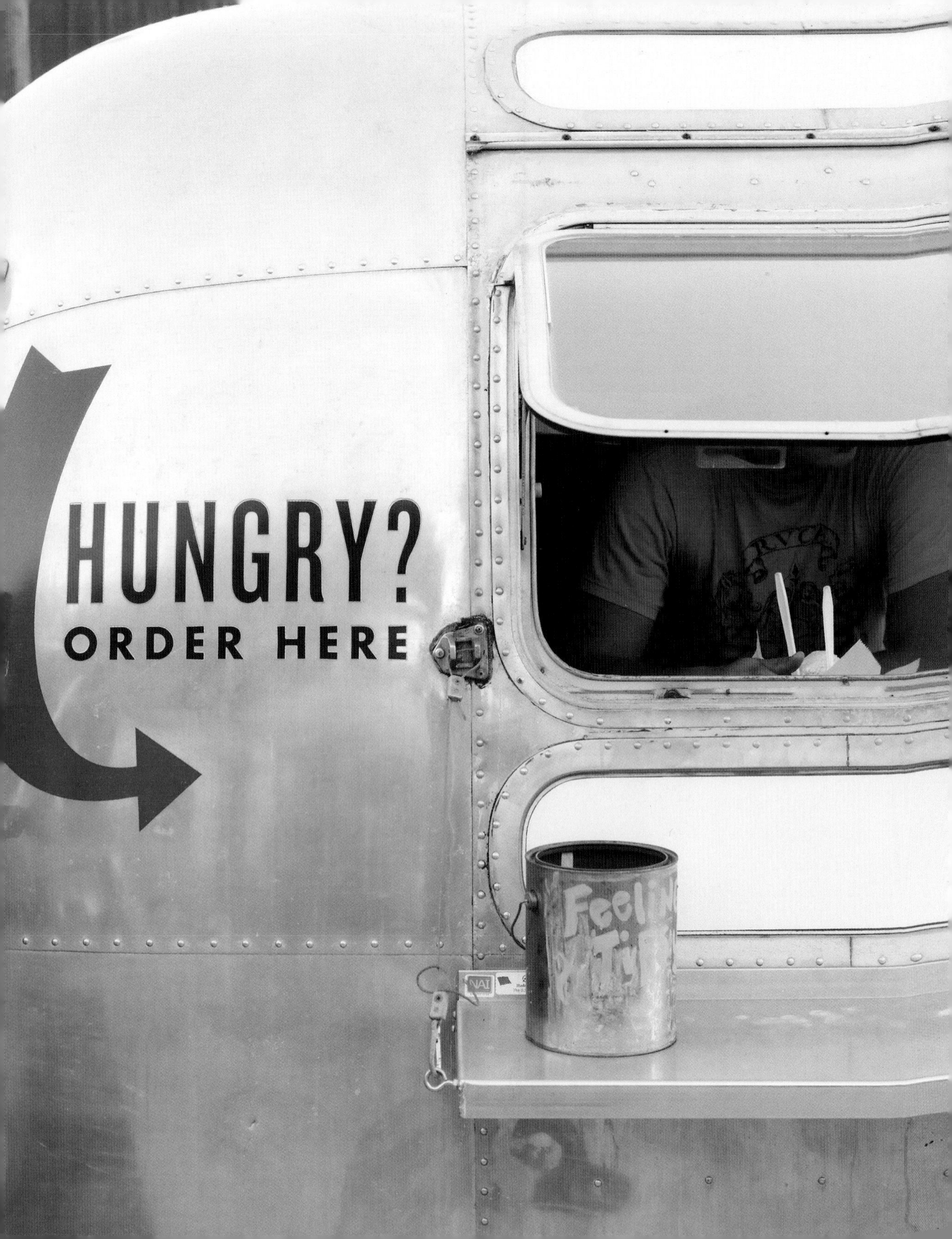
HUNGRY?
ORDER HERE

FOOD TRUCKS

Dispatches and Recipes
from the Best Kitchens on Wheels

HEATHER SHOUSE

Photography by Leo Gong and Heather Shouse

TEN SPEED PRESS
Berkeley

CONTENTS

ACKNOWLEDGMENTS

Thanks to Alexandra Sheckler for being the best research assistant I could have asked for; to my agent Jane Dystel for believing in my talents; to my editor Melissa Moore for her patience and persistence; to my designer Betsy Stromberg for building a beautiful book; to Leo Gong for his amazing photos; to Sarah Watts for maps that would make Rand McNally jealous; and to all of the truck, cart, and trailer owners for letting me into their lives for a bit. And above all, thanks to Mom and Dad, for everything.

INTRODUCTION

Forget everything you think you know about food trucks. During a year of traveling the country researching the topic, I stumbled upon a few truths: gleaming mobile kitchens run by trained chefs who have mastered Twitter can turn out disastrous food. Rickety carts with questionable permits might just turn out some of the best. The "roach coach" moniker doesn't apply to the majority of this country's mobile food operations any more than it does to the majority of this country's restaurants (well, save for the "coach" part, of course). And no, Kogi did not invent the food truck. But they just might have reinvented its wheels.

At least they got the world to sit up and take notice. The L.A.-based Korean taco truck was repeatedly cited as a source of inspiration by food truck owners I spoke to during my travels, and in the time since Kogi rolled out in late 2008, the buzz around food trucks has reached fever pitch. Favoring quirk over pomp, talented cooks and critically acclaimed chefs are ditching the brick-and-mortar standard for kitchens on wheels, churning out incredible food for a new breed of diners more interested in flavor than fuss. Just in time for the biggest recession this country has seen since the Depression, this alternative to the traditional restaurant model proved to

be a pretty smart business move for many talented cooks. What with rent or mortgage, tables and chairs, décor, front-of-the-house staff, a stocked bar, and additional labor, the average restaurant costs around $400,000 just to get the doors open. Most of the food truck owners I met across the country spent a fraction of that, more in the neighborhood of $20,000 to $50,000 to get up and running. Sure, there's the disparity in profits to consider, but for the most part these truck chefs are still making a decent living, while reaping the benefits of being their own boss and creating the biggest buzz the industry has seen since the advent of quick-serves.

In fact, the interest in food trucks has become so widespread that in September of 2010 Business.gov, the U.S. government's official website for small businesses, added a page titled "Tips for Starting Your Own Street Food Business," with links to state departments of health, zoning laws, and business permits. Navigating the red tape is often cited as the biggest hurdle for wanna-be food truck operators, so many of whom are itching to get into the game that several cities are being forced to reexamine their mobile food vending laws to satisfy the growing demand. Cities such as Los Angeles, where food trucks have long been legal, have seen mobile food vendor applications quadruple in the past two years, along with complaints from restaurants facing new competition. In response, city council panels have been set up specifically to keep the peace, setting limits on the number of permits issued and establishing new regulations on a continual basis. In areas where street food vending has historically been something of a non-issue, the city governments are scrambling to come up with regulations, as well as decide exactly where they stand on the issue. Case in point, Boston mayor Thomas Menino: to get his city up to speed with his neighbors to the south, New York and Philly, he hired a new food policy director in 2010 and launched a "Food Truck Challenge" to test the waters, with a goal of permitting thirty to fifty trucks by summer of 2011. Similarly, in June of 2010, Cincinnati approved a Mobile Food & Beverage Truck Vending Pilot Program to create twenty designated food truck parking spots in the downtown area; within a month all twenty slots were filled.

Keeping up with the regulation changes, the cities jumping on board with the movement, and the cities slow to come around (looking at you, Chicago) is as dizzying as tracking each new arena the popularity of food trucks seeps into. For the fall season of 2010, Food Network launched the show *The Great Food Truck Race*, a sort of street food take on the *Amazing Race*. On user-generated sites like Yelp, beloved trucks from various cities are holding their own with big-name restaurants. The annual National Restaurant Association convention (the biggest show in the industry) now has a section of the showroom floor dedicated solely to food trucks, with equipment companies, graphics specialists, and truck manufacturers chomping at the bit to sell their services to the next Kogi. Needless to say, these mobile kitchens have come a long way since the chuck wagons of the Wild West, the construction-site lunch wagons of the mid-1900s, and even the taco trucks that started popping up throughout the country in the 1970s. Taking many forms—a custom-welded pig-shaped rig complete with giant snout, a gleaming carnival on wheels manned by a crew sporting fake moustaches and turbans—this new breed of food truck often stakes out regular spots to set up shop for the day, but more recently, with the advent of Twitter, legions of chowhounds are kept in the loop with updates of the truck's travels.

But the food truck scene is not all gleaming mobile kitchens, newfangled technology, and accomplished chefs ditching fine dining for life on the road—time-tested global traditions continue with skewered chicken rotating over smoldering mesquite in a truck's trailer bed on Hawaii's North Shore, Czech dumplings and goulash simmering away in a tiny wooden cart in Portland, or a Sri Lankan immigrant swirling lentil crepe batter onto his mobile griddle in New York City.

In selecting the carts, trailers, and trucks that appear in this book, I traveled to areas with a high concentration of street food (with a couple of exceptions for stumbled-upon lone stars in New Hampshire, Kansas City, and even Marfa, Texas). Arriving in cities like Los Angeles and New York, which are nearly drowning in food truck options, I set about with copious notes in hand, consulted with area experts, and did a lot of walking and a lot of talking, with the principal goal of finding trucks and carts that were (a) serving delicious food, and (b) run by people with a story to tell. (In fact, I found so many fantastic eats that I included the extras as Side Dishes, which are sprinkled throughout these pages.) These meals on wheels turned out to be some of the best food I've eaten in my life, more memorable than multicourse tasting menus served in the ivory towers of haute cuisine, and the people behind these foods were often more inspiring than any "celebrity chef." For the street cooks who are first-generation Americans, their livelihood is a connection to their community, their cart or truck serving as a hub for conversation and, of course, eating; they are also a sign that a particular region of India, Eastern Europe, or Mexico has arrived in the States, with its definitive foods in tow. And for the young American cooks striving to make a name for themselves, the common thread is the same: with passion, commitment, and hard work, anyone can scrape out a living serving delicious food—no restaurant needed.

WEST COAST & PACIFIC

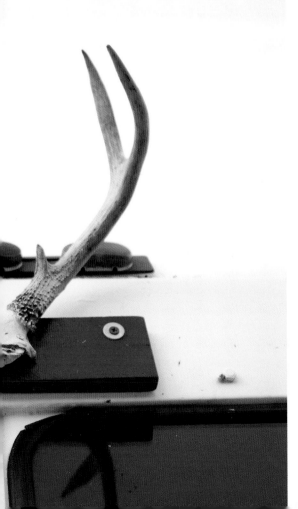

B y most accounts, Los Angeles is ground zero, the historical entry point for taco trucks on American soil. Brief history lesson: L.A. was actually a Mexican territory from 1821 until the end of the Mexican-American War in 1848. And even though the U.S. took control after the war, Mexicans reestablished themselves in L.A. in a big way after the Revolution of 1910, with an influx of immigrants larger than any Mexican migration up to that point. The Latino community has grown steadily since, and now accounts for half of L.A.'s population.

By the mid-1970s, East Los Angeles was the bull's-eye of the city's Latino community, with the highest concentration of Mexican immigrants in the country. Suddenly the landscape was dotted with tables topped with hot plates set up along the road, makeshift carts selling freshly cut fruit and corn, and delivery trucks outfitted to turn out tacos and more. With the taco truck industry in L.A. ballooning, regulations had to be enforced. The L.A. County Department of Public Health started the permit process in the late 1980s, requiring sanitation licenses and inspections similar to those a restaurant faces. Immigrants concerned about their own legal status, not to mention their truck's, continued to operate off the books. As of 2010, the department has 3,820 licensed trucks on record, but Erin Glenn, CEO of the Asociación de Loncheros, an advocacy group for and of taco truck owners, estimates that the number is closer to 7,000. "Clearly, they're not all reg-

FOOD TRUCKS

istered," Glenn says. "But our concern is to assist as many as we can. Taco trucks are part of the landscape here. Outside of being traditionally Mexican, it's traditionally Angeleno as well."

In 2008, the Los Angeles County Board of Supervisors passed an ordinance stipulating that a food truck couldn't park in a spot for more than an hour at a time. The Asociación de Loncheros organized a march to draw attention to the case, and with the help of a volunteer legal team, the ordinance was found unconstitutional the day before it was to take effect. Some of the longstanding taco truck owners have said, off the record, that the recent attention L.A.'s food truck scene has received thanks to the influx of gourmet trucks has brought unwanted scrutiny from the county and city. Some would say that's a good thing, but regardless, the divide between L.A.'s traditional taco trucks and the new concept trucks roaming the streets is fairly vast, and it isn't all based on competition. In fact, the target market has little overlap—one audience develops a taste for a taco truck out of convenience and routine, while the other actively seeks out a roving truck using social media, with the thrill of the chase adding up to at least half of the flavor. "There's this guerilla-style revolution taking place with all of the new concept food trucks popping up, but it's important not to forget that tacos came before Twitter," says Javier Cabral, an East L.A. native and creator of the food blog Teenage

Glutster (www.teenageglutster.blogspot.com). "I mean, they're cool to try, but when you need it, the O.G. taco truck will always be there. It will never be roaming, it will not have anything over $5, and it will always be reliably delicious."

Still, the success of Kogi, the undisputed juggernaut of L.A.'s new breed of food trucks, not only spawned a legion of imitators (Kalbi BBQ, Bool BBQ, Don Chow Tacos, and even Calbi, a partnership truck with the Baja Fresh corporation), but it also opened the floodgates to an alternative for chefs without the dough for a traditional restaurant. Jonathan Gold, the Pulitzer Prize–winning food critic for the *LA Weekly*, estimates he's been eating off trucks roaming his city for thirty years. While he tends to get more excited about discovering a new regional Mexican truck than some slick new fusion truck, he understands the business behind the boom. "If you're an interesting young chef who wants to get his ideas out, you can slave away on somebody's line and hope one day to enrapture enough people to invest in your concept," Gold says, "or, you can figure out a concept and have your vinyl stickers plastered on a food truck and roll out for a mid four figures. You decide."

Taco Truck Starter Guide

With an estimated seven thousand tacos trucks to choose from in L.A., you could eat at a different one every day for twenty years and never have to repeat a meal. So where to start? This list, for one. It's a carefully curated selection of trucks that have carved out a niche for themselves with one or two specialties, usually menu items that represent the region of Mexico the owner hails from. Once you start to associate the names of towns plastered on the trucks with the food likely to be inside of them, you're on your way to decoding the system.

Aguascalientes
(Olympic Blvd. between McBride and McDonnell Aves., Los Angeles)

The demand for *suadero* and *al pastor* at this four-year-old operation eventually outgrew the truck, so once the sun disappears and the street lights flicker on, a sturdy card table goes up on the sidewalk just in front of the rig and the real show begins. In a giant vat heated from a serious tabletop burner below, hunks of beef brisket simmer in bubbling fat, juiced with lime and seasoned only with salt. Just next to the *suadero*, a towering rotisserie spit turns a cone-shaped assembly of *al pastor*, layers of pork fat alternating with thin slices of the meat itself, seasoned with onion, lime juice, salt, and adobo, the sauce of canned chipotles. Gas-powered flames lick the sides as it rotates, caramelizing the pineapple juice running down the sides. The meat is carved to order, falling onto tiny tortillas, and the crowd that gathers throughout the night alternates between the tart *al pastor* and the oil-slicked *suadero*, comfortable that they don't have to choose between the two.

Cemitas Poblanas Junior's
(Olympic Blvd. at Rowan Ave., Los Angeles)

Okay, so the name game might not actually apply here. It's true that the Pueblan owners specialize in *cemitas*—toasted sandwiches of meat, avocado, chipotle salsa spread, an herb called *papalo*, and Oaxacan string cheese on a sesame seed roll—but that isn't actually the star of the show. Seek out instead the *mulitas* and *memelas*, the former a taco sandwich of sorts, made from two corn tortillas topped with cheese, slathered with beans, smashed together around your choice of filling (go for the *chicharrón*, crispy pork skin that adds a bit of salty crunch), then thrown back onto the griddle with a good dose of oil to crisp up. The *memelas* are actually a Oaxacan classic, similar to *sopes* and *huaraches*, but the masa is stuffed with lard-cooked

If you know what's good for you, you'll focus on working through the thousands of traditional taco trucks that cement L.A.'s reputation as the American capital of Mexican food. Still, the lure of the newfangled trucks is too great to ignore. And there are a few of these Twitter-embracing newcomers worth tracking down. For those who typically satisfy their breakfast cravings at a greasy diner, **Buttermilk** changes the game. The brainchild of Gidget-cute twentysomething Gigi Pascual, Buttermilk serves the most important meal of the day morning, noon, and night. The menu is thorough and creative, from silver-dollar red velvet pancakes to Hawaiian breakfast sliders, soy sauce–scrambled eggs tucked into a Hawaiian roll with caramelized onions and Portuguese sausage. Still, it's the classic combo of fried chicken and a syrup-soaked waffle that brings the late-night crowds to their knees.

A French take on fried chicken, the herbes de Provence-scented bird that celeb chef Ludo Lefebvre hawks out of his **Ludo Bites** truck causes almost as much frenzy in L.A. as . . . well, anything Ludo does. The culinary darling known for pop-up restaurants and competing on Top Chef Masters rolled out a state-of-the-art rig in ➡

beans before it's flattened into an oval, tossed on the griddle to toast, and then topped like a tostada. This truck is unique, using yellow masa for the *memelas*, giving them an earthier, whole grain–type heartiness.

El Gallito (3800 E Olympic Blvd., Los Angeles)

There are a dozen Gallitos in this local chain, but this is the only one with a taco truck parked outside, the ultimate proof that food served out of a truck can completely surpass the same food made in a brick-and-mortar kitchen. For many of the truck's patrons, the draw is the outdoor patio anchored by a central bar and a stage that hosts live bands on weekends (*banda* bands, no less; louder, wilder, and more dastardly youth-oriented than a reserved mariachi). But for those who think with their stomachs, it's the lure of the goat that brings them to this truck. *Birria de chivo* is the specialty here, and the traditional Jaliscan goat stew lives up to its reputation, the shredded meat as tender as a ripe tomato, with a heady perfume of smoky roasted chiles mingling with toasted cloves and fresh oregano. Fold a few forkfuls into a warm tortilla, sprinkle on chopped white onions and cilantro, give it a good squeeze of lime, then dip the end into the cup of consommé alongside, being careful not to lose the mother lode in the broth. Now repeat.

La Isla Bonita (4th St. and Rose Ave., Venice)

Venice Beach is known for a few things, among them meatheads with more muscles than brain cells and fortune-tellers whose crystal balls are as weathered as their shtick. But a legend among lunchers is tucked a couple of blocks away from the beach: Antonio Gonzalez's twenty-five-year-old "Beautiful Island" taco truck, hand-painted with an aquatic theme that could earn it a cameo in *The Little Mermaid*. The décor is a good clue as to the specialty, and Antonio's success supporting eight kids with his truck is a testament to the quality. With plenty of turnover, the seafood that stars on tostadas and in cocktails is bought fresh each morning, always disappearing by the 4 p.m. closing time to ensure the same routine the next day. Sea bass works on a slightly different schedule, marinating in salt and lime juice for twenty-four hours before meeting up with tomatoes, onions, and cilantro for the ceviche tostada. Bigger appetites reach for giant Styrofoam cups of the *campechana*, a seafood cocktail with the chilled tomato flavor of gazpacho, the tangy heat of serrano chiles and lime juice, and a medley of shrimp, sea bass, octopus, crabmeat, and imitation abalone (standard throughout L.A., as the real stuff is incredibly expensive). Most of the lunch crowd lingers around the truck, apparently anticipating the need for round two, but even those who grab and go never quite make it to the beach without stopping for a few bites.

Mariscos 4 Vientos #3 (3014 E Olympic Blvd., Los Angeles)

There's such a festive vibe around this seafood truck that you'd think you stumbled onto a birthday party. Actually, everyone is just excited to find ocean-side classics on a street with no ocean in sight. Up first are the delicious *tacos de camarón*: plump shrimp tucked into a tortilla and fried into a crispy pouch, then doused with a garlicky red salsa, elevating the crunchy taco to excellence. Save room, though, because the shrimp get put to yet another use in *tostadas de aguachile*, a take on ceviche that relies on both the heat of chiles and the acid of lime juice to "cook" otherwise raw shrimp. Here, the large, split shrimp are impeccably fresh and briny, tossed in their tangy marinade with slivers of red onion, then piled onto an avocado-lined tostada. About the only way the meal can get better is if you become enough of a regular that you can do what the genius next to me did: hand a six-pack of Corona to the guy in the truck and have it handed back as *micheladas*, beer spiked with limey hot sauce, each bottle garnished with a fresh shrimp.

Mariscos Jalisco (3040 E Olympic Blvd., Los Angeles)

There's nothing like a little healthy competition to inspire greatness. Only a block away from Mariscos 4 Vientos #3 you'll find this similar truck offering a nearly identical menu to a nearly identical legion of regulars. Deciding between the two is a problem we would all be so lucky to have, and the solution is to frequent them both. The man behind the stoves here is Martin Ramirez, a native of the Jalisco city San Juan de los Lagos and something of a local legend when it comes to trucks specializing in these crispy shrimp tacos (Martin calls them *tacos dorados de camarón*, golden shrimp tacos). Apparently, Martin worked for a number of other trucks in L.A., including Mariscos 4 Vientos #3, and he claims that once they learned his recipe they let him go. He says that they still don't have the touch, something he employs via a delicate seasoning of the shrimp (an altered recipe from the original that he now keeps under wraps) and a chunky red salsa flecked with chopped cilantro and plenty of raw onion.

El Matador (1174 N Western Ave., Los Angeles)

Parked just off the freeway under a glowing street lamp in an auto shop lot is the twenty-five-year-old Bullfighter truck, run by a family from Mexico City whose chipotle and *chile de arbol* salsas are so popular that they can get away with charging extra for a little cup of the stuff. Buy a bucket, as these two *salsas rojas* will haunt you when you get home, lingering in your

summer 2010, focusing solely on chicken. Juicy, crispy, salty, herbaceous chicken.

Sumant Pardal may not be as recognizable as Ludo, but this veteran of West Coast Indian restaurants (he's opened a dozen in the thirty years he's been in America) is a character all the same. Catch him at his **India Jones Chow Truck** on a bad day and you might get a grumpy Sumant, complaining to anyone who will listen about L.A.'s food truck regulations. Regardless of Sumant's mood, try the Frankie, an Indian street food classic. Flaky roti is tossed onto a hot griddle, brushed with beaten egg, flipped, brushed with egg again, then flipped until it's essentially an egg-encrusted roti. Go simple with paneer for the filling or more aggressive with cumin-flecked lamb; both are rolled up inside the egg-coated roti with onions, cilantro, and tamarind chutney.

For Southern Indian with a hippie vibe, **Dosa Truck** feeds the need. Brooklyn transplant Leena Deneroff rolls her truck into one of the spots in her rotation (primarily in slick-hip Silverlake) and immediately gets to work adorning the truck façade with brightly colored Hindu objects, including a tiny Ganesh figure in the window to greet customers. Spirituality aside, the ginger limeade and

CONTINUED ON PAGE 14 ➜

garam masala–spiced fries are transcendent on their own, and the dosas are good, smaller versions of the South Indian lentil and rice crepe.

Just as deft at bringing an ethnic staple to the masses is **Nom Nom**, a cute truck with a cute name started by a cute trio of friends who met at UCLA's Hapa Club, a meet-up group for Asian and Pacific Islanders of mixed heritage. For newbies, a helpful sign offers Banh Mi 101 via a visual breakdown of the classic Vietnamese sandwich. Traditional fillings range from lemongrass chicken to sweet and sticky barbecue pork, but there's also a tofu option–this is L.A. after all.

But before you go thinking the whole town's gone soft (or is it crunchy?), enter the **Grill 'Em All** guys. Taking their name from Metallica's epic debut album Kill 'Em All, this heavy-metal hamburger truck gained national recognition for taking home the title in the Food Network's first season of *The Great Food Truck Race*. The show's finale pitted Grill 'Em All against fellow Angelenos Nom Nom, but the burger barons won out. Diehards who've been following the truck long before the TV show swear by the Waste 'Em All burger, a juicy grilled patty smothered in a mess of beer-soaked onions and softened Hatch green chiles, crowned with pepper jack to crank up the heat. ➔

mind as the perfect match for that bag of chips in the cupboard. Back at the truck, use the juicy *al pastor* taco as the palette for the salsas; the hunks of flavorful pork have just the right tang, and those slightly charred edges mingle perfectly with bits of nearly liquefied fat. Keep in mind this is a nighttime operation—the only reason to show up early is to get your oil changed.

Ricos Tejuinos (2940 E Olympic Blvd., Los Angeles)

Okay, so the specialty of Ricos Tejuinos isn't made on site, the legalities of the operation are questionable, and you're only likely to find it parked here Fridays through Sundays until around 4 p.m. But believe me when I tell you there's something special being sold out of the bed of this 1966 white Ford pickup truck, easy to spot thanks to a giant rainbow patio umbrella jutting out of the back. The old man sitting in a lawn chair propped up in the truck bed might not want to give you his name, but he does want to sell you *tejuino*, a specialty of Jalisco that straddles the line between drink and dessert. This corn concoction is made by boiling masa with brown sugar and then letting the mixture ferment, which gives the tart drink a slightly funky edge, revved up by a generous dose of rock salt and a scoop of lime *nieve*, a sorbetlike sweet whose name means "snow." Eating one as a follow-up to a couple dozen shrimp at the nearby *mariscos* trucks on a hot day, you could just about convince yourself you were on vacation.

El Super Taco (4474 Whittier Blvd., Los Angeles)

In small letters across the front of this unassuming white truck you'll see one word: *pescuezos*. Literally translated, it means "necks." More important, it refers to chicken necks, coated in salty lemon-spritzed batter and fried to a crisp, then tucked into a soft, warm corn tortilla and doused with a bright red *chile de arbol* salsa. Jose Albizo started selling these *pescuezos* the first week he opened his truck in 2000, parked exactly where it sits today, mainly because the area had plenty of recent immigrants who, like him, came from Mexico City. If you're new to the neck, take a cue from the regulars lingering around cleaning the bones like lions, and remember that these delicacies are more about the crispy skin than any (nonexistent) meat, and that you will have to use your fingers and get a little messy. Get a few crunchy bites in and alternate with a bit of tortilla—try and get everything in one bite and you might just break a tooth.

Tacos Arturos (400 S Fair Oaks Ave., Pasadena)

If someone sends you looking for the El Gallito truck and you find this one in its place, don't be alarmed: you're in the right place. Mechanical problems seem to have put El Gallito under, but the same owner and staff bought the Arturos truck so that the show could go on (although as fast as these things can change, if you wind up seeing the El Gallito truck instead, you're still in the right place). The draw here is tacos made with carne asada, simply seasoned, nicely tender skirt steak with lightly charred edges and plenty of juice. But somewhat more exciting than the taco itself is the massive spread of stuff to pile onto it: a brilliant *salsa roja* with heat from arbol chiles and tartness from tomatillo, stewed pinto beans, caramelized onions, and blackened jalapeños, all lined up along a railing on the front of the truck like an all-you-can-fit-into-a-tortilla buffet.

Tacos El Korita (Rowan Ave. at Olympic Blvd., Los Angeles)

When you spot a hand-cranked tortilla machine inside a taco truck, that's a good sign that someone is paying attention to quality, and at this East L.A. mainstay, the tight focus on the little things adds up to an all-around solid experience. Now, some might say that a burrito is the gringo way to go, but one look at the massive spread of primo toppings running nearly the length of the truck and it's clear that a little taco tortilla isn't going to go very far. Choose the good-and-greasy *al pastor* and you'll be handed a thirteen-inch flour tortilla crowned with a mound of glistening, achiote-streaked pork, open-faced and ready for you to dress. Pile on grilled onions, a delicious charred tomatillo salsa, pico de gallo made with *nopales* (cactus paddles), and the lime-green avocado-based salsa synonymous with taco trucks; only El Korita's stands out as a chunky version with a good kick of heat. Once your masterpiece is complete, hand it back through the window and let the pros roll it up nice and neat so you don't lose a drop.

Not surprisingly, these trucks are constantly on the move. To find them, track their tweets:
@buttermilktruck
@ludobitestruck
@indiajonesct
@dosatruck
@nomnomtruck
@grillemalltruck
Enjoy the new breed of trucks roaming L.A. ◉

Antojitos Mi Abuelita

FIND IT: 6135 Vineland Ave., North Hollywood, California

Hortenzia Hernandez stands just a bit taller than the counter of her kitchen workspace, raising her elbow high in the air each time she brings the stone pestle in her hand down into a mortar, grinding the toasted chiles, sesame seeds, peanuts, and chocolate into a thick paste so dark red it's nearly black. After she smashes in ripe plantains, the base for her *mole negro* is complete, so she turns her attention to the *mole verde*. After tossing pumpkin seeds into a pan on the stovetop to toast, she plucks the leaves from a mess of parsley and cilantro stems, adds them to a mountain of radish greens and spinach, and then starts to peel back the husks of the tomatillos sitting in a pile like little presents waiting to be unwrapped. Hortenzia is Oaxacan, and this routine is not unlike the one her mother, her grandmother, and countless Oaxacan women before them have methodically moved through in the dark hours before sunrise since this culinary tradition began. But while her ancestors had the comfort of home kitchens for their weekly *mole* ritual, Hortenzia does her work in a truck, making some of Mexico's slowest foods mobile.

In her early sixties, Hortenzia really doesn't have to work anymore. Her husband Luis makes a living from the sign shop he runs in North Hollywood, and her daughter Olga owns a party supply store next door that does a solid business in piñatas and balloons. But Hortenzia doesn't like her family to eat fast food for lunch, so shortly after their businesses opened a few years ago, she started showing up at the shops around noon with homemade specialties in tow. Occasionally she brought crunchy, blistered tortillas about a foot around called *tlayudas*, slathered with refried beans and topped with Oaxacan string cheese, shredded lettuce, and sometimes strips of *cecina*, a salted, dried pork tenderloin. Other times lunch consisted of *pambazos*, sandwiches that layer refried beans, chorizo, and crumbly queso fresco onto hearty bread that's been dipped in guajillo chile sauce until the split roll is soaked through and stained crimson, then toasted to crisp up the edges. The tripe stew menudo was another specialty in Hortenzia's rotation, and quarter chickens doused in *moles* started showing up on weekends. Inevitably, all of this home cooking caused a stir, especially among Olga's husband and his friends, who started hanging out around the little strip mall, clamoring for Hortenzia's food. Hortenzia embraced her following with a little capitalism, setting up a table on the sidewalk where she began selling the Oaxacan and Mexico City specialties she lugged from her home kitchen. Soon, her supply couldn't keep up with demand, and Hortenzia wanted to go legit with a full-fledged truck, permit and all. Her son stepped up to finance the project, and in the summer

of 2008 a gleaming kitchen on wheels showed up in the parking lot; the little sidewalk table was worked into the covered seating area set up for diners.

Antojitos Mi Abuelita was the name bestowed upon the truck by Hortenzia's children, *mi abuelita* being an affectionate phrase for "my little grandmother" and the *antojitos* referring to the snacky foods on the menu like the *tlayudas*, *pambazos*, quesadillas, and flat griddled ovals of masa known as *huaraches*. Although Hortenzia is originally from Oaxaca, she and her family moved to Los Angeles from Mexico City in the late '90s, and fellow transplants from both of her hometowns have sniffed her out as one of their own, showing up at the truck to suss out the specialties. Business has steadily grown, with Fridays through Sundays resembling the bustling but laidback feel of a block party. Traditional Mexican folk music is piped out of a small stereo, and families eye the tables for a place to sit while a constant stream of plates heaped with tender chicken drenched in *mole* and steaming bowls of menudo are handed through the truck window. Hortenzia's daughter Olga and a family friend now work the truck as well (with Olga popping into the party shop to ring up the occasional order), and the hours have expanded from 9 a.m. to midnight on weekends and 11 a.m. to midnight during the week.

Her work on the *moles* behind her, Hortenzia stands over a cooler propped up on a table, scooping out sweet snowlike *nieve* in flavors like *pitaya* (dragon fruit) and *leche quemada* (burnt milk). She explains in Spanish that while the hours are long, she enjoys the work and the idea of passing down the recipes to her daughter, plus with her family all in one spot and the house nearby for rests, the fifteen-hour days don't take as much of a toll. "The customers say, 'Oh, it's so good, thank you so much,' and it's worth it," Hortenzia says. "A man even came one time and he offered me money for my salsa recipe, but I said no. He said, 'It's so special, what do you put in it?' and I said 'Nothing. I just make things my way.'"

Kogi

KEEP UP WITH IT: www.kogibbq.com or twitter.com/kogibbq

He's been called a genius, a visionary, a groundbreaking chef. His story has been told a thousand times by a thousand people, and sometimes the myths, the legends, and the truths get tangled up in the poetic pixie dust of it all. But Kogi's Roy Choi isn't the one casting spells—he's a bluntly honest quick-talker who drops f-bombs as often as he stamps out cigarettes, and he moves with a saggy-pants swagger that goes hand in hand with his line cooks calling him "Papi," his forearm tattoo that reads "Kogi *Por Vida*," and his cred as the creator of Korean-Mexican fusion. To be clear, he's a taco truck chef. But he's a *Food & Wine Magazine* Best New Chef taco truck chef whose fleet of four Kogi trucks reportedly did $2 million in sales its first year on the streets. Roy has plenty to say about plenty of things, including his desire to tell his own story instead of hearing others tell it. So here it is, from drug-induced hallucinations to getting salsa to sing like Britney Spears.

ON BECOMING A CHEF:

"When I was about twenty-two to twenty-five I was a fuck-up. I was hanging out in Koreatown drinking every night, getting into fights, doing horrible things. By the time I was twenty-five I was a true deadbeat. I owed a lot of money to people, I was doing a lot of bad things, I was strung out. I moved around on friends' couches. I was coming out of something one morning in 1995 and I was watching *Emeril*. He walked out of the TV, grabbed me on the shoulder, shook me, and asked, 'What the fuck are you doing? Taste this, smell this, eat this, look how beautiful this is.' And he's like, 'Get off the couch.' So that day I got up, took a shower, and since then it's been on. I just buckled down and worked odd jobs and paid all my debts. I went to a local culinary school, I applied to the CIA, and I got on a Greyhound bus and started working in Manhattan. I went to the bookstore every day and read about cooking. Then I got my acceptance to CIA, and when I got there, everything clicked. It was like everything connected and finally made sense."

ON THE IDEA:

"Of course there's the story of [founder] Mark [Manguera] drinking Champagne at 4 a.m. and wanting something to eat, then having this idea. But what happened was he called me and we had a cup of coffee in Koreatown, and he was like, 'Yo, until you find another job, what do you think about helping me out with this?' And I wasn't doing anything, so we bought $300 worth of food, tinkered around with the recipes, and within a month we found it. He came to me with 'Korean barbecue meat inside a tortilla,' and from there it all kind of came to me spiritually. I grew up on the streets of L.A. eating tacos and eating Korean food at home, so when I made this taco it just became a lyric to me, a flow, it just came together. I thought about Mexican chiles and lime and about the pickled salads you get at a Korean barbecue right before you eat the meat. I thought about the cilantro-onion mix you get at taco stands. I thought about the tortilla and how I always wished tacos would be [made with] tortillas [that are] just a little bit crispy with oil but still pliable. I thought about Korean meat being double cooked and charred and caramelized. Then it all just came together."

ON TEAM KOGI:

"We fuck around a lot, but we're not fucking around. We're a tight, focused militia. We attacked people on so many different fronts that they couldn't figure out which way we were coming from. Mark is the master of schmooz-ing. He can make you do anything. He's a hustler, always crackin' deals. He lives the part wherever he goes, like Leonardo DiCaprio in *Catch Me If You Can*; he can make the teller at the bank smile. From that, he's always opening doors for Kogi. [Co-founder] Caroline Shin-Manguera handles the books, and she established the service end of who we are. She was the order keeper in the beginning. With her Four Seasons background, no matter what was happening on the outside she was calm. It was like you walked into the Four Seasons, like, 'Welcome. Thank you for coming.' And [market-ing director] Alice Shin being a semi–food blogger herself, freelancing for SeriousEats.com, she just reached out to food bloggers, writing things with heart and with a fiction mind. It was like reading short stories: the prose and diction on our website wasn't what you'd expect from a taco truck."

ON THE EARLY DAYS:

"The first two weeks no one bought tacos. We went in front of all the biggest nightclubs in Hollywood. So our core business was between 1:45 to 2:30 in the morning, when there were literally two thousand people funneling out of the clubs. Imagine if you're young and you go to clubs every weekend, and every time you come out all you see is a row of carts selling dirty dogs. Then you see this taco truck, but with us in it. This is exactly what happened every night: 'Yo, there's motherfuckin' Asians in the truck. Check it out, there's motherfuckin' Orientals in that taco truck.' And we were like, 'Just eat it, check it out,' targeting the mother hen of the bunch, giving him the taco for free, and they'd be like 'Holy shit, yo, yo, come here.' And they'd buy, like, fourteen for the girls. And that's how Kogi started. Those guys buying for the girls, then the girls getting into it, then the other guys seeing the girls in miniskirts eating our tacos and then getting their own."

ON THE POWER OF THE INTERNET:

"Kogi was a forgotten memory at two in the morning. It was nourishment, this wonderful, beautiful taco going to runaways and hookers. So even though it was getting out to people, it wasn't getting any real attention. Then some of the girls from the club were like, 'Oh, you gotta come to UCLA. We'll tell all our friends.' We went there on a Thursday night and we had food for, like, 150 people. We rolled up into an area that was like off-campus dorms, all high-rises, co-op housing. It was almost like if you imagine old projects with people hanging out the window looking down. All of the windows had heads sticking out of them and there were six hundred people on the streets, all with iPhones and BlackBerries and laptops and cameras. And that was it. That was the moment we became famous."

ON THE FOOD:

"The key was that we put a taco in their mouths that was the most delicious fucking thing they'd tasted. Like hearing rap music for the first time. It just came on the scene so fresh. Our best sellers are the blackjack quesadilla and the *kalbi* taco, short rib marinated in this emulsion of soy sauce, garlic, onions, sesame oil, Asian pears, kiwis, sesame seeds, orange juice, orange zest, ginger, a touch of lime juice, black pepper, and salt. That same meat also gets mixed into mini burgers for the sliders, then topped with sesame mayo and *salsa roja*, which has, like, twenty different ingredients, mainly guajillo and California chiles. I do four different salsas, and right now I'm really feeling the Azul, our blueberry salsa. It has blueberries, opal basil, habanero chilies, roasted garlic . . . it's a little complex. Alone, it's like listening to something a little bit rough, like Nine Inch Nails. Together with the food, it sounds like Britney Spears."

"We're not what a lot of people may think we are. We're not this marketing juggernaut that is ten steps ahead of everybody else. We're complete nomads that are free in what we do. My philosophy is I'm willing to walk away from all of this, Kogi, right now and start something fresh tomorrow. With that philosophy, it drives us to go for broke every day. I don't give a shit if Kogi goes away. It's about the food and the energy. If people aren't feeling Kogi anymore, I'm not going to twist it to try to make it fit. If Kogi isn't relevant anymore, I'll just stop. I'm a cook; I'll come up with a whole new thing and a whole new flavor."

Kimchi Quesadilla Serves 4

1/2 cup unsalted butter

2 cups chopped kimchi

4 tablespoons canola oil

4 (12-inch) flour tortillas

4 cups shredded Cheddar-Jack cheese

8 sesame or shiso leaves, torn

1/4 cup toasted sesame seeds

Melt the butter in a sauté pan over medium heat. Add the kimchi and cook, stirring, until caramelized and slightly charred, about 10 minutes.

Add 1 tablespoon of the canola oil to a large nonstick pan or griddle over medium heat. Place one of the tortillas in the pan and sprinkle 1 cup of the cheese on one half of the tortilla. Add about a quarter of the caramelized kimchi, a quarter of the sesame or shiso leaves, and a quarter of the sesame seeds. Fold over to create a half-moon. Continue to cook until the bottom of the tortilla blisters like a Neapolitan pizza. Flip the quesadilla over and cook the second side until it reaches the same doneness. Transfer to a plate, cut into triangle-shaped pieces, and serve.

When an unlicensed street food vendor known as "the Tamale Lady" has nearly as many Yelp reviews as The Dining Room at the Ritz Carlton, it's clear that you have an interesting culinary community on your hands.

Virginia Ramos, a.k.a. the Tamale Lady, operates on foot, not on wheels, but the Mexican immigrant recalls that when she started her side job in the early 1990s, the only other mobile food vendors were other Latinos operating taco trucks. Today, San Francisco's street food scene has changed considerably, and as this book was going to print there was so much interest in curbside dining that city officials were holding public hearings with restaurant owners, cart operators, and members of the police force to figure out how to navigate the massive spike of interest in mobile food vending. For established restaurants with plenty of capital, fancy trucks, and a foothold in the business community, the leap to going mobile is fairly easy. For creative cooks looking to build some buzz and make some dough by hawking their homemade soups or made-to-order curries, the red tape can be daunting.

Part of the confusion and complication seems to stem from the fact that San Francisco has two different agencies issuing permits: the police department oversees mobile food vendors on public property, while the Department of Public Health is responsible for vendors working on private property. Not surprisingly, vendors cite instances in which the right hand

FOOD TRUCKS

doesn't know what the left hand is doing. Still, around 150 trucks and carts, both public and private, are operating legally, with a few taking advantage of organizations formed in recent years to help vendors get street legal. In 2008, Matt Cohen formed Tabe Trucks, a food truck consulting company that essentially gets ideas up and running, complete with design, branding, truck build-out, and permit navigation. By early 2010, the demand from small cart operators for guidance led him to start the San Francisco Cart Project, an online headquarters for the Bay Area's mobile food vendors. There, they can utilize the message board to voice concerns and ask questions, as well as purchase permit documentation for a nominal fee. The organization La Cocina performs a similar service, although its mission is aimed at women of color and immigrant communities. In addition to providing an incubator kitchen for these talented cooks, La Cocina helps its clients navigate the legalities of starting a food business, both stationary and mobile.

Across the Bay in Oakland, the 2010 Eat Real Festival featured ninety of the scene's most diverse and interesting food trucks and carts. More than 100,000 fans showed up as proof of a paying public that supports the mobile movement, and the smart ones figured out that the only way to beat the lines was to get your hands on some food, jump in another line, and eat the first plate while waiting for the second. It sounds gluttonous, but this street food scene is insatiable.

San Francisco, California

Curry Up Now

KEEP UP WITH IT: www.curryupnow.com or twitter.com/curryupnow

A lot of people hear about L.A. food truck juggernaut Kogi and think, "Cool," but their thought process typically doesn't go much further than that. But when husband and wife Akash and Rana Kapoor heard about Kogi, after thinking "Cool," they then thought, "We could do that, but Indian."

But unlike Roy Choi, the culinary brains behind Kogi, the Kapoors are not trained chefs. What they are is Indian, and what they have is experience cooking the food of their homeland, eastern India. The couple grew up in Ranchi, the capital of Jharkhand, living two blocks away from each other before reuniting and marrying in California in the mid-1990s. Akash made the move to the United States first, selling cars and then working in credit consolidation and eventually starting his own mortgage company. Rana jumped in and helped with the mortgage business, but she focused her energy more on raising their three kids and cooking for her extended family, which included Akash's parents, making for a crowded dinner table. "Akash's mom is an excellent cook, a celebrity cook back home in India, and she has held cooking classes," Rana says. "We both enjoy cooking, but it's nothing professional. It's just what your gut instinct is. If you ask me what goes in my chicken tikka masala, today I put this in, but tomorrow is different. It's what your heart wants to cook. . . . I can't cook under pressure. It's gotta be fun."

And to Rana, a project like Kogi sounded like fun. So she persuaded Akash to buy a former burrito truck off Craigslist in late 2008 and, while he figured out the business end (including the name), she set about bridging the gap between Indian and Mexican cuisine. Taking a cue from the truck's former life, she filled giant fourteen-inch flour tortillas with chicken tikka masala, tucked paneer and cumin-spiced lamb into corn tortillas, and dressed her tacos with cilantro chutney rather than salsa verde. In a twist on the quesadilla, potato-filled paratha stands in for tortillas, and Indian-spiced meats like chicken tikka or *keema* (ground beef) get sandwiched in between with gooey cheese and caramelized onions. The Indo-Mex concoctions were purely Rana, but for the traditional Indian street snacks like samosa *chaat* (dubbed "deconstructed samosa" at Curry Up Now), the patriarch in the house was the consulting chef. "Akash's dad tested it all," Rana says. "Especially the *channa*, the chickpeas. Something like fifty to sixty times he tested it and perfected it. You just know the one that hits the chord. You gotta do that with your food, otherwise it doesn't do the trick."

Dad Kapoor's *channa* does the trick, especially piled on top of a smashed-up samosa and drizzled with cilantro and tamarind chutneys. His *channa*, deep and earthy with cumin but balanced with a good dose of ginger, also shows up alongside what's listed on the menu as "Trinidad & Tobago doubles," but could just as easily be credited to India as *chole bhature*. Whatever you call it, this classic snack, traditionally eaten for breakfast, is served out of trucks throughout Trinidad and Tobago, as well as in most parts of India. The puffy fried bread is either used to scoop up spiced chickpeas or, in a "double," used in pairs to sandwich the chickpeas. In the rented kitchen she uses for her prep, Rana makes a new batch of dough for the doubles each day, letting it rise overnight before it's transferred to the truck and fried fresh to order. Her rolling pin gets plenty of use, churning out beignet dough for "Desi donuts" (spiced like chai and dusted with powdered sugar and crushed pistachios) and also the paratha for her *kathi* roll, the Indian take on the burrito and the quintessential street snack in Kolkata. The thin, flaky wrapper is layered with egg and then stuffed with curry chicken, mint-cilantro chutney, and perfectly tart pickled onions. "So good. It's my favorite," Rana brags. "And I have to have it with the Desi hot sauce. No toning down the spices. We go all out. It's authentic street food. The only thing is we do an 'American hot' and a 'Desi hot,' which people call the 'killer hot.'"

Curry Up Now actually gets more requests for the "killer hot" than the American, primarily because Akash has been business-savvy enough to secure regular weekly spots at major corporations with a huge number of Indian employees. Software giant Oracle, based in the Bay Area suburb of Redwood City, employs about ten thousand Indian-Americans, and Rana and her truck are in the parking lot for lunch every Tuesday. Wednesdays she has standing gigs in the lots of Walmart.com and YouTube, Thursdays it's video game developer Gazillion, and Fridays it's Virgin Airlines' headquarters. Weekends the truck usually hops around the affluent suburb of Burlingame, a short drive from the Kapoors' house, and Mondays the crew regroups, spending most of the day prepping for the coming week. "I stopped counting how many hours I work, but it's way more than a full-time job," Rana says. "It's gratifying seeing people enjoying what you envision. It makes me happy, you know? I'm cooking, I'm at the truck meeting people, talking to everyone. That's what we do in India. You're talking through the window to your neighbor, to people on the street. I do that all the time and they think I'm crazy but I don't care. I love every bit of it."

(SAN FRANCISCO'S UNDERGROUND FOOD CART REVOLUTION)

A cluster of hipsters of all stripes streaming in and out of an art gallery on a Saturday night is a fairly common sight in San Francisco's Mission District. But at Olivia Ongpin's Fabric8 Gallery, there's also often a guy out front cooking Thai curries in propane-fueled woks mounted to a cruiser bike's sidecar. Next to him is another guy using a three-foot metal pipe as the bellows to stoke the fire inside his "FrankenWeber," a twenty-two-inch Weber kettle grill on wheels that he's turned into a pizza oven by constructing a concrete dome to contain the heat of flaming hardwood charcoal.

Magic Curry Kart and the **Pizza Hacker** are the most visually arresting of the carts that have been roaming San Francisco's streets since the scene took hold in 2009, but wind your way through Fabric8 (taking notice of the pop-surrealism art on the walls while you go, of course) and you'll land in a lush backyard that is turned into a veritable food-cart court nearly every week. Under the branches of a giant oak, using a small flood lamp for a work light, Curtis Kimball of the **Crème Brûlée Cart** looks every bit the part of a professional pastry

CONTINUED ON PAGE 26 ➜

chef, clad in starched chef whites and cartoonish toque, carefully sprinkling a fine layer of sugar onto palm-size vanilla custard cups and brûléeing them with a small torch. There's a line of about twenty people and it's nearing 10 p.m., but the cart closes only when the last crème brûlée is gone.

A rotating lineup of food carts bearing everything from barbecue to cookies is invited to Fabric8 on an almost weekly basis (www.fabric8.blogspot .com), so technically these mobile chefs aren't breaking any rules since they're on private property. But when a handful of the carts have teamed up for an impromptu food fest in a park, on a random street corner, or even in a back alley, that's when the fuzz has occasionally intervened. For the most part, the cart owners say that the city hasn't cracked down too hard by ticketing or fining, even though nearly all are operating without permits or licenses. Still, over the course of the movement, many cart owners have become a bit more careful where they go and when. Twitter has always been the preferred method of announcing pop-up locations, and the Health Department has no doubt figured out how to use their computer, but the roving crew seems undeterred, most intent

CONTINUED ON PAGE 28 ➜

Rana's Chicken Kathi Roll Serves 12

CHICKEN
1/3 cup vegetable oil
1 tablespoon minced fresh ginger, pressed to
    make a paste
1 tablespoon crushed garlic, pressed to make
    a paste
1 teaspoon red pepper flakes
1 1/2 teaspoons ground cumin
2 teaspoons ground coriander
1/2 teaspoon ground turmeric
1/2 teaspoon garam masala
2 pounds boneless, skinless chicken breasts
    or thighs, cut into bite-size pieces
3 small green chiles, coarsely chopped
2 onions, finely diced

4 Roma tomatoes, diced
Handful of cilantro leaves, finely chopped
Salt to taste

WRAPS
2 eggs
Salt and freshly ground black pepper
Red pepper flakes
12 white or whole wheat flour tortillas or
    frozen roti
1/4 cup chopped cilantro leaves
2 limes
Mint or cilantro chutney (available at most
    Indian grocery stores)

To prepare the chicken, heat a wok or large, heavy sauté pan for a few minutes over medium heat. Add the oil.

Add the ginger and garlic and cook, stirring constantly, for 1 minute. Add the dry spices and cook, stirring constantly, until the oil begins to separate, 2 to 3 minutes. Add the chicken, cover the wok, and cook, stirring occasionally, for 5 minutes. Add the green chiles, onions, and tomatoes and cook, uncovered, stirring constantly, for another 5 to 7 minutes, until the oil separates and the water evaporates from the chicken.

Turn off the heat and add the cilantro. Season with salt to taste. Using a slotted spoon, transfer the mixture to a bowl and set aside.

To prepare the wraps, beat the eggs with a fork in a small mixing bowl. Season with salt, black pepper, and red pepper flakes.

Heat a griddle or a nonstick pan (preferably the same size as the tortillas) over medium heat. Pour just enough of the beaten egg mixture into the pan to create a circle about the size of the tortilla, then immediately place a tortilla on top. Using a spatula, gently lift an edge of the tortilla; once you see that the egg has solidified on the underside and stuck to the tortilla, flip the tortilla to lightly brown the opposite side.

Transfer the tortilla to a square of wax paper, spoon about 3 tablespoons of the chicken mixture on top, sprinkle on some of the cilantro, and add a generous squeeze of lime juice. Drizzle with a bit of chutney, then roll the kathi like a burrito in the wax paper. Repeat with the remaining tortillas. Serve.

FOOD TRUCKS

Sam's Chowdermobile

KEEP UP WITH IT: www.samschowdermobile.com or twitter.com/chowdermobile

When five thousand people are clamoring to get into your restaurant every week, you might start thinking about expanding. Sam's Chowder House in Half Moon Bay, a coastal town about twenty-five miles south of San Francisco, has been packing them in since it opened in 2006, luring diners with New England classics and ocean views worthy of a tourism brochure. It's tough to beat clam chowder and lobster rolls on a waterfront patio, especially with an ice-cold beer in hand and the West Coast breeze a-blowin', but not everyone can make it to Half Moon Bay. For them, Sam's went mobile.

"It was the brainchild of myself and Paul Shenkman, who is proprietor of Sam's Chowder House," says Lewis Rossman, chef and partner at Sam's. "The volume we were doing at Sam's was just fascinating to us, so we were contemplating opening another restaurant, but we're relatively location-specific. There's nothing like eating seafood on the sea. So we started researching and we started hearing about this food truck movement. We found a truck with only 1,600 miles on it on Craigslist, and we asked ourselves, 'What are the items we're selling most of?' So we basically set up the truck to be able to do those items."

That means that since it started rolling in June 2009, the massive red truck slings New England clam chowder, crispy calamari, lobster rolls, and fish-and-chips—the Chowder House's greatest hits. Lewis also came up with a Baja-style fish taco exclusive to the truck, beer-battered pollock tucked into a corn tortilla along with mango relish, shredded cabbage, and a chipotle crème fraîche. Still, the best seller remains the chowder, clam broth thickened with cream and studded with chunky potatoes, littleneck clams, smoked bacon, and thyme. It's simple and it's stellar, just like the lobster roll, nothing more than bright red hunks of lobster basted in warm butter on toasted brioche.

The food doesn't need the ocean-side setting to taste good, which is key considering that the Chowdermobile spends most of its time in decidedly unglamorous business parks in suburbs like Brisbane and Burlingame or San Jose. That seems to be where the truck does steady business, with lines forming at lunchtime of nine-to-fivers sick of brown-bagging it. The truck also gets plenty of requests for private events, turning birthdays and weddings into clambakes and chowder fests. They've even turned the San Francisco 49ers parking lot into a New England–style tailgating party— Patriots fans not allowed.

on operating underground, both to sidestep the red-tape headache of going legit and also in the age-old San Francisco spirit of sticking it to the man.

Tracking the carts on Twitter takes little more than connecting the dots: start at feeds like @cremebruleecart, @magiccurrykart, and @pizzahacker.com and you'll quickly see other tweets from cart associates like **Gobba Gobba Hey**, **Sexy Soup Cart**, **Lumpia Cart**, **Gumbo Cart**, and **Soul Cocina** (technically not a cart, but in the same spirit nonetheless). Just remember that while most of the food tastes on par with that of the pros, these are not streamlined restaurant operations, so go with the flow, expect a bit of a wait, and don't go looking for a manager if you arrive to the front of the line to be met by that dreaded phrase, "Sold out." ◉

Sam's New England Clam Chowder Serves 6

2 ounces uncooked smoked bacon, chopped

2 tablespoons unsalted butter

1/2 onion, finely diced

1/2 stalk celery, finely diced

2 cloves garlic, chopped

1 tablespoon fresh thyme

1 bay leaf

2 pounds Yukon Gold potatoes, diced

1 (46-ounce) can clam juice, at room temperature

2 pounds shucked littleneck clams

1 1/2 cups heavy cream

Salt and freshly ground black pepper

In a large stockpot over medium heat, sauté the bacon in the butter, cooking until the bacon is browned. Add the onion, celery, garlic, and herbs to the pot and sauté until they become soft and moist but haven't yet caramelized, about 4 to 5 minutes. Add the potatoes and clam juice. Cook until the potatoes are tender, about 15 minutes.

Turn off the heat and stir in the clams and cream. Season with salt and pepper to taste and serve.

Spencer on the Go

FIND IT: Folsom St. between 7th and Langton Sts., San Francisco, California
KEEP UP WITH IT: www.spenceronthego.com or twitter.com/chezspencergo

Escargot drenched in garlic butter, wrapped in puff pastry, and stabbed with a skewer seems like the type of thing you'd find being passed around on silver trays at a party where more people spoke French than didn't and owning a home on the Riviera was more common than owning all of your own teeth. But thanks to a long-running joke that finally became reality, you'll actually find these little lollipop-like escargot puffs being sold out of a gleaming silver truck in San Francisco's South of Market District, several blocks away from the Mission. "I was joking with a guy who has a taco truck and I said, 'I'm going to compete with you and sell lobster right next to you,'" says Laurent Katgely, chef-owner of the truck Spencer on the Go. "We joked about it for a while, but the more we did and the more I talked to friends, the more they said it was a good idea. So I just stopped joking about it and did it."

Laurent already had a successful bistro, Chez Spencer, that had been plugging along in the Mission since 2002, but he's never really been one to sit still. He was born in Grenoble, known as the capital of the French Alps, but his dad had a habit for picking up odd jobs, and picking up to move toward them. Laurent, his brother, and his sister all dropped out of school in their early teens, and Laurent ended up in a program for "bad kids," a sort of vocational school where grammar and math were pretty much incidental and the real focus was on practical work experience as a hairdresser, mechanic, or baker. Laurent could handle that, but when he landed in the restaurant program, he was more impressed with cute hostesses and regular paychecks than he was by the classical French cooking techniques he was learning.

Still, whether or not he was psyched about cooking, he was good at it; it came naturally to him. After his required year in the military, he headed back to the kitchen, this time in Paris working his way through the ranks at a Michelin-starred restaurant. He left to follow an Irish girl to Dublin, where he lasted a year before heading to Venezuela. He stayed there about a year before moving on to Guatemala, where it was two years before he took off again and eventually wound up in Los Angeles. At every stop along the way he knew he could make money cooking, and he stuck to the kitchen.

"I was sous chef most of the places I worked," Laurent says. "But then I got the head chef offer for Pastis in L.A., and I got more confident." He took the job, but he soon parlayed that confidence into a move to San Francisco, where he eventually opened his own restaurant, Chez Spencer, named for his then two-year-old son. Spencer on the Go is really just an extension of

the bistro, selling French classics that Laurent road tested at his sit-down restaurant first. Like those escargot puffs, the fat slabs of foie gras torchon you'll get from the truck are the same as you'd be served at Chez Spencer, sprinkled with gray sea salt and served on a slice of baguette toast. Only at the truck, it's handed over in a paper boat and you can munch on it from a little café table while watching a classic or foreign flick projected onto a white sheet tacked up to the fence. For the most part, the menu is doable without the fork and knife required at Chez Spencer, but that's been something of a learning process. "In the beginning, spring 2009, I was doing everything to order. The first night was a complete disaster," Laurent says. "We had three hundred people here in line. It was insane. I was yelling at people . . . it was *not* fun. I wanted to take off. Just leave. So we made some adjustments. Street food has to be fast. Me, I was seasoning to order, sautéing skate cheeks to order. I decided we can't do that in a truck on a tiny little range."

But what they *can* do is make use of the steam table for warming halibut soup with saffron aioli and use the convection oven to bake up potato gratin and warm chocolate pudding. For the most popular menu item, the lamb cheeks, the meat is seasoned with herbes de Provence and then braised for two hours with red wine, port, orange juice, and lamb stock until it could basically fall apart if you stare at it too hard. The hunks of tender meat get dressed with a mustard vinaigrette and butter lettuce before being piled onto a baguette-like roll Laurent gets from "a French guy, a typical French baker with a big beard that's all dusted white when you see him. He sleeps in his flour. No, really. I saw him a couple times and he's asleep in his flour bag. He's great. He just does what he loves."

Braised Lamb Cheeks Sandwich Serves 4

8 lamb cheeks	2 cups lamb stock
Salt and freshly ground black pepper	4 crusty sandwich rolls (ideally baguette)
1 cup herbes de Provence	Dijon mustard, for serving
¼ cup olive oil	

Season the lamb with salt and pepper and rub each cheek with the herbes de Provence.

Heat the olive oil over medium-high heat in a large, deep sauté pan or a stockpot. Add the lamb cheeks, in batches if necessary to avoid crowding them, and sear, turning halfway through to brown both sides. Once the edges are golden brown, add the lamb stock, turn the heat to low, and simmer about 90 minutes, until meltingly tender.

Once the meat is cool enough to handle, shred it into small pieces and set it aside.

When ready to serve, slice the rolls in half and warm them slightly in a warm oven. Spread Dijon mustard to taste on each roll and pile on the warmed shredded lamb cheek.

RoliRoti

KEEP UP WITH IT: **www.roliroti.com**

Tourists hit the Golden Gate Bridge and Fisherman's Wharf. Chowhounds make a beeline for the Ferry Building Marketplace, where the goods at Cowgirl Creamery and Boccalone Salumeria turn otherwise normal human beings into lions at a feeding frenzy and bleary-eyed locals stand forty deep for a hit of Blue Bottle's coffee. But no line is longer than the Saturday lunch queue at RoliRoti.

"I go as fast as I can go, but still people are sometimes in line for an hour," says Thomas Odermatt, grinning as he furiously slices crackly skinned porchetta, piles the glistening pork onto a slice of ciabatta, slathers onion marmalade on another, and smashes a handful of peppercress into the middle before closing up the sandwich. "I can only make about 250 of these each Saturday, though, so when I run out I feel bad, but I just can't do more."

The demand trumps the supply every time, and Thomas is fine with that. The porchetta was an afterthought anyway. RoliRoti trucks (there are three) were built to cook chicken. A *lot* of chicken. About 120 all-natural California chickens rotate on massive skewers that run almost the entire length of the trucks. Propane-fueled heat crisps the skin and coaxes out juices that fall to the griddle below, coating awaiting fingerling potatoes with fatty goodness perfumed with rosemary, thyme, and oregano. It's a rotisserie grill on wheels and business is booming, good enough that Thomas dispatches his fleet to nearly a dozen farmers' markets throughout the Bay Area. But RoliRoti's success wasn't born out of the blue: it was inherited.

Otto Odermatt was one of thirteen kids, raised in a poor mountain town in the Swiss Alps. Otto really wanted to be a baker, but there was no apprenticeship available. There was, however, a slot at the butcher shop, and, as Thomas says, "You don't learn a second trade. You learn one trade and become the best of the best."

So Otto did. Eventually he was deemed a *Metzgermeister,* or master butcher, and his shop in the small town of Hombrechtikon has survived more than five decades on his dedication to the craft. Still, Thomas wasn't interested in hacking meat. He was drawn to farming, and after high school pursued an organic agriculture degree in Switzerland, which then took him to California, where he considered importing olive oil. "But then something happened," Thomas says. "I felt that olive oil wasn't going to work, and I knew that a mobile concept was the way to go. Growing up in the butcher shop and growing up farming, I put one and one together and decided to make simple food with top-notch ingredients from local farms."

The insistence on high-quality meat came from his father, but it was his mother Maria who spawned the idea that would become the business's namesake. "We have a rotisserie grill at the butcher shop, and my mother cooked with it," Thomas says, "but only on Saturdays." Chickens and potatoes, both prepared to Maria's specifications, were the only offerings when RoliRoti launched in 2002. Around 2005, those porchetta sandwiches were added to the menu. "My father came to San Francisco for my wedding and said, 'I cannot bring anything from Switzerland, but I'll make porchetta when I arrive,'" Thomas recalls. "It was so good I realized I must make this at RoliRoti, but it took me a year to perfect it."

Thomas says the key is to use a whole pork loin with the skin on and score the skin so that the fat "pops" while it cooks, essentially basting the meat. A rotisserie is ideal, but a regular oven will do in a pinch. Also, it probably helps to have an eighty-eight-year-old master butcher on speed dial should you have any questions, but his tried-and-true recipe is a pretty good stand-in.

Otto Odermatt's Porchetta   Serves 10 to 12

For the porchetta at the RoliRoti truck, Thomas uses a deboned pork middle, cutting out about half of the belly fat and leaving about ¹/₂ inch of fat on the loin. If you're unable to find pork middle (a special request item, for sure), he suggests using a skin-on pork belly and wrapping the loin inside of it. Thomas also uses his signature rotisserie. Using a home version would be ideal, but this recipe has been adjusted so that it can be made in a standard oven.

2 tablespoons finely chopped lemon zest

2 tablespoons freshly squeezed lemon juice

2 tablespoons minced garlic

2 tablespoons pinot grigio or other
  dry white wine

1¹/₂ tablespoons chopped fresh rosemary

1¹/₂ tablespoons chopped fresh sage

1 tablespoon chopped fresh marjoram

2 tablespoons fennel seeds, toasted and
  lightly crushed

4 bay leaves, toasted and ground

3 tablespoons kosher salt

2 tablespoons freshly ground black pepper

3- to 4-pound pork belly

2-pound pork loin

Thomas's Balsamic Onion Marmalade
  (recipe follows), for serving

Preheat the oven to 425°F.

In a small bowl, combine the lemon zest, 1 tablespoon of the lemon juice, the garlic, pinot grigio, all of the herbs, 2 tablespoons of the salt, and the pepper to make a marinade.

Lay the pork belly out on a clean surface, skin side down, and rub the marinade all over the meat. Place the loin at one edge of the belly, coat it thoroughly with the marinade as well, then roll to completely encase the loin with the belly. Tie with butcher's twine, using one loop on each end and one in the middle so that it keeps its shape. Score the skin in a crosshatch pattern, being careful to pierce the meat only about ¹/₈ inch deep so that the loin won't dry out.

Make a paste out of the remaining 1 tablespoon lemon juice and 1 tablespoon salt. Rub the mixture on the outside of the porchetta and place it on a rack in a roasting pan. Transfer to the oven.

Roast the porchetta, watching it carefully, just until the skin takes on some color and starts to crisp, about 10 minutes. At that point turn the oven down to 300°F and cook, checking the internal temperature every 20 minutes, until the center reaches 135°F, about 2 hours. Remove the porchetta from the oven and let rest for 10 minutes before slicing and serving. Top with the Balsamic Onion Marmalade (see page 34).

Thomas's Balsamic Onion Marmalade

Makes about 2 cups

1 tablespoon vegetable or canola oil

4 yellow onions, thinly sliced

1/2 teaspoon ground cloves

1 teaspoon salt

1 teaspoon freshly ground black pepper

3 tablespoons brown sugar

Zest from 1/2 orange

2/3 cup balsamic vinegar

Heat the oil over medium heat in a large skillet. Add the onions and cook, stirring occasionally, until they are soft and caramelized, about 20 minutes. Add the cloves, salt, and pepper, stirring to coat.

Reduce the heat to medium-low and add the brown sugar and orange zest. Cook, stirring frequently, until the onions start to shrivel. Add the vinegar, reduce the heat to low, and cook for 1 1/2 hours, stirring occasionally. Adjust the seasoning to taste and serve warm. Leftovers can be stored in the refrigerator, tightly sealed, for about a week.

Tanguito

FIND IT: **2850 Jones St., San Francisco, California**

At Fisherman's Wharf, you can fulfill your wildest dreams of perusing the racks of "I Escaped from Alcatraz" T's at Crazy Shirts, check out a cable car made of matchsticks at Ripley's Believe It or Not! Museum, and settle in for a plate of fried shrimp at Bubba Gump. And if there's still time, don't forget the wax museum, Hooters, and Hard Rock Café, oh my! Okay, so it's no news flash that the wharf is a giant tourist trap, but that only means that finding a reason to go there is that much more important. Somewhat hidden (although in plain sight from the F Line streetcar station on Jones Street) amid this massive display of chain consumerism is a slightly ramshackle truck called Tanguito. There's a handwritten sign advertising Argentinean specialties, photos of those dishes that look like they were taken with a disposable camera, a few picnic tables under an awning that extends from the truck's windshield, and a brightly painted mural on the back of the truck that you can really only see if you wedge yourself between Tanguito and the six-foot fence that it's parked in front of. None of that is important. What is important are the flaky empanadas, the chimichurri-drenched sausage *choripan* sandwich, the massive grilled beef ribs, and the juicy Argentinean beef burger.

"We bought the truck from an Egyptian guy in the fall of 2008, and I know we need to fix up the front of the truck, but we just don't have the time or money," says Tanguito's owner, Steven Rodriguez Mares. "But it's more important to us that our truck is clean and that the food is good."

That it is. Steven picked up pointers at the stove from his mother growing up in Buenos Aires, while his father ran a bar and grill called Las Marinas. However, he's quick to remind anyone who will listen that he's not a chef. He cooks food the way he likes to eat it: simply seasoned with salt and pepper, with a minimal number of ingredients. Steven, who moved to the United States in 2000, had never worked in a kitchen (although he did work as a server for about a year), and until the food truck idea came to him he supported his wife, Bettina, and his two daughters by driving a taxi, which he still does from about six at night until two in the morning, five days a week.

"We are open only during the day right now, and no, we aren't making any real money, but it doesn't really matter to me," Steven says. "I found something that my family can all do at the same time. The children can be here, Bettina is here . . . I love it."

As he says this, the Saturday afternoon rush is dying down and Bettina is inside the truck assessing the stock of empanadas, her contribution to the menu, while eight-year-old Zoe and three-year-old Lara sit quietly on little stools in front of the truck's reach-in cooler, coloring pictures of horses and rainbows. Steven says Zoe likes to help and sometimes pitches in by cleaning shrimp; she once made paella with only a little help from Dad when it came to igniting the grill. Fire is a borderline obsession of Steven's. When he talks about how he swapped out the truck's flat-top grill for a gas-powered grate grill, his eyes light up as he mimics the flames needed to cook his signature beef ribs. Steven also handles the burgers, hand-cuts the fries, grills the Italian-style sausage for the *choripan*, and prepares shellfish paella in a wok in about twenty minutes. And even though the truck was Steven's big idea, Bettina decided that if they were going to serve food from their homeland, they needed empanadas. "In Argentina, they have an empanada shop on every block, and when you want them you can just go there or they'll even deliver," Bettina says. "So actually, when I lived there, I never made them myself. But when we moved to America, Steven's mother gave me a classic Argentinean cookbook because she knew I would have to cook here, and I took the dough recipe from that, but for the fillings there are no recipes. It's just common sense, very simple, what we like to eat. How we cook on the truck is how we cook in life, so of course we cook for people the same way we would cook for ourselves. What other way?"

FOOD TRUCKS

Beef Empanadas   Makes about 12 empanadas

4¼ cups all-purpose flour, plus more
    for dusting

1½ teaspoons salt

½ cup margarine, at room temperature

¾ cup water

2 tablespoons corn oil

3 onions, diced

3 cloves garlic, minced

1 pound ground beef

½ teaspoon freshly ground black pepper

1 tablespoon chopped fresh Italian parsley

1½ teaspoons chopped fresh oregano

½ cup diced roasted red bell pepper

¼ cup chopped green olives

2 hard-cooked eggs, chopped

1 tablespoon raisins (optional)

1 egg yolk, lightly beaten

Preheat the oven to 450°F. Grease a baking sheet and sprinkle flour over it.

In a large mixing bowl, combine the flour with 1 teaspoon of the salt, 6 table-spoons of the margarine, and the water, stirring with a spoon and then using your hands to thoroughly blend the dough. Roll the dough out to a thickness of ¼ inch, then spread the remaining 2 tablespoons margarine on the dough's surface. Lightly sprinkle the dough with flour, fold it in half and then in half again, and then roll it out again to a thickness of ¹⁄₁₆ inch. Cut out about 12 circles from the dough using a 5-inch ring mold.

Heat the oil in a large skillet over medium heat, then add the onions and the garlic. Stir in the ground beef and season with the remaining ½ teaspoon salt, pepper, parsley, and oregano. When the beef is lightly browned, add the bell pepper. Increase the heat and cook, stirring constantly, until the beef is fully cooked. Let cool and then stir in the olives, hard-cooked eggs, and raisins. Put 2 tablespoons of the filling in the middle of each dough circle and fold the dough in half to form a half-moon, pressing the edges together firmly and pinching them all around or pressing them with the tines of a fork to seal. Place the empanadas on a the prepared baking sheet and brush them with the egg yolk. Bake until golden brown, 15 to 20 minutes.

Oahu, Hawaii

L unch wagons, as they're known, are so cemented into Hawaiian culture that if you ask a native to recount his or her first meal at one, the response usually starts with, "Well, my dad had this one favorite . . ." Even city officials (whose Department of Health records for mobile food vendors go back only to 1996) recall the trucks as "being around forever," tracing their origins to the early 1900s, when mobile canteens cruised the island's many military bases to feed soldiers. By the 1960s Honolulu started to emerge as Oahu's business hub, with enterprising home cooks loading classic Hawaiian "plate lunches" onto delivery trucks and driving them to construction sites to feed hungry workers responsible for building up the downtown area. Over time, as nine-to-fivers started to fill the jobs being created, they, too, got in line for home-style eats either rooted in Hawaiian tradition (kalua pork, *laulau*, poi) or influenced by Hawaii's sizable Asian population (pork katsu, teriyaki beef, chicken long rice, Korean-style short ribs). These plate lunches look exactly the same today as they did decades ago: two heaping scoops of white rice and a scoop of macaroni salad topped with whatever protein floats your boat. Somewhere along the way a small salad crept into the container, done at some trucks as a cabbage-lettuce blend, at others as a few leaves of iceberg drizzled with Thousand Island dressing.

By the 1990s tourism had taken the lead as Hawaii's main source of revenue, and as buses loaded with camera-toting tourists eventually headed

FOOD TRUCKS

beyond the high-rise hotels on Waikiki to the beautiful beaches of the North Shore, shrimp farmers began to figure out that selling their catch whole-sale wasn't the only market. Dilapidated shuttle buses, many retired from resorts or the airport, got tropical makeovers on the outside and jury-rigged kitchens on the inside. Many of these shrimp trucks set up only a few feet from their shrimp ponds, between the coast and Kamehameha Highway, the main artery from Honolulu to the North Shore. The Bonzai Pipeline at Ehukai Beach had already been discovered by international surfers seeking massive waves during the 1960s, and these penny-pinching drifters proved to be loyal customers for shrimp trucks when tourist season was at its low (quick surf lesson: Hawaii's waves are biggest in November and December).

After recording about fifteen years at a steady number, Department of Health supervisor Peter Oshiro saw Hawaii's lunch wagons nearly double from 2007 to 2008, followed by another 30 percent increase from 2008 to 2009, with a current count of over two hundred. Speculation among truck owners is that the recession inspired many would-be restaurateurs to think smaller and go mobile. But ask Macky Chan of the North Shore shrimp truck Macky's and he points to his truck's appearance on *Lost* as key to the spike. Egocentric? Maybe, but sixteen million viewers can't exactly hurt business.

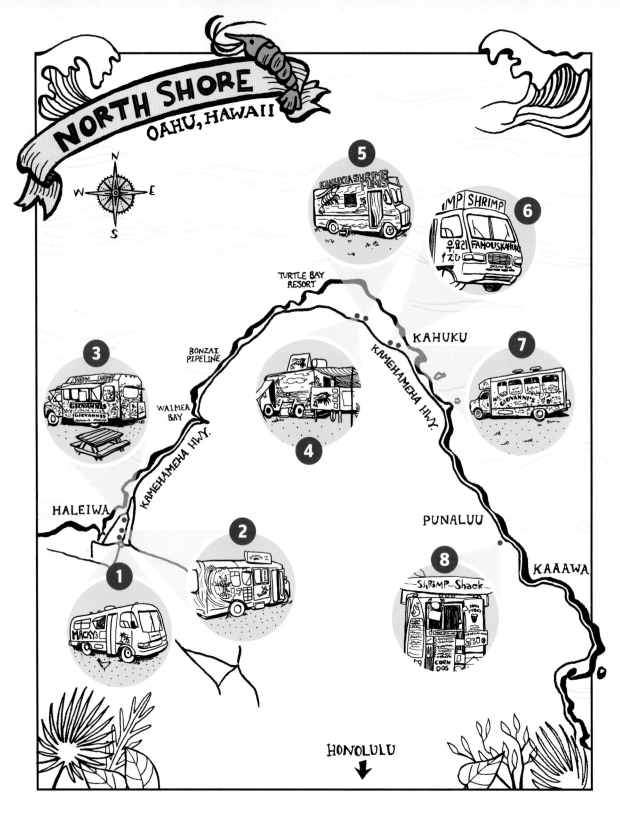

North Shore Shrimp Trucks

❶ Macky's Kuhuku Sweet Shrimp (66-632 Kamehameha Hwy.; see page 42)

❷ Big Wave Shrimp (66-521 Kamehameha Hwy.) Just next door to the hippified One Love Surf Shop you'll find more good vibes at this chill shrimp truck, a colorful converted tour bus run by Thai native Kawita Stacy, who's as sweet as she is hospitable. Towering trees, a few picnic tables, and a front-row seat to Haleiwa's main drag makes for a nice spot to spend an hour crunching on crispy coconut shrimp, then slurping up sweet shave ice.

❸ Giovanni's II (66-460 Kamehameha Hwy.) The newer Haleiwa sibling of the Kahuku institution shares a serene shaded lot with a couple of other food trucks, including Opal Thai (see Side Dish, page 48), which gives Giovanni's a run for its money when it comes to bustling business. Giovanni's might be a newer spinoff, but it's battered and plastered with graffiti just the same, and the garlic-laden shrimp is a dead ringer for the tasty stuff the original has been serving for years (although if you're in these parts, you might as well keep going south to Macky's).

❹ Tony's Kahuku Shrimp (56-775 Kamehameha Hwy.) Somewhat overshadowed by nearby Fumi's and nearly hidden by its own tarp shelter covering a handful of picnic tables, Tony's has a decade of experience to its credit, and the Taiwanese father-daughter team running it makes every effort to stand apart from the crowd. Regulars bring beer to fan the flames from the sweet-and-spicy "lava" shrimp, which, like the entire lineup here, are served head on and in the shell for extra flavor. Not hungry? Cool off with lychee iced tea or homemade pineapple ice cream.

❺ Fumi's Kahuku Shrimp (56-777 Kamehameha Hwy.) The romantic sunset splashed across the side of this truck takes a bit of poetic license on the real deal, but at least you know exactly what you're getting when it comes to the shrimp—it comes from the ponds adjacent to the parking lot. Unlike most of its competition, Fumi's takes the time to devein (a bonus for the squeamish), plus they offer a marriage of popular styles with their garlic-spicy shrimp. For something subtler, go for the stuff that's peeled and sautéed with fistfuls of fresh ginger slivers.

❻ Famous Kahuku Shrimp Truck (56-580 Kamehameha Hwy.) About a tail-toss away from the throngs crowding Giovanni's you'll find this local favorite, a bit more low-key and staffed by folks who seem genuinely appreciative of your business. Maybe that's why they let patrons mix-and-match, handing over plates half piled with garlic shrimp and half piled with a chile sauce–glazed spicy version. Both are good, but the plump guys that are lightly battered in the style of Chinese salt-and-pepper shrimp are the standout.

❼ Giovanni's Aloha Shrimp (56-505 Kamehameha Hwy.) Just past Romy's shrimp ponds and their roadside shrimp hut (not on wheels, so not in this book) you'll spot this graffiti-splattered truck, perpetually mobbed by tourists who've heard about the media darling and come for a taste. Going on nearly two decades, Giovanni's is the original truck of the North Shore shrimp scene, slinging a few hundred plates of fat, garlic butter–drenched crustaceans daily. The "hot & spicy" is no joke, so go at your own risk.

❽ Shrimp Shack (53-360 Kamehameha Hwy.) Driving south down the "windward," or eastern, side of the island the crowds thin, the air feels even fresher, but the food options become few and far between. Enter Irene Theofanis's surfboard-clad, banana-yellow shrimp truck, beckoning to travelers with its upscale menu of beer-steamed mussels, rock crab cakes, and mahi smothered in grilled onions. Snap out of the food coma with a Kona Iceberg, fresh-brewed coffee poured over vanilla ice cream.

Macky's Kahuku Sweet Shrimp

FIND IT: 66-632 Kamehameha Hwy., Haleiwa, Hawaii

"Go big or go home." So proclaims the sticker slapped onto a battered surfboard leaning up against a truck parked along Kamehameha Highway, the main artery of Hawaii's North Shore. The slogan is referring to waves, of course, the bigger the better here on the island home to the famed surf spot known as the Bonzai Pipeline, host to the sport's toughest competitions each winter when twenty-foot waves roll in.

Macky Chen doesn't surf. But he knows surfers, knows their lingo, and knows how they like their shrimp. Macky runs one of the dozen or so shrimp trucks that dot the Kamehameha Highway, some of which have been feeding surfers and tourists alike since the '80s. Trucks have come and gone, but Macky's—a relative newcomer open only since 2004—has a cult following throughout the island of Oahu. A second-generation shrimp trucker and the son of a shrimp farmer, Macky abides by two laws: the secret is *not* in the sauce. And the shrimp, like the waves, have gotta be big.

Once the Taiwanese military got their required service out of him, Macky's father, Ming-Cheng Chen, decided he'd had enough of his homeland and set sail for Hawaii with his family in tow. This was the mid-'90s, and the Hawaiian aquaculture business had been booming for a decade: the world wanted seaweed and shrimp, and Hawaii knew just how to raise them. Ming-Cheng decided that a bit of reading material, advice from friends, and some start-up money was all he needed to dive headfirst into the aquaculture world. And just like that, he was a shrimp farmer.

Chen-Lu Shrimp Farm (Macky's mother, Hualien Lu, is the other half of both the farm and its name) sold its first crop in 1995, carving out a niche by raising only Pacific white shrimp and only selling them live. To hear Macky tell it, "Pacific white have to be raised in saltwater, and no matter what people tell you about freshwater or prawns or anything else, you don't believe them, because these shrimp have meat that's sweeter and more tender than anything. It's a very different flavor, so you don't need seasoning; you don't even need to cook it."

Funny thing about those surfers and tourists: they like their shrimp cooked. So after nearly a decade of Ming-Cheng haggling with wholesalers over the price per pound and Macky manning the nearby shrimp stand—bagging up big, fat Pacific whites to hand over to Hawaiian housewives stocking up for dinner—the matriarch of the family laid out her own plan: cook the shrimp and sell it. Sure, the competition among North Shore shrimp trucks is stiff, but so is the shrimp farming business. And those other guys don't have Chen-Lu Pacific whites and Hualien Lu's way with cooking them.

The Chens got their hands on an old shuttle bus that barely ran, but it didn't really need to. They outfitted it with a full kitchen—range, fryer, fridge, sink—found a spot to park it, popped out a side window to serve as the pass-through for finished plates, and plastered the menu onto the door. Alongside two-foot-tall letters that read "Macky's," a giant red hand-painted shrimp looms over the window for placing orders, almost daring customers to request it and its kind. Macky's Kahuku Sweet Shrimp opened for business in 2004 ("It's Chinese tradition to name a business for the son," Macky explains, "but really it is their truck first"). The next year the crispy coconut shrimp won the Battle of the North Shore Shrimp Trucks, a not entirely friendly competition organized by Turtle Bay Resorts. Legend has it (according to Macky, at least) that after this newcomer walked away with first prize, pressure from an established shrimp truck or two convinced Turtle Bay Resorts to retire the contest. In essence, Macky's is the one and only champion of the Battle of the North Shore Shrimp Trucks.

The attention that followed—and soon swelled, thanks to a cameo on the TV show *Lost* and a nod as Best Shrimp Truck from *Honolulu* magazine—translated to sales of roughly eighty to a hundred pounds of shrimp a day. Realizing that his wife's cooked shrimp might just be his golden ticket, Ming-Cheng sold the farm in 2005, but those Pacific whites are still the only shrimp you'll find on Macky's truck.

All five shrimp plates Macky's serves come with the standard Hawaiian setup: two mounds of fluffy white rice, fresh pineapple, and a green salad drizzled with what's generally referred to as "Oriental dressing," a concoction of sesame oil, soy sauce, and ginger. Choices enter the equation only when it comes to how you like your shrimp. Macky says the diehards order theirs boiled and unseasoned ("Maybe they're shrimp farmers testing us. Who knows?"), but he prefers his "spicy-hot," sautéed in Hualien's secret hot sauce, a distant cousin to Szechuan chile paste. Lemon-pepper remains something of the redheaded stepchild of the bunch, bringing up the rear as the flavorful-but-tame option for the AARP set. That battle champion coconut shrimp is the only fried option—the shrimp are soaked in coconut milk, dredged in a mix of flour and shaved coconut, then dropped in a roiling vat of vegetable oil—so that tends to be the choice for irie surfers. And finally there is the iconic garlic-butter shrimp, the variation found in every shrimp truck doing business in Hawaii, and which is most often linked to homesickness among expats and nostalgic rhapsodizing among tourists returning to the mainland. Any version you'll come across has essentially the same ingredients: garlic, butter, and, of course, shrimp. But as Hualien Chen knows, it's what you do with the shrimp that sets you apart.

(SIDE DISH)

Not many people want to interrupt their Hawaiian vacation with a trip to a boring shopping mall ("you can buy shoes back home, dear"), but there is one reason to make a detour to the Waikele Shopping Center: a red-and white-striped trailer slapped with giant lettering that reads "HOT MALASADAS." *Malasadas* are Portugal's answer to the doughnut, holeless and amazing, yeasty and eggy like brioche inside but with an exterior that gives way with a crunch similar to that of a croissant. Leonard Rego's grandparents came to Hawaii from Portugal in the late 1800s, and half a century later Leonard started his own bakery, selling these Portuguese sweets at his mother's suggestion. His son, Leonard Jr., runs the business today, and it was his idea to roll out the **Leonard's Malasadamobiles**, one of which roams (see www.leonardshawaii .com for locations) and the other of which is parked at the mall daily (94-894 Lumiaina St., Waipahu). The *malasada* fryer is constantly sizzling, turning the little puffs of dough golden brown before they're scooped up by a wire basket and set aside for final flavoring. They can be injected with coconut, vanilla, or chocolate custard, but they're better intact, tossed in plain sugar or given a dusting

CONTINUED ON PAGE 44 →

of cinnamon. I fell in love with the *li hing mui* variety, where the *malasada* is rolled in salty dried plum powder. It's not for everyone, but mix-and-match boxes come by the half dozen, so you can afford to take a leap on one. ◉

Macky's Garlic-Butter Shrimp Plate Serves 4

10 cloves garlic, minced

1 tablespoon vegetable oil

1/4 cup unsalted butter

2 pounds Pacific white shrimp or other jumbo saltwater shrimp, deveined, with tail and shell on

4 teaspoons garlic salt

4 cups cooked white sushi rice

1 small head romaine lettuce, chopped

1/2 small head red cabbage, chopped

1 large carrot, shredded

2 tablespoons prepared ginger-sesame salad dressing (any brand)

4 fresh pineapple wedges

Heat the garlic and vegetable oil in a sauté pan over low heat, stirring occasionally to make sure the garlic doesn't burn, until a deep brown color, about 20 minutes.

Melt half of the butter in a large sauté pan over medium heat. Add half of the shrimp and cook until bright red, about 3 minutes per side. Remove from the pan and set aside. Repeat with the remaining butter and shrimp. Sprinkle each of the two batches with 2 teaspoons of the garlic salt and toss to coat. Spoon the browned garlic into the pan with all the shrimp and toss to coat.

Divide the shrimp among 4 plates. Add to each plate two 1/2-cup scoops of rice and a small pile of the romaine topped with an equal amount of cabbage. Sprinkle the shredded carrot on the cabbage and top the vegetables with the salad dressing. Garnish the plate with a pineapple wedge. *E 'ai ka-kou!* (*Bon appétit!*)

Soul Patrol

KEEP UP WITH IT: **twitter.com/pacificsoul**

If you were the executive chef of one of Hawaii's most popular fine dining restaurants—a revolving restaurant on the twenty-first floor, no less, with 360-degree views of Waikiki Beach—and you were adored by the media, making a six-figure salary, putting your kid through private school, and flush with benefits, would you leave it all to start a food truck? Sean Priester would, and did. And he's banking on the island's best fried chicken to sail into success.

"I started as the chef at Top of Waikiki five years ago, I proved myself, and there was a point last year that I realized I was done proving myself," Sean says. "I've been cooking in Hawaii for the past twenty years, and in the last ten or so my voice began to develop. One of the things Charlie Trotter wrote in *Lessons in Excellence* was every chef needs to find his voice, and I just found mine."

He found it in Soul Patrol, the white box truck he stumbled onto in 2009. Sean's friend Utu Langi has headed up an organization known as H5 (Hawaii Helping the Hungry Have Hope) since the mid-'90s. Utu and a few friends cruise areas thick with poverty in a fully stocked lunch wagon, delivering hot meals to the hungry. One day in early 2009 Sean went along for the ride and came back with a newfound reverence for Utu's mission, but also bitten by the lunch truck bug. After joining Utu on a few more outings, Sean couldn't stop talking about how cool it would be to do this for his full-time gig. "And then what happened was Utu bought another wagon, and he just said, 'Here's your lunch wagon.' At the time I was fully employed as the head chef at Top of Wakiki, and I was totally uncomfortable and overwhelmed with leaving. I guess I asked for it, but I didn't think I was actually gonna get it."

At first, Sean tried to figure out a way to do both his fine dining gig and his lunch truck at the same time, getting "creative" with scheduling and pushing his bosses at Top of Waikiki to the limits of their flexibility. After about three months of this, plus weekend mornings cooking at a farmers' market stand under the name Pacific Soul, it was pretty clear that Sean's days of serving his food on fancy china were over.

"I've cooked everything, from Hawaiian regional cuisine to progressive American, you name it. But I only just realized that I've always had this essence of the South in there, making gnocchi out of sweet potatoes, throwing greens underneath fish. I've always wanted something more traditional and Southern," Sean says. "I'm an Army brat, but my parents are

When locals get tired of the standard plate lunch fare synonymous with wagons, they seek out one of the three **Simply 'Ono** (www.simplyono.com) trucks. These clunky warhorse trucks are nothing fancy to look at, but it's what's inside that keeps diners on their toes: prime rib with jus and horseradish sauce, cool crab club sandwiches, lamb French dip, and international comfort food from corned beef and cabbage to cheesy lasagna. The rotation of daily specials comes from the years Harris Sukita and Cora Stevens spent cooking at the Kahala Hilton, formerly one of the island's premier hotels. When the hotel closed in 1995, Harris talked Cora into going into the lunch wagon biz. It's been fifteen years of success since Simply 'Ono launched, and along the way Harris and Cora became a couple (regardless of Cora's insistence that she thought Harris was a "male chauvinist" back in the hotel kitchen), and they've also become surrogate parents to hordes of college kids who flock to the truck in search of comforting home-style eats. The day's menu always balances something slightly fancy with good old down-home cooking, and Fridays feature Hawaiian classics like kalua pig, shoyu chicken, and chicken long rice—a compromise the couple made to not stray too far from their roots. ◉

from South Carolina, and while I didn't know it was a part of me, I embrace that as you see it now."

"Embrace" is putting it mildly. Soul Patrol is 100 percent Southern staples: barbecue spareribs with a perfect pink smoke ring; po' boys stuffed with crunchy battered shrimp; Carolina-style pulled pork with the same vinegar tang Hawaiians have come to know by way of Filipino adobo; chili made from black-eyed peas; moist cornbread slathered with honey butter; and, of course, the buttermilk fried chicken that's won more local acclaim in the year since Soul Patrol launched than Sean has seen his entire career.

There's no question Sean is cooking the best soul food Hawaii has ever seen, but it's figuring out the truck game after stepping down out of the ivory tower that's taking some time. He still sticks to his mission to work with H5 providing meals to the hungry, but the bulk of his time is spent navigating the streets of Honolulu and hoping Hawaiians eventually embrace Twitter the way chowhounds on the mainland have. Slowly but surely, the word is spreading, and as Sean gets faster and more consistent with his Tweets, he's elated to pull into a spot and find a few people milling about, just salivating to get their hands on that fried chicken.

"I spent a lot of my career just wanting to be a great chef. Not a great black, soul food, Southern chef, but just a great chef," Sean says. "But it turns out when I talk about my cooking, I think of my grandfather's pot of field peas and neck bones and rice. I remember going to his house and experiencing that food, and there was something very spiritual about it. I didn't quite understand it at the time. I knew it was good, but now I know what it means."

Soul Patrol Buttermilk Fried Chicken Serves 8 to 10

2 quarts buttermilk

5 cups water

1 cup kosher salt

2/3 cup sugar

1/4 cup lemon pepper

3 tablespoons minced fresh rosemary,
  plus more for sprinkling

1 1/2 teaspoons minced fresh sage

5 pounds chicken legs and thighs

Lard or canola oil, for frying

3 cups flour, seasoned with salt and pepper

Sea salt, for sprinkling (optional)

Combine the buttermilk, water, salt, sugar, lemon pepper, rosemary, and sage in a large nonreactive bowl or container with a lid. Add the chicken to the brine, cover, and refrigerate for at least 24 hours, and preferably for 48.

When ready to cook the chicken, pull the pieces, one at a time, from the brine and slide your thumb between the meat and the bone, gently separating the flesh a bit from the bone where you can. This ensures the chicken will cook through to the bone. Return the chicken to the brine until the lard is ready.

Heat the lard in a deep fryer to 350°F.

Spread the seasoned flour in a shallow dish. Pull the chicken from the brine, one piece at a time, coat with the seasoned flour, and carefully drop into the oil. Fry for 12 minutes, remove with a slotted spoon, and transfer to a paper towel–lined plate to drain. Taste, and if more seasoning is desired, combine equal amounts of the rosemary and salt and sprinkle on the chicken.

Ray's Kiawe Broiled Chicken

FIND IT: Saturday and Sunday mornings at Haleiwa Super Market
(66-197 Kamehameha Hwy., Haleiwa, Hawaii)
KEEP UP WITH IT: rayskiawechicken@hawaii.rr.com

On the mainland, kids sell chocolate bars to raise money for football uniforms or sleepaway camp. In Hawaii, they sell *huli huli* chicken, rotisserie-cooked chicken named for the motion *huli huli*, or "turn turn." Ray Tantog has always been one to support a cute kid who has come knocking on the door, but after buying a poor excuse for a proper *huli huli* chicken, he marched over to the school's football coach to announce that he could do better. A man of his word, he did, and he became the school's chicken supplier for its fund-raiser by the following week.

Ray has always been an all-around handy guy, mechanically inclined, tinkering with projects that would impress even skilled tradesmen. At the time of the infamously inferior football team chicken of the 1980s, Ray was working in refrigeration. In his spare time he made *huli huli* chicken for family and friends, cooking the birds on a little rotisserie on wheels he built himself. It was quite a leap forward from the *huli huli* method he learned as a teen when his family arrived in Hawaii from the Philippines. "Way back in 1949, we used to put the chicken on a stick and roll it by hand over a fire we dug in the ground in the backyard," says Ray. "We started using the rotisserie around 1955, '57, with the long metal skewer on the ground over the fire and the end in a bicycle sprocket, with one person on the side cranking it."

By the time Ray took that fund-raising gig, his homemade rotisserie was a four by four-foot self-contained smoker of sorts, with three metal skewers that could hold a dozen fryer chickens, fueled by *kiawe* charcoal, a hardwood mesquite relative native to Hawaii that burns hotter and longer than typical charcoal briquettes, with no chemical additives. After word spread that Ray's Kiawe Broiled Chicken was putting out the juiciest birds in town, he and his rig were in high demand, so he put his six kids to work helping. It was clear that his small grill on wheels wasn't going to cut it keeping up with school fund-raisers, backyard luaus, and church celebrations, so Ray crafted an ingenious rotisserie out of a sixteen-foot flatbed trailer, fabricating massive metal skewers equal to its width and fitting their end grooves with a chain powered by a reduction gear motor. The *kiawe* lump charcoal burns in the base of the flatbed as the chickens slowly travel from one end of the trailer to the other, the coals carefully tended by Ray so that the highest heat is near the front, crisping the skin and sealing in the juices, and a slightly lower heat throughout helps ensure a fully cooked

(SIDE DISH)

Want to stand out in a sea of North Shore shrimp trucks? Cook Thai food. Sounds simple, but that decision has brought success for Opal Sirichandhra since he opened **Opal Thai** (66-460 Kamehameha Hwy.) in Haleiwa in 2006. The Bangkok native had more than a decade of cooking experience in the Bay Area before taking a vacation to Hawaii, falling in love with its similarities to Thailand, and →

bird. Ray figured out the sprocket and the timing of his contraption so that it takes twenty-five minutes for each rod of chicken to reach the end of the line, the exact amount of cooking time it needs to reach perfection.

Over the years Ray added a thirty-foot trailer to the fleet, which he uses for events calling for around 1,500 chickens (Japanese churches are his best customers for the big rig). The original trailer he started with is still in rotation, used primarily for regular Saturday and Sunday gigs at a grocery store parking lot in Haleiwa, where the sweet smoke of *kiawe* wafts through the sleepy town before its surfers even crawl out of bed. And for events where fewer than five hundred chickens are on order, Ray wheels out his custom-built wagon, a crafty setup with a sneaky hidden burner that rolls out from behind a gate, cooks up the chicken, then rolls back into its storage spot as smoothly as a drawer on casters. He's mastered each of these machines, but as he gets older, his children's role in the family business has increased. Still, he's quick to point out that only his sons Dino and Jesse can be trusted to man the flames.

Ask Ray about any of his inventions and he's happy to talk for days. Ask him about his chicken, though, and he clams up tighter than a witness pleading the fifth. "I just use my own spice, salt, paprika, just rub it on with no liquid, just season it, you know? But I've used the same chicken since I started, fryer chickens, three or four months old. Older chickens are tough," Ray explains.

He's reluctant to go on, mainly because he doesn't think the secret lies in the chicken. For a man who's been building his own mobile cooking devices for fifty years, it's the method that makes the difference. "People have taken my spice and done it themselves and they say it's not the same. I know that. I'm waiting for a franchise. Not KFC, RKC. I want to put it in a brick building like Taco Bell and have my big rotisserie in the center. As soon as people walk in the door, that's the first thing they see."

relocating to the island. There he met his wife Aoy, also Thai but from Chiang Mai, and the couple started cooking a small lineup of Thai noodle and rice dishes in a propane-fueled tabletop wok set up under a ten-by-ten-foot tent along the side of the road at Sunset Beach. Their street food gig lasted about a year, until they left for the mainland, where Aoy gave birth to their son, Lio. They returned four years later with a California taco truck in tow and secured a spot in a shaded lot in Haleiwa, where three other trucks, including one of the famous Giovanni's shrimp trucks, compete for customers. As the only Thai truck on the island, Opal has become a destination, earning legions of loyalists with bright green papaya salad and a delicious pad Thai, seasoned with a touch of the smoky roasted Thai chiles that Aoy's mother sends her from Chiang Mai. Mom also sends packages of a homemade curry blend from a family friend, and Opal swears it's a key to his truck's success, pointing out that even if Hawaiians don't know the difference, he does. ◉

Haili's

FIND IT: Auahi St. between Ward Ave. and Kamakee St., Honolulu, Hawaii

There was a time when the waterfront at the southern tip of Honolulu was packed stern to stern with fishing boats, docked to unload their haul just after sunrise, then heading back out to sea by sunset. Their customers were wholesalers, restaurateurs, and families with many mouths to feed, and among those lined up to negotiate prices on skipjack tuna and squid was Peter Haili. In the late 1940s he got to the docks before the sun did, loading the day's buy onto a rickety cart and wheeling it a few hundred feet to his modest fish store, one of a handful of businesses there in the Kaka'ako area. Peter sold the fish whole and filleted, diced up tuna for poke, and turned the scraps—the head, bellies, and innards—into palu, which sport fishermen used as bait. Gradually Peter's wife, Rachel Ching Haili, set out nibbles of her home-style cooking for customers. There were maroon-colored strips of jerkylike aku, salted and air-dried tuna. Neat little bundles of pork shoulder and butterfish were wrapped in taro tops and ti leaves, steamed to perfection, and called laulau. Ground taro root was cooked down into poi, a purplish-gray pudding eaten alongside meals throughout the island for centuries. And like many Hawaiians with Asian roots, Rachel channeled her Chinese ancestry to make the mother of all Asiawaiian comfort foods: chicken long rice, a tangle of clear noodles and gingery chicken tossed in the bird's rich cooking broth. That little counter was soon overflowing, and somewhere along the way Peter's fish shop became Haili's Hawaiian Foods.

According to the Haili girls—there are five: Rachel, Donna, Sandra, Roberta, and Lorraine, all in their sixties and seventies—their parents officially started the business in 1950, a couple of years after Peter began his nameless fish operation. The girls helped out as the business grew, forming an assembly line in the garage to wrap laulau, scampering up the coconut trees in the yard to gather supplies for pudding, but standing out of the way when their father filled the imu with hot lava rocks, the underground oven doing its job to gently smolder kalua pig. Haili's became an institution for Hawaiian culinary traditions that fell to the wayside as time-consuming preparations were no longer a priority.

As the fishing industry began to dry up and downtown commercialized, the look and feel of Kaka'ako changed, but Haili's didn't. The little store plugged on, catering backyard luaus and finding a bit of extra money from a lunch wagon Rachel ran at Kapiolani Community College in the 1970s, which she eventually sold to focus on being a grandmother. After both she and Peter passed away, the children's commitment to the business was stron-

(SIDE DISH)

There's not very much of interest in the area just north of Honolulu airport, just a few budget hotels, generic office buildings, and the occasional fanny pack–clad tourist wandering around complaining that he should have sprung for a place on the beach. But that's exactly why people get so excited to discover the **Jawaiian** lunch truck (669 Ahua St.), usually stumbled upon accidentally by visitors lured by the rhythmic reggae beats and the smoky ➡

ger than ever, but times had changed. Kaka'ako was now the Ward Center area, named for a sprawling development of chain stores and restaurants. The adjacent Ala Moana Center had opened in the late 1950s as an open-air marketplace for fishermen to do business, but by the late '90s, the market stalls were long gone and small retailers had been gobbled up by designer chains like Prada and Louis Vuitton. Clearly there was money to be made in this pocket, and a little store like Haili's just didn't fit in anymore. In 2008 the family was told that the lease they had held for fifty-nine years would not be renewed, as the behemoth Japanese supermarket Marukai Corporation would be taking over the entire block. "Originally the Ward family owned all of this area, and they were a very humble family," says Donna Haili, the oldest of the sisters at seventy-three. "They wanted the local people to have something of their own, but this is general growth now. So the local families get pushed out."

The sisters wanted to stay connected to the area, but rents were astronomical. Based on the memory of their mother's little blue lunch wagon of the '70s, they acquired a lunch wagon, gave it a colorful decal wrap, and in summer of 2009 they parked it just across from a megaplex movie theater, in the shadow of a Buca di Beppo. Undaunted, the Hailis turned their little strip of sod into a tranquil oasis, complete with tables and chairs, traditional music, and a few tiki torches for spirit. Most of the classics the store sold for decades are now served out of the truck, best sampled via the Big Kahuna plate lunch, an assortment of kalua pig, laulau, chicken long rice, tuna poke, lomi salmon, poi, and haupia, or coconut pudding. For its first few months the lunch wagon was the Haili's only outlet, but eventually they also secured a small storefront in the Kapahulu neighborhood. "The lunch truck has been a transition for us, a way of letting our costumers know that we are still here," Donna says. "We may be on a smaller scale, but we're not going out entirely."

scent of jerk chicken. Jamaican-born Cassie Simmonds is in his sixties but looks like he's in his thirties, and the activity that keeps him young happens behind a beaded Marley curtain that separates the customers from what's cooking: spoon-tender pork shoulder soaking up curried coconut milk, flaky snapper swimming in tart *escovitch* sauce of vinegared onions and peppers, and, of course, that jerk chicken, which Cassie marinates overnight and grills behind his truck on a charcoal-fired smoker. He spent nearly thirty years in Miami, cooking at a range of restaurants before finally making it to Hawaii, but he talks about Jamaica with such love that it seems he never left. Still, when he's in the island zone, bobbing to the music, stepping out of the truck to hand off homemade lime ginger beer to customers while checking on his fiery chicken, it's clear that he couldn't have picked a better name for his current lot in life. ◉

Haili's Ahi Tuna Poke Serves 8

2 pounds sashimi-grade ahi tuna, cut into bite-size cubes

1/2 cup soy sauce

1 tablespoon sesame oil

1 fresh chile, seeded and minced

1/2 cup minced green onions

1/2 cup slivered Maui onion

1 1/2 teaspoons minced fresh ginger

Combine all the ingredients in a large bowl and stir to combine. Cover and refrigerate for an hour before serving in individual bowls with spoons. The poke can be stored in the refrigerator for up to 2 days.

PACIFIC NORTHWEST

CZECH OUT CZECH FOOD

When Portland is your neighbor, the food cart shadow looms large. Although at one time Seattle was almost neck and neck with Portland in mobile food vendors, the land that gave birth to grunge and coffee culture moved much of its dining and drinking indoors, safe from the weather that earned this town the nickname "Rain City." The infamously drizzly days might have chased a few carts off the streets, but most Seattleites point to tightened regulations in the late 1990s as the noose that strangled the street food scene. Up until then, espresso carts were as much a part of Seattle as Nirvana and the Generation X slackers made famous in Cameron Crowe's *Singles*. More than a dozen cart manufacturers were based in the area throughout the 1980s, fulfilling the demand from local upstarts like Seattle's Best Coffee (an indie way back when, but now owned by Starbucks), which ran thirteen coffee carts during that turbo-charged era, only to close them one by one as the regulations on sidewalk vending shifted.

Today, of the three hundred licensed mobile food vendors in King County, only thirty-four have permits from the Seattle Department of Transportation to operate in the city of Seattle, and the Health Department only permits them to sell coffee or hot dogs. A handful of newer food trucks and trailers, like Skillet, Marination Mobile, and Halláva Fafafel, operate by sticking to private property, just so they don't have to secure right-of-way permits from the Department of Transportation. Larry Smith, compli-

ance officer for the Department of Public Health, admits that "in the past, the city of Seattle did put restrictions on street use, and to accomplish a vibrant street food scene these need to be changed."

Luckily, there are a few people in the city government who are intent on seeing things change; they don't just want to bring back those espresso carts synonymous with Seattle, but they're determined to diversify beyond coffee to get the city up to speed with its progressive neighbor to the south. Gary Johnson of the city's Department of Planning and Development is heading up a project called Vibrant Street Food, and at the time this book went to press he was preparing legislation that would do three things: lift restrictions to allow all types of food to be served from carts; eliminate the need for a vendor to get permission from business owners in the area in order to operate on the sidewalk; and designate official vending zones where food trucks can park and do business. "It's not a done deal until our council approves, and we're getting significant pushback as the initiative is starting to feel more real to people," Johnson says. "But street food vending adds an element of interest and color that attracts people." And if Johnson gets his way, Seattle will get that element back.

Skillet

KEEP UP WITH IT: www.skilletstreetfood.com

Friday night moviegoers at Seattle's Thornton Place Cinema skip the popcorn and head for the parking lot instead. There, clusters of diners gather to compare bites of hand-formed gnocchi tossed with Oregon corn and hunks of sage-perfumed pancetta, and debate a movie's merit over swigs of minty cantaloupe lemonade. This isn't an elevated take on tailgating; the food is being cooked to order inside a gleaming silver 1962 Airstream trailer adorned with a flying cast-iron pan and a single word: SKILLET. This roving restaurant is the starting point of the line that snakes through the movie theater parking lot this Friday night, but it's up to chef Joshua Henderson where diners will be able to catch it tomorrow.

Henderson's resume is not unlike that of any hot, young chef of the week: he bounced around in kitchens while his friends went to college, figured out cooking was his calling and set out for the Culinary Institute of America. He worked his way through kitchen stations of respected restaurants, rose to head chef of the Avalon in Beverly Hills, and was lured away by a gig as a private chef, cooking meals out of an RV for photographers needing sustenance while snapping *Vogue* magazine covers and fancy car ads.

The next chapter in the evolution of an established chef might be to open his own restaurant, but Henderson left L.A. and moved back to his hometown of Seattle, where he found a mid-century Airstream trailer on Craigslist. He spent six months rigging it with a twenty-four-inch grill, a deep fryer, a fridge, and enough hand sinks and hot water to pass a health inspection. And after he passed, he found a place to park his Airstream and opened for business.

Seattle's street-use regulations say that a mobile eatery can operate on private property with no hassle. So, since launching in January 2008, Henderson has simply found businesses that want more business. It didn't take long for word to spread that this wasn't your average taco truck (a menu that includes a sandwich of fennel-roasted pork shoulder with lemon aioli and charred onions will do that). As Henderson puts it, "We're not street food. We're more like a restaurant that serves food on the street, trying to stretch the shortsighted idea that street food has to be a two-dollar taco."

Skillet charges around ten bucks for rotating specials, garnering grumbles from some street food fans used to those two-buck tacos, but Henderson holds himself to the same standards as any respectable chef cooking modern American food, creating seasonal dishes for a menu that changes every few weeks. The one signature customers won't release from their death grip is his burger, scrawled on the chalkboard menu as, simply, "The Burger." This isn't just some simple patty on a bun. Oregon grass-fed ground beef is formed into a hefty round, grilled to a bright-pink medium-rare, then stacked on a brioche bun with arugula and Cambozola, a soft-ripened triple-cream Gorgonzola cheese. Getting the burger recipe from Henderson was no trouble, but he clammed up when asked for the burger's pièce de résistance: bacon jam. Now, you can buy a jar of Skillet's bacon jam from the truck or have it shipped to you via the website, or you can accept that the approximation given here is close enough and just make it yourself. In fact, the renegade in Henderson would probably respect you more if you did.

"The Burger" Serves 4

1¼ pounds ground beef (preferably organic)

Sea salt

½ cup Bacon Jam (see below)

4 brioche buns, split and toasted

8 slices Cambozola or other soft blue cheese (about 1 ounce each)

1 cup torn arugula leaves

Prepare a grill for direct cooking over medium-high heat.

Form the ground beef into 4 equal patties and season generously with the salt. Grill the burgers, turning once, for about 3 to 5 minutes per side for medium-rare.

While the burgers are cooking, spread the bacon jam onto the toasted buns.

Transfer the burgers to the buns and then top each with 2 slices of the Cambozola and about ¼ cup of the arugula. Serve at once.

Bacon Jam Makes 1 cup

2 pounds good-quality bacon, diced

1 small yellow onion, diced

2 tablespoons balsamic vinegar

2 teaspoons brown sugar

1 teaspoon chipotle chile powder

1 teaspoon allspice

1 teaspoon freshly ground black pepper

½ teaspoon salt

Place the bacon pieces in a large sauté pan or cast-iron skillet over medium-low heat. (You're cooking the bacon over lower heat than normal to render out as much lard as possible without browning it.)

While the bacon is still rendering, spoon about 1 tablespoon of the bacon fat into a separate sauté pan and add the onion. Cook over medium heat for about 15 minutes, stirring often and deglazing the pan occasionally by adding just a bit of water while scraping the caramelized bits from the pan with a spatula or wooden spoon. Once the onions are a deep brown, add the balsamic vinegar, brown sugar, chile powder, allspice, pepper, and salt and cook for 2 minutes more.

Add the onion mixture to the pan with the bacon, turn the heat to low, and continue to cook, stirring occasionally, until most of the moisture has been absorbed (Josh says he cooks his for 6 hours).

Remove the mixture from the heat, spoon into a jar with a tight-fitting lid, and place in the refrigerator overnight or until the mixture has set to a jamlike consistency. Store in the fridge for up to 2 or 3 weeks (longer if left unopened). Use as you would any condiment, as a topping for sandwiches, or slathered liberally on burgers.

Maximus/Minimus

FIND IT: **2nd Ave. and Pike St., Seattle, Washington**
KEEP UP WITH IT: **www.maximus-minimus.com**

You can't miss it: it's the giant metal pig parked on a busy corner in down-town Seattle. Even in the shadow of Pike Place, the oldest farmers' market in America and Seattle's number-one tourist destination, the colossal oinker that is Maximus/Minimus is impossible to overlook. And that was precisely the point when Kurt Beecher Dammeier parked it there in the spring of 2009.

The fact that this swine-shaped food truck exists at all is thanks to an adversion to golf. Born into a wealthy family whose successful print-ing business was worth $85 million when he sold his stake in 1998, Kurt Beecher Dammeier could easily have retired at thirty-eight. "I couldn't play golf the rest of my life. I was just not at all ready to be done," he says. "So I got to go out to a second career where making money wasn't the main objective, where I didn't fall into it but I had to pick it."

And so he picked food. Soon after he got out of the family business, he set up his own company, Sugar Mountain Capital LLC (yes, named for the Neil Young song), became the largest shareholder in Pyramid Brewer-ies, and snatched up a Seattle mini chain of gourmet takeout shops called Pasta & Co. In 2003, he opened Beecher's Handmade Cheese in Pike Place Market, an artisan cheese company that produces half a million pounds of cheese a year and has scored awards from just about every association that gives them. (The heat-and-eat mac and cheese is so popular that Kurt was asked to prepare it with the Grand Dame herself on *The Martha Stewart Show* in 2008.)

And in the midst of the breweries, the gourmet takeout, and the cheese, Kurt managed to open a restaurant, Bennett's Pure Food Bistro in Washington's wealthiest town of Mercer Island. A cookbook followed, which the self-described "creative director and I guess chef" worked on from the test kitchen at Sugar Mountain's downtown office. It's an impres-sive command center, a company of 150 jeans-clad employees who greet Kurt with reverence reserved for *Mad Men*'s Don Draper. When Kurt's not popping into marketing meetings or fielding calls on new shipping options for cheese, he's tinkering around in the gleaming test kitchen. "Oftentimes if I'm bored or have something I want to work on, I'll cook lunch for my staff," he says. "So I did this braised pork topped with braised onions and this sauce I was making for Bennett's, kinda spicy with beer, peppers, fruit juices. One day someone said, 'Man I wish there was a place close by that sold this because I'd like to eat this three times a week.' I said, 'So would

I,' and I got to thinking, 'Wait a minute, we're a restaurant company. We could do that.'"

The idea came right around the time the recession hit, so to keep prices low and suit the casual nature of a pulled-pork sandwich, Kurt, in an "aha!" moment, decided that a mobile eatery, with its low overhead, was the way to go. And since he's never been one for moderation, the brazen businessman enlisted a local industrial designer, Colin Reedy, to turn an Alaskan hot dog truck into a giant pig. Using fiberglass and aluminum, Colin concocted a 34 by 14-foot gleaming porker with a windshield for eyes, wheels for hooves, and an awning that pops up off the right side of its belly to serve as the order window. Internally, the pig houses a kitchen much like you'd see in a small restaurant, with a double fryer, a couple of heat lamps, a griddle, a four-burner stove, a fridge/freezer combo, a long prep counter, and a three-compartment sink. It's manned by a couple of fresh-faced kids executing Kurt's vision, slapping together pulled pork sandwiches for downtown workers grabbing a quick lunch. The name, Maximus/Minimus, was the jumping-off point for a menu Kurt describes as "yin and yang," in which the basic braised and pulled pork comes spicy, i.e., "Maximus," or somewhat sweet, with a Minimus sauce tamed by tamarind, molasses, and honey. The theme continues: pulled pork's best partner, vinegary slaw, is also offered two ways, the Maximus, with the bite of radish and the smoky heat of chipotle, and the Minimus, sweetened by honey mustard, dried cranberries, and fresh mint. Bracingly sharp ginger lemonade is dubbed the Maximus of drinks, while the sweetly tart hibiscus punch bears the title of Minimus. Chips, however, are equal opportunity, and perhaps the best thing on the menu: a crispy medley of sliced beets, potatoes, thin rounds of carrot, fresh green beans, and whole jalapeños, gutted of their seeds. Pulled hot from the fryer's rice bran oil, the veggie chips are sprinkled liberally with a Maximus/Minimus spice blend that is, of course, on its way to being packaged and sold at a store near you.

Lunch crowds are steady, but the businessman in Kurt believes the whimsy of eating in the elements, standing next to a massive conversation starter or not, will wear thin come cold weather. And so the pig goes into hibernation from November through March, coming out for the occasional catering gig or to feed hungry families at the Mercer Island football field where Kurt coaches his kid's team. It returns to a parking lot less than a block from Sugar Mountain headquarters in spring, where Kurt and his employees make good on their promise to eat those pulled-pork sandwiches three times a week. "We do okay, but in terms of success, I can say it's been successful in getting a lot of free lunches to my employees," he laughs. "But we still have a long ways to go, figuring out how to turn this pig into a business."

Maximus/Minimus Pulled Pork Serves 6 to 8

3¹/2 pounds pork shoulder

1 cup firmly packed brown sugar

¹/4 cup dried oregano

¹/2 cup chili powder

2 tablespoons garlic powder

1 tablespoon cayenne pepper

4¹/2 tablespoons kosher salt

Prepared barbecue sauce, for serving

6 to 8 sandwich buns, toasted

Trim the fat from the pork, leaving a ¹/2-inch fat cap.

In a small bowl, combine the brown sugar, oregano, chili powder, garlic powder, cayenne pepper, and salt. Rub the entire roast with the mixture, massaging it into the meat. Cover and refrigerate overnight.

Prepare a charcoal or gas grill for direct cooking over high heat. Preheat the oven to 325°F.

When the grill is as hot as possible, place the roast in the center. If you are using a charcoal grill, place the roast on the grill directly over the white-hot coals. Cook each side of the roast just until it is well browned but not burned, moving the meat to a new spot on the grill each time you turn it, 10 to 15 minutes total.

Remove the roast from the grill and place in a large Dutch oven or heavy pot. Cover and place it in the oven. Cook until the pork pulls apart easily with a fork, about 3 hours.

Break the meat into small chunks using two forks. Mix with your favorite barbecue sauce and divide the pork among the sandwich buns.

Halláva Falafel

FIND IT: 5825 Airport Way S, Seattle, Washington
KEEP UP WITH IT: www.myspace.com/hallava

On a ragged industrial stretch of Seattle's Georgetown neighborhood, a simple signboard along the side of the road demands "EAT," scrawled just above a gnarly-horned black ram and a small arrow. That arrow points to an adjacent lot, to a sun-yellow truck sporting that same ram and the words "Halláva Falafel." The gravel lot holds a motley lunchtime crew of clean-cut airplane techs from nearby Boeing Field, dusty laborers on break from surrounding factories, a few burly members of the Magic Wheels Motorcycle Club next door, and a handful of hipsters coming and going along this small stretch of salvation, which includes a café, a vintage shop, and dive bars with names like Nine Pound Hammer. Rick Baker is in the thick of it all, a one-man show taking and filling orders, working smoothly and calmly, nodding his head to the Danzig song blasting from a small radio inside the truck. The metal anthem "Mother" screams out its chorus of "Muhhhthurrr/Tell your children not to walk my way." Scruffy, tattooed, and generally stubborn about everything from the food he serves to how fast he serves it, Rick has earned the nickname Beet Nazi for good reason. "You're not allowed to *not* have beets," he says. "That's the way I make it. The falafel comes with fucking beets, a Russian beet relish, and I'm going to do a new menu that says that clearly so these people don't think the toppings are optional. Fuck that."

He's dead serious. The man is passionate about the sandwich he's created, from the salted cucumbers, another required topping ("They're Armenian and they're wild, which is a totally different thing than some regular old cucumber"), to the freshly fried falafel ("I don't like fava beans or the color they turn falafel, so I use garbanzo, but the key is a ton of fresh parsley when you're grinding the beans"). The result is a memorable explosion of flavors, textures, and temperatures, the warm falafel, cool toppings, and cumin-heavy spice blend combining with perfect synergy.

Reversing the Burger King motto and making it *his* way is Rick's method of quality control. "Let's say you heard about this sandwich, then you come here and tell me how to make it without all the stuff on it . . . it will be a mediocre sandwich. Not happening," he says. "Once they've had it the right way, I might allow them to modify it, but nobody does. Probably 99.9 percent of people eat it and like it and come back. One guy said it was Americanized, but he thinks falafel is microwaved balls and tahini and tomatoes and shit. He doesn't know the possibilities."

But Rick does. Originally from Tacoma, a blue-collar city about a half hour southwest of Seattle, he wound up in Russia after a string of events unraveled from a trip his father, a photography teacher, took there with a group of students. Pops returned with a sort of foreign exchange student, Yuri. But the trouble was, Yuri spoke little English and the Bakers spoke no Russian. Rick decided he wanted to "get in his head and know what he was thinking," so he learned Russian, which he found easy, comfortable even. So comfortable that he soon decided he wanted to become an interpreter, so off to Moscow State Linguistic University he went. Shawarma shops were as common as hot Russian girls, and Rick was attracted to both. In time, it was his attraction to interpreting that waned, as he decided it was "not very fun. You're just a conduit. It's not like you're someone's advocate, looking out for them. You're just repeating what the other person says, but in another language."

Eventually he wound up in Israel, where he went "just to live, to check it out." Again, falafel and shawarma became part of his daily diet, and he learned to discern the good from the really good. Time passed, Rick grew restless, and he found himself back in Washington, working at a scooter shop in Seattle. He came across an ad for a Bajaj, a three-wheeled scooter from India, sort of a motorized rickshaw used to haul goods and people, and he instantly decided he wanted to build a business around it, mainly because "it's the coolest thing ever." Based on his opinion that Seattle was hurting for some good falafel, he put together a plan for his falafel Bajaj biz and submitted it to the city health department. Turns out, only coffee and hot dogs are permitted on carts that aren't covered. So Rick shifted his focus to a former DHL delivery truck, borrowed some money from a friend to buy it, then maxed out his credit cards for the supplies to turn it into the mobile kitchen it is today, complete with a deep fryer for falafel, a rotating rotisserie spit for shawarma, an oven for warming the pita he sources from a Middle Eastern bakery, and a prep counter where he concocts sharp *tzatziki* (yogurt sauce), a tomato-zucchini spread, a mayo-thick curry sauce for the shawarma, and, of course, those fucking beets.

His lunch crowd is so good that most of the year he's only open from about 11 a.m. until he's out of falafel, typically around 2 p.m. He sells close to eighty sandwiches a day, making a dent in paying back the $30,000 investment that still makes him wince to say aloud. The falafel sandwich, loaded up as it is with toppings, and the shawarma, a two-hander filled with a full day's supply of spit-roasted lamb-beef blend, both go for $6.50, the top end of what Rick feels he can charge in good conscience. "I can't really charge more. . . . I mean, the name of the truck is Halláva, which is a Russian word that basically means 'unexpected deal,' something you say when you go to a party and there's a bunch of free food, or when you buy one and get one free."

He's just sold his last falafel of the day, so he pauses to tell a girl who looks like she walked ten miles to get here, "Sorry, all out." She has the look of Dorothy when, after a long journey to Oz, she discovers that the wizard has no power at all. "Call me next time you're on your way and I'll save one for you," Rick says as the dejected girl walks away. After this brief demonstration of his softer side, he returns to the conversation, not missing a beat. "Yeah, so Halláva, pronounced khal-AH-vah, with the accent on the second 'a,' but the problem is that a lot of people don't understand linguistics and see the stress mark," he says, making an accent in the air for emphasis. "So people think it's Helluva, and it drives me crazy, because that would be such a stupid name. I mean, it is a helluva good sandwich, but give me a fucking break."

Rick's F@*#ing Russian-style Beet Salad
Serves 6 to 8 as a side dish

You can use this as a condiment on sandwiches, or, if you're serving it as a side salad, you could add 3/4 cup chopped walnuts, 3/4 cup Russian-style farmer's cheese (similar to cheese curds), or 3/4 cup chopped prunes.

2 or 3 fist-size beets (about 2 pounds total)	2 teaspoons freshly ground black pepper
6 to 10 cloves garlic, minced	2 tablespoons sour cream

Place the beets in a large stockpot, add enough water to cover them by a couple of inches, and bring the water to a boil over high heat. Once it's boiling, let it continue to boil until a fork slides into the beets with little resistance, about 30 minutes. Remove the beets from the water and rinse with cold water. Once they're cool enough to handle, lop off the ends and peel them. Next, shred them (a food processor makes quick work of them).

In a bowl, stir together the shredded beets with garlic to taste and the black pepper. Stir in enough sour cream to turn the salad a nice violet color, but not pink. (If it's pink you may have overcooked the beets, not drained them well enough, or used too much sour cream.) Serve as a side salad or use as a condiment.

Marination Mobile

KEEP UP WITH IT: www.marinationmobile.com

"Weather forecasters have the easiest job in Seattle. Nine months out of the year you're hanging out surfing the web, then, 'Oh, it's my turn to speak? Cloudy with a chance of showers!' And that's pretty much it."

That's Kamala Saxton, and she's not exaggerating. Weather history will tell you that it rains in Seattle more than 50 percent of the time, meaning this is not the kind of city that brings to mind hopping patios and picnics in the park. Still, Kamala opened a Korean-Hawaiian food truck in Seattle during the summer of 2009, with a plan to stay open twelve months out of the year with nothing more than an awning over the order window to shelter customers. "I didn't say I was the smartest person in the world," Kamala laughs. "But I'm hedging my bet on the fact that Seattleites aren't chickens. I'm hedging my bet on my community and their toughness."

A look at the line gathering under the Safeco Field pedestrian walkway before a Mariners game on a drizzly Thursday night could be proof of that toughness, or it could just be a testament to the Aloha sliders and kimchi fried rice bowls this massive, gleaming truck (nicknamed "Big Blue") has quickly become known for. Marination Mobile's menu is a direct descendent of Kamala, who is part Korean and part Hawaiian. But manning the grill to execute Kamala's creations is business partner Roz Edison, who adds to the multicultural mashup as a Chinese-Filipino born in Greece and raised by a Japanese mother. The duo met at Boston's prestigious Match Charter Public School, where Roz was teaching after earning an education and business degree from Harvard and Kamala was consulting after wrapping up business school at Silicon Valley's Menlo College. After Boston, both moved around a bit but eventually landed in Seattle. And how did two business smarties end up running a food truck? "I lost everything in the market," Kamala says. "I had $8 left and had to find some place that would accept a postdated check for lunch. Ultimately I felt so out of control, so far removed from my money that people on Wall Street were making poor decisions with, so I became my own hedge fund manager, hedging my bets on this city and our work ethic."

She presented the idea to Roz, who went to work on financial spreadsheets, loan applications, and truck sourcing while Kamala went to work on recipes, bringing in a few Seattle cooks for support. The Aloha sliders she came up with are derived from Hawaiian-style kalua pork, but given the impracticalities of going legit and burying a pig in a hole lined with

Craving Cuban? Pedrito Vargas was too, so he christened a converted delivery truck into **Paladar Cubano** (8953 Aurora Ave., North; www.pedritovargas .com/paladarcubano.html) and started serving toasted pork-packed sandwiches, *tostones* (fried green plantains), and crispy yucca in Seattle's Greenwood neighborhood. Pedrito hands over the goods with a signature "Thank you, my friend," but you can repay the kindness by checking out his Latin timba band, Grupo Ashé, at their next gig around town. ◉

banana leaves and filled with lava rock, the pork shoulders are wood-smoked in a commissary kitchen (a home base required for all Seattle food trucks). After a lengthy smoke, the tender meat makes its way onto the truck, where it's piled onto Hawaiian sweet rolls (think egg bun with added sugar) along with a scoop of signature Asian-leaning slaw: cabbage and carrots hot-wired with Sriracha, lime juice, sesame seeds, and cilantro.

Korea enters the picture via the tacos. *Bulgogi*-style beef short ribs and *kalbi*-style pork get classic ginger-soy marinades, with a bit more heat via red chile paste for the *kalbi*. The meats share grill space with ginger-miso chicken, and all three get tucked into soft corn tortillas and topped with that crunchy, tangy slaw. Almost everything that doesn't get slaw is served with kimchi, that funky, flavorful, fermented Korean cabbage concoction of endless variation. "Every Korean church has the go-to Korean elders, typically women, who make kimchi, and each church always claims to make the best," Kamala says. "I tracked down my favorite kimchi to a church in the Seattle area, but after long deliberation the elders decided the volume of kimchi that we go through was too much for them to make. But they sent me to a distributor in Tacoma that's Korean church-lady approved!"

After getting a blessing any kimchi would be proud of, the sour-spicy stuff has been put to good use, incorporated into the menu as a quesadilla, sandwiched between tortillas hugging tight to gooey jack and cheddar laced with *kochujang* (red pepper paste). It's also the star of a fried rice bowl so addictive it could be classified as a narcotic. "We take the kimchi, dry it out, then we create our own kimchi paste from it," Kamala explains. "So when it's ordered, the kimchi paste is folded into cooked rice as it's seared to create little crunchy bits. Then bits of fresh, not dried, kimchi are folded in, and it gets a beautiful fried egg on top, fresh-cut green onions, and nori (dried seaweed)."

As popular as the Korean-derived eats at Marination are, it's been Kamala's personal mission to turn Seattleites on to her homeland's most beloved shelf-stable staple: SPAM. Ever since the rectangular-shaped spiced pork product showed up on the island shores during World War II, Hawaiians have been gobbling it up like nothing you've ever seen—they're the reigning champ for SPAM consumption per capita in the United States. Kamala sells SPAM sliders, small hamburger-like patties of grilled SPAM on Hawaiian sweet rolls dressed with the signature slaw and a sauce known as "Nunya" (as in nun-ya business—the sauce is so popular that Kamala is looking into bottling and selling it, along with a couple of the meat marinades, so the recipe is top secret). But the SPAM creation closest to Kamala's heart is *musubi*, a mound of sushi rice topped with a slice of SPAM, all tied up into a compact little bundle with a ribbon of nori. Throughout Hawaii you'll find *musubi* wrapped mummy-tight in cellophane, sitting on counters of convenience stores just waiting for hungry school kids and surfers to grab one on the go. "SPAM is killing my people one *musubi* at a time," Kamala laughs. "I mean, clearly the stuff has mega-sodium, but man is it good! Seattleites just don't know what they're missing." If they can brave the weather to track down Marination, they'll catch up.

SPAM Sliders Makes 4 small sandwiches

At Marination they dress the SPAM sliders with their signature "nunya sauce" and slaw with a pickled ginger vinaigrette.

1 (12-ounce) can SPAM

¼ cup panko (Japanese bread crumbs)

1 egg

½ small onion, minced

Salt

1 teaspoon freshly ground black pepper

4 Hawaiian sweet rolls, split

Use the grinder attachment on a stand mixer to grind the beautifully pressed can of SPAM (if you don't have the grinder you can use the beater for this). Once SPAM is ground, add the panko, egg, onion, salt, and pepper then form them into patties. Place the SPAM patties on a flattop or in a sauté pan and sear until golden brown on each side. Serve each patty sandwiched in one of the rolls.

Bring up the topic of food trucks anywhere in the country and inevitably Portland is heralded as a Shangri-La. As the bull's-eye of the Pacific Northwest's progressive living movement, the city of a half a million has plenty of green spaces, bike lanes, public walkways, an admirable recycling program, restaurants supporting local farmers, hip bars, alternative strip clubs, and, last but not least, more food carts than they know what to do with. In other cities you might have a mix of trucks, carts, and trailers, but in Portland it's all about carts—nearly 500 of them, in fact, as of mid-2010. There are four different classifications to the little boxes on wheels or hitch carts you'll see on the streets. The majority are either "Class 3" or "Class 4," the only real difference being that Class 4 carts are permitted to cook meat, not exactly a requirement in a town so vegetarian-friendly that the phrase "vegan barbecue" isn't laughed at.

This liberal mecca becoming synonymous with street food was no accident. Encouraged and supported by the local powers that be, the number of food carts in Portland has hovered in the high three hundreds since the early 2000s. When 2009 saw a spike of nearly a hundred new carts hitting the streets, it was pretty clear that Portlanders considered this industry integral to their experience. So much so that when the Portland Plan launched in 2010, the twenty-five-year city plan included food carts among topics like economic development, historic resources, and sustainability.

Through surveys, community workshops, and public hearings with the Portland City Planning Commission, the organization committed to supporting and growing Portland's green-and-hip reputation.

In the past few years Portland's food carts have settled into spots alongside one another, joining forces to become a dining destination as opposed to splitting up throughout the city and decreasing their foot traffic. Environmental health supervisor Jon Kawaguchi points to the downtown parking lot at Southwest 5th and Stark as the first cluster of carts, with records showing Saigon To Go and King Burrito operating there in 1997. Brett Burmeister of the exhaustive blog www.FoodCartsPortland.com agrees, citing that intersection as one of the first to really grow from one or two carts to more than a dozen. "Downtown you've always had the taco carts, hot dog carts, the small push carts, and the Asian carts, but within the past six years it really took off," Burmeister says. "Now Portland has started to embrace these pods, where a private investor rents out spaces in his parking lot so that instead of having one or two of these carts on the edge, you have ten to fifteen all together, and in all sorts of different neighborhoods, not just downtown." Roger Goldingay is one of those investors. A self-described "real estate rehabilitator" for nearly thirty years, Goldingay bought a plot of land on the corner of North Mississippi and Skidmore a few years ago, tore down the dilapidated building sitting on the property, paved it with permeable asphalt, added tables and chairs, and invited ten food carts to the pod he dubbed Mississippi Marketplace. "I was looking at the food cart scene in Portland, which isn't always user-friendly because you buy food and you stand on the sidewalk where people jostle you. There's no place to get out of the weather, no restroom facilities where you could wash your hands," Goldingay says. "I just thought the whole scene was not as nice as it could be, so I wanted to develop a community gathering place, make a positive impact, and draw people to the neighborhood. And people seem to have really taken to it. We've got food carts, beer from the adjacent bar on the lot, the outdoors. This . . . is totally Portland right here."

Potato Champion

FIND IT: SE 12th Ave. and Hawthorne Blvd., Portland, Oregon
KEEP UP WITH IT: www.potatochampion.com

Must be last call. Every few minutes another crew of buzzed hipsters staggers into the Portland food truck "pod" known affectionately as Cartopia, claiming a spot at a picnic table after making the rounds to the seven mobile eateries ringing the lot. Raven-haired roller derby girls weave through the crowd on skates, earning the attention of a gang of bike messenger types, the kind that wear heavy chain-link locks as belts and leave their pant legs rolled up long after they've hopped off their fixed-gear bikes. Scoping goes hand in hand with eating here, and for the under-forty set that prefers whiskey to wine, Johnny Cash to Coldplay, and DIY to ING, there's no better place for either.

Among this hourly wage crowd of waitresses, thrift store cashiers, and record shop stockers, local musicians and artists blend in seamlessly. The mop-topped drummer for the electro-rock trio Reporter seems to know at least half of the hundred or so in this weekend-night crowd, but not just because of the band's growing popularity. Mike McKinnon is the fry guy, the owner of the Potato Champion trailer, and the driving force behind turning a parking lot on Portland's Southeast Side into the most happening hotspot in the city's rowdy late-night scene.

"Ever since I spent some time in Holland and Belgium in 2001, I['ve been] obsessed with late-night *frites* places," Mike says, keeping one eye on his growing line and one on the Amélie lookalike manning his fryer. "I always bitched about it with my friends, 'Why doesn't Portland have a fry place?' It's stupid, because there are so many bars, so we obviously really needed a fry place."

After about seven years of lamenting, Mike put up and shut up. He set about the first order of business: coining the name "Potato Champion" in honor of Antoine-Augustin Parmentier, an eighteenth-century French chemist who managed to convince his countrymen that potatoes didn't cause leprosy, as was widely believed, and that the spuds should be eaten instead of just tossed to hogs. With a name like that, there was no turning back; Mike found a little trailer on Craigslist and spent his days fixing it up into a frymobile and his nights perfecting the Belgian-style *frites* that kick-started his obsession. With only the lingering taste from his travels and a bit of pizzeria experience, he went through months of trial and error before arriving at the perfect result. Russets are his go-to potato ("they don't brown up too much and they have the right sugar/starch content"),

and he only fries in rice bran oil ("high smoke point, awesome flavor, a little expensive but lasts longer"). And in true Belgian *frites* fashion, the fries get a double-dip—first a quick blanch in the fryer and then a minimum twenty-minute rest, followed by a longer fry just before serving. A scoop of the perfectly crisp, golden-brown beauties overflows from a paper cone, with a small cup of dipping sauce alongside. The nine different condiments are one part nod to Belgian tradition (Dutch mayo, peanut sauce) and two parts experiments in Portlanders' sense of adventure (tarragon-anchovy mayo, rosemary-truffle ketchup). Mike has a seemingly endless supply of creative sauces up his sleeve, but the fourteen by sixteen-foot trailer has barely enough room to hold the necessities as it is. On a Friday and Saturday night combined, about a thousand pounds of potatoes are sold out of that little truck, and thanks to Mike's hugely popular addition of the Canadian classic poutine to the menu, those fries have to make room for electric tabletop warmers that hold ten quarts of free-range chicken gravy and ten quarts of meat-free gravy (he can't ignore Portland's hefty vegetarian population). A handful of fries topped with a ladle of gravy and a sprinkling of cheese curds can undo just about any damage done during the night's double-fisted drinking adventures, or at least help counter tomorrow's revenge.

Catering to the night owls was always the business model of Cartopia's oldest food truck, El Brasero, a friendly family-owned trailer that deals in Mexican standards, but when Mike rolled into the lot with Potato Champion in spring of 2008 he set up a tented eating area, complete with heat lamps to combat Portland's cool and drizzly weather. Shortly after, Dustin Knox opened Perierra Creperie adjacent to Potato Champion and built about a dozen wooden picnic tables for the lot, which soon became home to a total of seven different food trucks, all banding together to stay open until at least three or four in the morning to lure the postbar crowd. Wood-fired pizza, N'awlins po' boys, steak burritos, sweet or savory fried pies, gourmet crepes, and even spaghetti bolognese are up for grabs, but if the size of Potato Champion's line is any indication, Portland's best drinkers are a lot like Belgium's.

Potato Champion Poutine Serves 4

FRIES

5 Russet potatoes

Rice bran oil, for frying

GRAVY

1 yellow onion, chopped

1 small shallot, minced

3 cloves garlic, minced

3 tablespoons balsamic vinegar

1 tablespoon freshly ground black pepper

$1/4$ cup unsalted butter

$1/4$ cup all-purpose flour

1 quart chicken stock

Salt

1 cup cheese curds or queso fresco

To make the fries, cut the potatoes into sticks about $3/8$ inch thick. Rinse with cold water to remove the excess starch, then pat dry with paper towels. Let them continue to dry while you heat enough rice bran oil to cover the fries in a large, heavy stockpot or tabletop fryer to 325°F. Carefully drop the fries into the pot and fry for 5 minutes. Remove using a wire basket or slotted spoon, transfer to a paper towel-lined plate, and let them sit at room temperature for 30 minutes.

To make the gravy, add the onion, shallot, garlic, vinegar, and pepper to a large stockpot and simmer, reducing until the onions are translucent, about 5 minutes.

While the mixture is reducing, make a roux by melting the butter over medium heat in a small sauté pan and whisking in the flour until completely dissolved and the roux takes on a pale golden color.

Add the stock to the onion and shallot mixture, bring to a boil, and then whisk in the roux. Reduce the heat to low and simmer for 30 minutes. Season with salt to taste.

For the second potato fry, bring the oil up to 375°F and fry again until lightly browned and crisp.

To assemble, douse the hot fries in warm gravy and top with the cheese curds.

(SIDE DISH)

In the pastry department of legendary Bay Area restaurant Chez Panisse, Jehnee Rains developed a crush on pristine fruits in their peak season. After transplanting to Portland, she fell in love again, only this time with a 1973 Airstream trailer parked behind a one-room A-frame restaurant called **Suzette Crêperie** (2921 NE Alberta St.). After taking over Suzette from the original owners in 2009, Jehnee got to work inside the Airstream-turned-kitchen and overhauled the menu, setting it to the seasons. With two crepe irons, one stand mixer, and limited storage space, batches are small and the product is fresh. Somehow Jehnee still finds the room to make multicomponent crepes that are more like composed desserts than the standard Nutella-filled jobs. Expect creations along the lines of this fall special—a lemon butter–filled crepe topped with sautéed apples, cider caramel, and a scoop of trailer-made crème fraîche ice cream. Order at the trailer, watch Jehnee at work, then take your eats inside to enjoy alongside a glass of wine or local beer. ◉

Nong's Khao Man Gai

FIND IT: SW 10th Ave. and Alder St., Portland, Oregon
KEEP UP WITH IT: www.khaomangai.com

They call Thailand "the land of smiles," which sounds great on the back of a tourism brochure. The slogan might be shtick, but not for Nong Poonsukwattana, a pint-sized twenty-nine-year-old who looks something like a squirrel storing nuts when she's grinning—which is most of the time. She's happy because her plan worked. Nong set out to "be kick-ass" at making one dish and one dish only, following in the footsteps of many street food vendors in her home country who do one thing and do it very well. Her thing is *khao man gai*, or chicken with rice. Sounds simple enough, right? Wrong.

The process of making *khao man gai* the right way is intense. Nong's way is beyond intense, partly because she's doing everything from prep to service in an eight by eight-foot cart, and partly because she's intent on being "kick-ass."

"I put the best that I can into this, use the best ingredients even though I have to go out of my way to get them every morning because I don't have the storage," Nong says. "I do this because this is me. This cart is everything I worked for, saved all my change for over the last six years since I've been in America."

Following a boy she married in Thailand who headed to Portland for college, Nong left her family home in Ratchaburi, a town about three hours from Bangkok known for its floating market of vendors in small boats. The marriage didn't work out; Nong tells a story that goes from hilarious to horrible in which her ex-husband decides he wants to be the first famous Thai rapper, "the Thai 50 Cent," but ends up having an affair with the MC he was working with. Nong divorced him but decided to stay in Portland, waitressing from 10 a.m. to 11 p.m. every day in Thai restaurants. "I didn't understand. I had pad Thai and said, 'This is not pad Thai.' I had yellow curry and said, 'This is not yellow curry,'" Nong says. "But I was FOB, fresh off the boat. So I had to listen to the Thai people already here in America, and I had to believe them that Americans won't understand or won't like the Thai food, and they didn't know where to find the ingredients anyway. Some even say if you make the food too spicy customers will sue you. But all of that changed when I went to Pok Pok."

Pok Pok is the brainchild of chef Andy Ricker, an American obsessed with Thai food who returned to Portland from travels in Asia intent on recreating the dishes he fell in love with. Pok Pok started as a small shack of sorts but has grown into a multiroom restaurant and a Portland destination; Ricker was even nominated for a 2010 James Beard Award for Best Chef: Northwest. "Andy wants to make the food he ate when he was in Thailand, and he believes that other Americans want to eat that too, so Pok Pok is a different reflection of Thai restaurants, from the other side," Nong says. "That's why they get all the media coverage, why they won *The Oregonian*'s Restaurant of the Year, and I thought, 'I can work in any of the kitchens I was in before, but I don't want to. I want to work at the best.'"

And so she did. Nong already had about ten grand saved with the idea of opening her own place, and she intended to work at Pok Pok for three months to pick up some pointers. She wound up staying for a year, until a kettle-corn cart pretty much dropped in her lap, and with the Pok Pok crew's blessing and connections, she converted the tiny wooden box into Nong's Khao Man Gai, opening in April of 2009. She knew she was limited by the size of her cart, so she did what many Bangkok street vendors do and focused on one dish, her favorite: *khao man gai*. Running through her mental Rolodex of her aunt's recipe, versions she'd had in Thailand, and information she found online, Nong "practiced, practiced, practiced" before selling her first dish. The result is a $6 lunch you'll never forget. Wrapped in a neat little origami-like bundle of white butcher paper, the chicken on rice is presented like a gift, with a small bowl of squash-studded chicken broth alongside for sipping in between bites. Nong starts with the chicken, trimming the excess bits and tossing them into a skillet to render the fat with banana leaves for aroma. Meanwhile, the whole chicken (small birds Nong gets from nearby Draper Valley Farms) is simmered with garlic, ginger, and more banana leaves for about thirty-five minutes, while the little bits of chicken fat that rise to the top are skimmed off and later mixed with sugar and salt for a rub that coats the chicken after it's cooked. And the fat rendered in the beginning of the process gets added to shallots, garlic, and ginger for a mix that Nong stirs into the rice while it's cooking, using the simmering broth from the chicken rather than water for the rice. (She says the rice is the hardest part, requiring constant attention and stirring to take on the right consistency.)

Seeing as how she makes only one dish, Nong is hesitant to give up the exact recipe her entire business depends on, but she will share the soup recipe, as well as break down what goes into the *nam jim*, the sauce people pour over the *khao man gai* as if their life depended on it. Fermented soybean paste, fresh ginger, garlic, pickled garlic, thin soy sauce, Thai vinegar, black sweet soy, and a simple syrup made from palm sugar and water. "But the key is everything in the sauce, the paste, the vinegar, even the soy, is the best quality. If you want to be kick-ass, you use the best to be the best."

(SIDE DISH)

Eggs, bacon, and toast will be breakfast of the past once you try the preferred eye-opener of Iraqi Jews. Called *sabich*, this breakfast wrap combines garlicky hummus, grilled eggplant, and hard-cooked egg in a pita, and the converted camper dubbed **Wolf & Bear's** (SE 20th Ave. and Morrison St.; www.myspace.com/wolfand bearskitchen) is the only place in Portland to find one. "Bear," or Jeremy Garb, grew up eating *sabich* in his native Israel, and these days, with the help of girlfriend Tanna TenHoopen Dolinsky (a.k.a. "Wolf"), he recreates the specialty with raw onions, potent mango pickles, fresh parsley, crunchy cucumbers, and a perfectly pliable pita. Add a few squirts of the bright green hot sauce known as *zhoug* and grab a cup of Fair Trade coffee for a Middle Eastern breakfast of champions–transplanted to Portland and best enjoyed on a creaky metal loveseat swing in a gravel lot. ◉

(SIDE DISH)

City regulations might stand between you and your beer truck dreams, but you can still enjoy a cold one with your street food. When Roger Goldingay built the lot known as **Mississippi Marketplace** (North Mississippi Ave. and Skidmore St.) in 2009, he made room for ten food carts and the German-style bar Prost. Aside from Bavarian-style beers (tough to find in a town that loves its hoppy microbrews), the real draw of this Teutonic pub is the spacious back deck and a flexible policy that allows you to raid adjacent food carts for Nuevo Mexico's sopaipillas or Ruby Dragon's veggie curry, then bring the haul back to Prost to wash it down with a proper *hefeweizen*. Now that's fusion. ◉

Nong's Winter Squash Soup   Serves 4 as a starter

4 white peppercorns, plus ¹/₂ teaspoon
    ground white pepper

3 sprigs fresh cilantro, chopped, plus
    8 cilantro leaves

1 cup chicken stock

2 cups water

4 cloves garlic, minced

2 cups peeled and diced winter squash

3 tablespoons thin Thai soy sauce
    (preferably Healthy Boy brand)

2 tablespoons dark Thai soy sauce

Using a mortar and pestle, crush the whole white peppercorns with the cilantro sprigs.

In a soup pot over medium-high heat, bring the chicken stock and water to a boil, then add the white pepper mixture, garlic, and squash.

Return the mixture to a boil and add the soy sauces. Cover and let cook until the squash is fork-tender, about 7 minutes.

Turn off the heat, garnish with the cilantro leaves and a sprinkle of white pepper, and serve.

Tabor

FIND IT: Stark St. just east of SW 5th St.
KEEP UP WITH IT: www.schnitzelwich.com

"You have to make sure you cross the river before the current sweeps you back to communism."

It's strange to hear these words coming from within a cheerful, candy apple–red food cart in one of Portland's busiest downtown street food spots. Karel Vitek, the man speaking, has crinkly eyes when he smiles, and as proof that he does that a lot, the creases seem permanent. But when he talks about his escape from communist Czechoslovakia, his eyes take on a detached thousand-yard stare. "Have you ever read 1984? That's the kind of feeling when you live in communism. You cannot leave, you cannot travel freely, education is unattainable. You . . . have to know somebody to get somewhere." He didn't know any somebodies, so in 1985 he escaped, choosing to move through Yugoslavia after determining that other routes were "virtual suicide. They . . . would shoot you immediately, or if they didn't shoot you, they would put you in jail for thirty years." And so he walked. And ran. And eventually, when getting to the Mura River that forms the border between Austria and Yugoslavia (now Slovenia), he swam. He arrived at the Austrian immigration office tired and hungry, but free, or at least close to it—he was sent to a camp where he and other escapees awaited sponsorship in the United States. He made a few friends, played chess, foraged for mushrooms in the nearby woods, and dreamt of what he was headed toward. After nine months, sponsorship came . . . from a Mormon family in Nebraska. "Was I bored!" Karel laughs. "I left them swiftly and went to San Diego, where I had friends from Czechoslovakia. There I was kind of a beach bum." Eventually, Karel found his way to Portland in the early 1990s, landing at Reed College. He sat in on classes, learning English and developing an interest in philosophy, which eventually led to a bachelor's degree from Portland State University. And what does a wannabe philosopher with plenty of stories to tell do next? Open a food cart, of course.

"For years friends told me I should open a restaurant. I said, 'Oh sure, sure, right,'" Karel recalls, rolling his eyes. "I met Monika, my wife, and we bought this cart in 2002. It was just sitting in our driveway. We'd wake up and look at it every day, like, 'Jesus, what do we do with this? What do we sell?'" He pauses, looks around, and lowers his voice. "I don't look down upon taco stands, but I wanted to do something more spectacular. . . . I wanted to bring Grandma's cooking to this little trailer. Nobody that knows

Waffles are nothing new in the world of food trucks, but when your waffle iron is powered by the sun, people tend to take notice. A joint venture of Portland Public Schools and the nonprofit energy education group SolTrekker, **Solar Waffle Works** (NE 23rd Ave. and Alberta St.) pulls more than half of the energy it uses from gleaming solar panels attached to the roof of its sea-blue trailer. Recent high school grads in the Community Transition Program take turns working the register, prepping waffle batter, and filling piping-hot waffles with whipped cream and toasted nuts, all the while gaining on-the-job experience and people skills intended to give them a leg up in the real world. The teens seem to appreciate the responsibility, and what's not to like when the perks include a free waffle each shift? ◉

this kind of food, it's time-consuming cooking, could believe it. Czechs would walk by and just go, 'This is impossible.'"

A nose that knows could probably sniff out Tabor from a block away. But even for those unfamiliar with this food, the aroma of potent garlic and smoky-sweet paprika are tough to miss. Depending on the day of the week, you might also catch a whiff of onions caramelizing, lacy potato pancakes frying in olive oil, or orange-scented beets simmering their way into borscht. But none of these have been photographed and blown up into a poster, the size of which is usually reserved for babes on Corvettes, and attached to the side of the tiny wood-paneled cart.

That honor is bestowed upon the "schnitzelwich," the crispy pork loin sandwich that earned national attention a few years after Karel opened Tabor in 2005. Slices of pork loin as thick as your thumb are marinated overnight in salt and vinegar, which tenderizes the meat, and plenty of garlic, which is just plain tasty. Karel dredges each loin in a mix of panko and dried ciabatta crumbs before pan-frying it to order. Monika slathers a ciabatta roll with both *ajvar*, a condiment of red bell peppers, eggplant, garlic, and chiles, and her signature spread made from horseradish, sour cream, and olive oil. Onions caramelized to near extinction and a leaf of romaine complete the package, so beloved that bumper stickers reading "Schnitzelwich for President" almost outnumbered Obama swag around election time.

As moving as the schnitzelwich is, it's technically a specialty of the Germans. The cooking that's truly aligned with Karel's DNA produces beefy, garlicky goulash ladled over puffy white dumplings. Occasionally, usually on Thursdays, it manifests in *halusky*, herbed noodle-like dumplings a German might call spaetzle. And every now and then, Tabor's shoebox-size kitchen turns out chicken paprikash, thighs simmered in a rusty-red paprika cream sauce until the meat falls apart with a gentle poke. As with many dishes handed down through generations, the recipe for Karel's paprikash didn't exist until I asked him to write it down. "If you are Czech, your grandma cooked different goulash, different paprikash, than other grandmas. Everything is custom-tailored to your street, your household," Karel says. "I grew up with *this* particular taste. Yes, I have looked in famous Czech cookbooks, but I would close the book and find the taste. I had the target all along."

Karel's Chicken Paprikash Serves 4

Ajvar is a red pepper spread found in some European and Middle Eastern grocery stores.

2 tablespoons vegetable oil

1 small yellow onion, diced

3 tablespoons unsalted butter

1 tablespoon Hungarian paprika

1¹/₂ cups plus 2 tablespoons water

¹/₂ teaspoon freshly ground black pepper

1 teaspoon salt

1 pound boneless, skinless chicken thighs, cut into 3-inch pieces

2 tablespoons all-purpose flour

¹/₄ cup heavy cream

¹/₄ cup sour cream

¹/₄ cup ajvar (optional)

Karel's Dumplings (see below), for serving

Heat 1 tablespoon of the oil over medium heat in a large sauté pan. Add the onion and cook, stirring every few minutes, until the onions are nice and brown and the oil has been absorbed. Add the butter and paprika, followed immediately by the 1¹/₂ cups water (paprika turns bitter when burned, so be sure to add the water quickly). Add the pepper and salt and turn the heat down to a low simmer.

Heat a large nonstick pan over high heat. Add the remaining 1 tablespoon oil and slowly place the chicken, one piece at a time, into the pan, being careful not to crowd (cook the chicken in batches if your pan isn't large enough so that the pieces doesn't overlap). Don't touch the chicken for 4 to 5 minutes, then turn each piece to allow the other side to brown. Once the pieces are brown, transfer them to the sauté pan holding the sauce and simmer for 10 minutes.

Meanwhile, in a small mixing bowl, combine the flour with the remaining 2 tablespoons water and whisk until smooth. Slowly add the flour mixture to the chicken mixture while gently stirring. Bring just to the boiling point, then turn off the heat. Gently stir in the cream, sour cream, and ajvar. Spoon over the dumplings and serve.

Drunks crave grilled cheese sandwiches, but drunks have been
known to burn things, namely
themselves. To the rescue is
The Grilled Cheese Grill (1027
NE Alberta St.; www.grilled
cheesegrill.com), a vintage Airstream that turns out a dozen
varieties of the kiddie classic and
stays open until 2:30 a.m. on
weekends to feed the need. And
to hammer home the nostalgia,
patrons take their meal onto a
rainbow-colored school bus to
eat from converted bus seats
and tables plastered with school
photos, characteristically taken at
the height of dorkdom. ◉

Karel's Dumplings   Serves 4 to 6

3¹/2 cups all-purpose flour, plus more as
   needed

1 teaspoon dry yeast

1 cup whole milk, at room temperature,
   plus more as needed

2 eggs, beaten

1 teaspoon salt

Mix 1 cup of the flour and the yeast together with a fork in a large mixing bowl, then
whisk in the milk. Let the mixture rest for about 1 hour.

   Add the eggs, mixing with a fork as you add them, then slowly add the remaining 2¹/2 cups flour. Knead the dough until it thickens, is somewhat springy, and no
longer sticks to your hands (add more flour or milk if necessary to get the right consistency). Divide the dough into two equal pieces and roll each piece into a log about
2 inches in diameter. Allow the dough to rise until the logs have doubled in size,
1 to 2 hours.

   Fill a large stockpot about ³/4 full with water, add the salt, and bring to a boil.
Carefully place each roll of dough into the pot. Let the water return to a boil, lower
the heat to medium, cover, and cook for 13 minutes. Using a slotted spoon, remove
the dumpling rolls from the water, and quickly stab each side a few times with a
sharp knife. Allow the dumplings to rest for at least 5 minutes. Slice the dumplings
crosswise into rounds ¹/2 inch thick just before serving.

Moxie Rx

FIND IT: **N Mississippi Ave. and N Shaver St., Portland Oregon**
KEEP UP WITH IT: http://moxierx.blogspot.com

When something that's seven years old qualifies as "old-school," you might be dealing with a relatively new phenomenon. But ask Portland food cart vendors whom they consider a pillar in the local scene and most will point to a teal trailer that's been parked in a grassy lot in the city's Northeast Side since 2004. It hides behind an iron rooster perched above a weathered wooden sign reading "Moxie Rx." Throw in the 1967 Kenskill camping trailer plastered with vintage bakeware, the attached eating area ensconced between a dirt floor and a rippling aluminum roof, the mason jars serving as flower vases, and the menu board advertising "elixirs" and "remedies" and you might feel as if you've stumbled into the lair of an Old West traveling medicine show. Only there's no snake oil here—Moxie's Nancye Benson rejuvenates hungover hipsters and half-dead hippies with potent cure-alls concocted from kale, mint, spirulina, ginger, echinacea, bee pollen, and just about any fruit or vegetable she can fit into a juicer. If it's good enough to keep Britney Spears and her back-up dancers on their toes and soothe John Mellencamp's trademark throaty voice, Benson figured it was good enough for Portland, too.

"I've been in the food business for a long time, catering and doing the personal chef thing, and was based in the San Francisco Bay Area for a while," Nancye says. "I worked for Britney Spears on tour, making drinks and food for her and the crew, and then I was John Mellencamp's personal chef for two years when he was traveling. But I decided I didn't want to tour anymore. It's really grueling, really long hours, and it's not very challenging as far as food is concerned."

So she returned to her home base of Portland and stumbled upon an opportunity when an Airstream creperie called Fold decided to move out of its lot (which Nancye's friend owns) and park itself in another spot across town. At the time, she was slinging coffee at a little local shop, but with some encouragement from her husband and the right trailer popping up for a good price on Craigslist, Nancye was suddenly a business owner. "This was 2004, so food carts were out there, but it was Asian food, tacos, and burritos, and I didn't want to do any of that stuff," she says. "I always loved the mid-century era and the earlier apothecary stuff, prescriptions, tonics . . . that kind of thing. And so one thing led to another from the concept to the name to the look, and I loved that I could do whatever I wanted. It was like an art installation."

But the artist wasn't content to simply doll the place up with vintage finds and sell juices. A convection oven in the tiny trailer—big enough to hold two half-sheet pans or about two dozen buttermilk biscuits—is in use long before sunrise and most of the day until closing time at 3 p.m. Those biscuits are so rich and buttery that when they're part of a cheesy breakfast sandwich with fluffy egg and applewood bacon, it's tough to tell where the Cheddar ends and the biscuit begins. That little oven is also responsible for perfectly sweet-and-sour date-and-goat-cheese scones, delicate raspberry crumble muffins, and ciabatta varieties like rosemary pecan and anise fig, small rounds that get split and filled with fruit and cheese before being pressed into panini. A tabletop waffle maker turns buckwheat batter into browned gold; yogurt, apple butter, and maple syrup seal the deal. Plenty of ingenious baking goes on in that thirteen-foot camper trailer, but there's just not enough counter real estate for an espresso machine. And because it's mobile, Moxie can't get a liquor license (regardless of the fact that the thing hasn't moved from its spot since day one). Coffee and booze are a restaurant's big moneymakers, so although one of Portland's most popular food carts seems constantly buzzing, business is far from booming.

"People are like, 'Oh man, I want to open a food cart, they're everywhere, everyone's making dough,' but for a lot of people it's barely a living," Nancye says. "It definitely sustains itself, but not necessarily me, and that's because of the way I did it. We have really high labor, we make everything fresh every day. A lot of the new trucks I'm reading about in other cities are fueled through restaurants. Border Grill, Spencer's in San Francisco, the Maximus guy in Seattle—that truck cost him $100,000 to put together—they have restaurants to cook out of. Here, I just can't store enough stuff."

And of course there's Portland's infamous weather to deal with: plenty of rain and drizzly, cold winters (well, cold by West Coast standards). In the past few years Nancye has done plenty to keep business coming through during the rougher months, from adding homemade eggnog and hot chocolate to the menu to turning part of Moxie's green space into a Christmas tree lot. She conceded in the winter of 2009–10, throwing in the towel from November through February while supplementing some R&R with occasional appearances at holiday bazaars, signature baked goods in tow. Still, she remains committed to her "art installation" spring through fall, her marriage to the little teal trailer intact. "I've asked myself a lot, 'Is this a business or is it my personal project?' But then I'll come in in the morning and I'm like, 'Oh, I love you.' I do. I love it, and it really gives me such joy. But yeah," she laughs, "this is clearly more of a personal project."

Moxie's Cold Cure-All Serves 1

Juice from 1/2 lemon

1 teaspoon freshly grated ginger

2 teaspoons agave nectar or honey

Pinch of cayenne pepper

1 dropperful Super Echinacea

Soda water, for serving (optional)

To make a warm tonic, combine the lemon, ginger, agave, cayenne, and echinacea in a mug, stirring to dissolve the agave. Add piping-hot water to fill the mug and let steep for a moment before drinking.

To make a cold fizz, combine the lemon, ginger, agave, cayenne, and echinacea in a tall glass, stirring to dissolve the agave. Add enough ice to fill half the glass and top with soda water.

FOOD TRUCKS

CARTOPIA
(SE 12th St. and SE Hawthorne Blvd.)

Unofficially known as the late-night pod, this cluster of carts on SE 12th St. and SE Hawthorne Blvd. draws a good mix early (most carts are open by sundown), but tends to turn into a hipster party once the night wears on. If you're a drunk twentysomething in Portland, chances are you'll end up searching for sustenance here. Cart owners know it, so most stay open until at least 3 a.m. most nights.

1 Perierra Creperie Creative Euro-style crêpes are made to order at this cute little trailer (which is owned by the guy who constructed Cartopia's picnic tables and heated tent structures to get business booming year-round). There are more than a dozen mouthwatering options on the menu, and that's just the crêpes; there are also shakes in flavors like lavender-basil-coconut milk. Branch out from classics like Nutella and bananas to the killer combo of figs, prosciutto, goat cheese, and honey.

2 Whiffies Fried Pies If you're asking, "What's a fried pie?" you must be a Yankee. This Southern staple resembles an empanada, and the hand-held filled pastries are fried to order. Whiffies offers both savory and sweet, so go ahead and be a glutton and start with the barbecue brisket, then finish with a marionberry. Seasonal selections come and go; look for the delicious pumpkin pies in fall.

3 El Brasero While they get props for being the oldest on the lot, nothing on this Anglo-Mex menu wins out over the other adjacent options. Still, vegetarians will tell you that the veggie burrito isn't half bad, and, given that Brasero usually stays open 24/7, a standard taco will do in a pinch.

4 Bubba Bernies Cajun/Creole is this truck's focus, but it's actually the consistency of the pastrami dogs and Philly cheesesteaks that have helped keep Bernie's afloat. For a warm dose of Southern comfort on a cold night, the brisket-studded black bean chili does the trick, while Portland's sizable vegan crowd benefits from specials like jambalaya with kale and veggie sausage.

5 Pyro Pizza It's not much to see a wood-fed oven in an artisanal pizzeria these days, but to see that kind of roaring fire from inside a food cart? Now that's impressive. Pyro's owners (who also run the popular downtown cart Give Apizza A Chance) somehow figured out how to build their cart around a hefty wood-fired pizza oven, and now they're kicking out bubbly crusted, 12-inch, whole wheat pies in traditional varieties like margherita and quattro formaggi (that's four cheese to you and me). It's an impressive pizza, and not just because it's made on wheels.

6 Potato Champion (see page 71)

NORTH STATION
(N Killingsworth St. and N Greeley Ave.)

One of the newest "pods" to open in Portland, North Station is anchored by **Pizza Depokos**, a converted gas station open from 5 p.m. to 9 p.m. nightly (except Sundays). Most carts open for lunch (around 11 a.m. to 3 p.m.) then again for dinner (around 5 p.m. to 8 p.m.), and very few are open on Sundays. Depokos's liquor license means that pod patrons can enjoy a meal from their favorite cart with a beer to wash it down, plus eat under the shelter of the attached garage should that infamous Portland rain start pouring.

❶ El Rancho The fish tacos, veggie burritos, and chilaquiles are the greatest hits.

❷ Saucy's BBQ Make a quick meal of a hotlink sandwich and crunchy, tart slaw.

❸ Sila Thai Thai standards with occasional standout specials from the board.

❹ Yogio It's easy to fall in love with this hot-pink cart based on its adorable design and concept alone: Korean bar snacks given the names of Rock (portable bibimbap), Paper (savory pancake with sautéed veggies), and Scissors (rice cake noodles in faintly spicy red pepper paste). All are crave-worthy.

❺ Scoop Artisan ice cream in seasonal flavors plus cider and caramel apples in fall and winter.

❻ Kettle Kitchen Going above and beyond the usual repertoire of chicken noodle and barley beef, this soup cart offers up a rotating array of flavorful bowls, from Indian curry soup studded with pink shrimp to chunky potato soup brightened by diced pickles. Don't miss the killer biscuits, especially the gorgonzola-black pepper.

❼ Starchy and Husk A clever name and an unusual concept have secured this cart a spot in the hearts of the local street-food cognoscenti. Mac and cheese brings the "Starchy" while roasted corn on the cob brings the "Husk." The '70s TV show references continue via menu items like the Gran Torino (squash and pancetta–studded mac and cheese) and the Huggie Bites (sweet potato hush puppies).

❽ Brother Bob's Bakery Straight-up homestyle baked goods.

❾ PDX 671 Taking its name from Portland's airport code and Guam's area code, this mash-up means you can expect interesting Chamorro food made with local ingredients. Titayas (grilled flatbread flavored with coconut milk) make for a nice breakfast snack, while crispy shrimp fritters known as bonelos uhang are delicious anytime.

❿ Brown Chicken Brown Cow One owner is from Austin, the other from Connecticut, hence the two specialties of this oddly named cart: breakfast tacos (Austin lays claim to them) and steamed cheeseburgers (a New England thing). Both are surprisingly satisfying, although purists might miss the char-grilled flavor on the burger.

⓫ Olympic Hot Dogs Red hots with various toppings plus a Tofurkey brat for veg heads.

MIDWEST

We have the classics: Italian beef, deep-dish pizza, hot dogs galore. We have the big-name chefs: Charlie Trotter, Grant Achatz, Rick Bayless. But we don't have food trucks. Not in the sense that every other major city does. Thanks to a tangled mess of red tape, Chicago's mobile food scene has long been limited to a handful of operators who aren't actually allowed to cook in their trucks. Instead, they prepare their food in traditional restaurants, load it onto a truck, then keep it warm via heat lamps while they set up camp in local parks. Not only is this far from appetizing for the city's culinary cognoscenti, but it's also not exactly brag-worthy for someone traveling around the country researching America's best food trucks. Seeing how cities like Portland, Austin, and L.A. have evolved and cultivated their food truck scene, then returning to my own city to find little more than roving heat lamps loaded with greasy food has been depressing, but the last year has brought a spark of hope that there might be change a-comin'.

In late winter of 2010 I received an email from Troy Johnson, a native of Chicago's South Side who was excited to learn I was working on this book. Johnson had spent the past year constructing his food truck All Fired Up, converting a former fire truck into a gleaming mobile kitchen and building a buzz by peddling his fried chicken and barbecue at nightclubs and events in the city's African American strongholds. Somehow he had slipped through the cracks and a health inspector licensed his truck to cook as an

FOOD TRUCKS

adjunct of a restaurant he took over, but after I profiled him in *Time Out Chicago* to get the word out, the city cracked down pretty hard, reigning him back in by prohibiting him to cook in his truck. Johnson was undeterred, and together we went on local radio to encourage Chicagoans to contact their aldermen to voice support for bringing our food truck scene up to a national standard. With the support of *Time Out Chicago*, the website www.StreetFoodNow.net was launched to serve as an HQ for the movement. Around the same time, local chef Matt Maroni was ramping up his own efforts to overhaul the city's street food regulations so that he could get his business, Gaztro-Wagon, up and running. Aldermen Scott Waguespack and Vi Daley backed a new ordinance that Maroni drew up and, at the time this book went to press, that ordinance is slowly but surely plugging its way through city council. If it passes, Chicago chefs will finally be able to join the mobile food revolution—and Chicago chowhounds will finally be able to take to their Twitters, track down the trucks, and hold their heads high that they're no longer left out of the club.

A few Chicago food trucks are already up and running, playing by the city's rules and preparing their food in commissary kitchens while waiting for new regulations to take hold. Technically, I aimed to only highlight trucks, carts, and trailers who actually cook on the street in this book, but hopefully by the time you read this you can add these to that list.

Chicago Start-up Guide

All Fired Up twitter.com/chgoallfrup
Troy Johnson's roving soul food station pops up at parties and parks serving crispy catfish, deep-fried chicken, and ribs barbecued in a smoker towed on the back of the truck.

Gaztro-Wagon twitter.com/wherezthewagon
"Naan-wiches" are the creation of truck chef Matt Maroni, who stuffs the thin, Indian-inspired breads with glammed-up combinations like wild boar belly with blue cheese, caramelized onions, date jam, and romesco sauce.

Happy Bodega twitter.com/happybodega
For now Amanda Cavazos is keeping it simple with baguette sandwiches, locally made granola bars, and Crop To Cup coffee, but she hopes to add scooped-to-order gelato and an expanded savory menu once she's legally able to.

Hummingbird Kitchen twitter.com/hummingbirdtogo
Because it operates just north of the city in the neighboring suburb of Evanston, this truck run by the restaurateurs behind Union Pizzeria and Campagnola doesn't have to play by the same rules that city trucks do. That means the organic local-beef burgers, pork Milanese sandwiches, and almond milk smoothies are made fresh onsite.

SOLDIER FIE...

$7 Eggplant Caponata
CAPERS, ZUCCHINI, FRESH MOZZARELLA

$7 Fidel "gastro"
PORK, HAM, PICKLES, MANCHEGO, MUSTARD

$8 Wild Boar Belly
DATES, BLEU CHEESE, ROMESCO, ONIONS

$8 Braised Lamb
APRICOTS, WALNUTS, QUESO PANELA, PEPPERS

$8 Duck Confit
MELTED LEEKS, BRIE, APPLE CHUTNEY

$8 Corn Beef Reuben
PROVOLONE, WARM CABBAGE SLAW, TOM, REMOULADE

$12 Lump Crab
FRESH MOZZARELLA, PORTOBELLOS, CHIMMICHURRI

$2 Plaintain Chips !!

$4 Sweets OATMEAL CREAM PIES
         FUDGE CREAM PIES
         CARAMEL POPCORN

PRICES DON'T INCLUDE TAX

NAAN WICHES

hummingbirdkitchen.com

Fresher Than Fresh Snow Cones

FIND IT: Sundays at 17th and Summit Sts., or first Fridays at 110 Southwest Blvd., Kansas City, Missouri

KEEP UP WITH IT: twitter.com/FTFsnowcones

When life gives you herbs, you make simple syrups. Or at least that's what Lindsay Laricks did, after moving into a house in Kansas City's West Side and discovering a backyard so overgrown that it was hard to make out the weeds from the herbs. The avid gardener went rooting around for the bad guys, plucked the life out of them, then split and replanted the good guys. Pretty soon she had herself a thriving herb garden, and after a trip to Austin, Lindsay decided she needed to reap what she sowed. "My boyfriend, Brady, and I went to Austin, and that's where I first discovered the food trucks phenomenon. I immediately fell in love," Lindsay says. "I thought it was the most fabulous thing. I said, 'Why don't we have anything like this in KC?' and Brady said, 'Lindsay, you could do this.'"

"I thought, 'Yeah, right, working full time,' but then I thought maybe I could if it was simple enough, and that word—simple—just kept coming up, and somehow it turned into simple syrups, something manageable I could do using what I already have plenty of, herbs."

And what to do with simple syrups? Pour them onto shaved ice and make snow cones, of course. Lindsay describes the summery American classic as "lovable, but disgusting if you break it down," referring to the artificial flavorings and colors that coat the ice, drip from the paper cone, and stain many a shirt. So she approached the snow cone from a natural, sustainable point of view, combining her homegrown herbs with fellow organics, from fruits to coffee to tea. While Lindsay was tinkering around infusing herbs into syrups and researching Hawaiian shaved ice machines, she also had her hands full as creative director for a local ad agency and with the letterpress and design company, Hammerpress, that she and Brady Vest run in Kansas City's art-rich Crossroads District. Still, one look at an adorable 1957 Shasta trailer on eBay (the compact style known as the Canned Ham) was all it took to turn an idea into a business.

During Fresher Than Fresh's first summer, in 2009, Lindsay split her time between her day job and the trailer, using weeknights to concoct syrups like blackberry-sage, clementine-thyme, and watermelon-basil and weekends to hawk her snow cones parked in a fitting garden setting, just across the street from the popular locavore restaurant Blue Bird Bistro. It was an instant hit, with Lindsay turning down private event requests left and right because there just weren't enough hours in the day. After spending a winter thinking about the trailer's popularity, she took a leap, quit the agency, and started the 2010 season full-steam, immediately booked for most of KC's hippest happenings, from craft fairs to dance performances to art walks.

So what will she do in fall when the cold rolls in and appetites for snow cones have waned? "To be honest, I don't really know where it's going, but I know I'm doing the right thing . . . it's just so lovely and it makes people happy, it makes *me* happy. The gut feeling that this is what I should be doing overpowers the fear of the unknown."

(SIDE DISH)

Forgive the trip down memory lane, but of all the food trucks I've been to, none holds a place in my heart like the battered old **Jerusalem Café** (Westport Rd. between Mill St. and Pennsylvania Ave.) truck in Kansas City. Since 1993 this gyro and falafel operation has come to the rescue of many tipsy locals, who stumble out of Westport bars and right up to its window to order a packed pita sandwich slathered in hummus and finished with flame-red harissa (it's open 11:30 p.m. to 3:30 a.m.). Even before I was old enough to join the goons myself, I'd hang out in the parking lot where Jerusalem does business, my dorky friends and I striving to be as cool as Westport itself, the epicenter of the only late-night action in town. The truck's owner, Fred Azzah, a native of Jerusalem, opened his brick-and-mortar café just a block away in 1990, but somehow the same crispy balls of chickpeas and shavings of greasy gyro meat just don't taste the same sitting down. And as I learned by the mid-'90s, they taste even better when they're all that stands between you and that massive Sunday morning hangover. ◉

Blackberry Lavender Ice Pops

Since most people don't have a commercial Hawaiian shaved ice machine, this recipe has been adapted to make ice pops. Use molds or ice cube trays with standard wooden ice pop sticks, plastic spoons, swizzle sticks, or even chopsticks.

2 heaping cups blackberries
1 cup sugar
1¹/₂ cups water

2 tablespoons fresh or dried culinary
 lavender buds
6 tablespoons freshly squeezed lemon juice

Combine the blackberries, sugar, water, and lavender in a saucepan over medium-high heat. Bring the ingredients to a boil, reduce the heat, and simmer for 8 minutes.

Mash the ingredients with a potato masher to extract as much juice as possible from the berries.

Let the mixture cool in the refrigerator for about 30 minutes. Remove from the refrigerator and add the lemon juice.

Using a fine-mesh strainer, strain the mixture into a large liquid measuring cup (or something similar with a pour spout). Discard the solids. Evenly divide the liquid among whatever pop molds you are using. Cover the molds with foil and poke sticks through the foil to secure them in place. Freeze for at least 4 hours before serving.

Streetza

KEEP UP WITH IT: www.streetza.com or twitter.com/streetzapizza

A couple of guys roaming the streets at 2:30 in the morning, drunk enough to be roaming the streets at 2:30 in the morning, are bound to come up with a few crazy ideas. And when they're in search of sustenance but winding up empty-handed and hungry, those ideas might turn to how to solve the problem. For Scott Baitinger and Steve Mai, the solution became giant slices of pizza, fresh from the oven, handed through the window of a tricked-out ice cream truck parked only steps from Milwaukee's booming bar scene on Water Street. "We had a couple of taco trucks you'd run into here and there, but really no one was doing any other food out of trucks," says Scott. "We looked into it, and for the most part there weren't any regulations prohibiting it. It was just that no one had done it yet."

So they did. Scott was, and still is, working as the creative director at an ad agency while Steve was managing a pizzeria with about ten years of restaurant experience under his belt. The two got their hands on an old ice cream truck and decided to convert it into a pizza truck themselves, "making every single mistake possible," Scott says. Electric pizza ovens and electric appliances meant they needed a massive generator, one that the Department of Transportation vetoed just by looking at it. They had no choice but to dismantle the entire truck, sell the parts on Craigslist, and start from scratch. They learned their lesson, moving on to propane-fueled ovens with slate decks, and after finally getting the truck street legal, they started partying. Friends and family came by Scott's house, where the truck was parked, to sample pie after pie, commenting on cheese blends, tomato sauce sweetness, topping ratios, crust crispness, and just about every other element that goes into making the perfect pizza. In the end, Scott and Steve settled on what they call "something in between New York and Chicago style, with doughiness on the inside, a bit like deep-dish, but with a crispy crust like New York." Through trial and error they developed a multistep dough method in which they halt the proofing process by sticking the dough in the fridge, accelerate it on the proofing rack for a bit, stop it again to transfer it from the commissary kitchen to the truck, and then proof it a bit more on the truck just before it's stretched and slid into the oven, where 10 minutes at 650°F puffs it up to a nice golden brown.

Streetza rolled out for business in May of 2009 with a menu that's partly standard pizzeria (pepperoni, sausage, veggie, plain cheese) and partly gourmet. The latter includes special slices of the day inspired by world travels

Pulling up in a sweet ride has been one way to get noticed since *Rebel Without a Cause* was in theaters. Brothers Vijay and Manoj Swearingen know that, so when they decided to become mobile food vendors, a standard step van wouldn't do. Instead, they purchased an NEV (Neighborhood Electric Vehicle), a battery-powered car that can be charged using a standard outlet and tops out at around 25 mph. Made by Global Electric Motorcars, a division of Chrysler, the tiny, rounded, eco-friendly car looks something like the egg-shaped spaceship Mork arrived in from Ork, if that spaceship were transformed into a mobile kitchen, complete with gas grill and fridge. **Pita Brothers** (www.twitter.com/pitabros) launched in the summer of 2009, cruising into downtown Milwaukee for breakfast, heading to the Third Ward around lunchtime, and hitting Marquette's campus for dinner. As their name implies, the menu revolves around thin Lebanese-style pita, used to wrap fillings ranging from falafel with hummus to steak with bacon drizzled with Southwestern ranch. They're flavorful and filling, but much like in the movies, sometimes what's inside the ride is secondary. ◉

(a trip to Romania turned into a combo of smoked ham, fresh corn, and sun-dried tomatoes); suggestions from Twitter followers (the "Tweetupgirls Heartbreaker Slice" gets artichoke hearts, grilled chicken, and basil); and odes to local legends (a 1989 Wisconsin State Fair champion chili appears on a pizza instead of tomato sauce and gets topped with Cheddar, sour cream, and red onions). Wisconsin cheeses are pretty much required around these parts unless you want to get chased out of town by an angry mob, and Streetza goes even further by supporting local crops with a seasonal Farmers' Market slice. Hometown pride gets broken down block by block via eight different Neighborhood Slices, including the Brewer's Hill, topped with hunks of brats simmered in Blatz beer, and a nod to the tony North Shore with smoked salmon, crème fraîche, fresh dill, and a dollop of black caviar.

Since the mobile pizza kitchen has hit Milwaukee's streets, only a couple of other food trucks have followed suit, meaning that Streetza gets prime pickings when it comes to spots in front of those same bars Scott and Steve stumbled out of before their "aha moment" really took root. That's not to say that feeding the drunks means you can't occasionally still be one, but when investors are knocking on your door and you just inked a deal to put forty-eight trucks in the Midwest within two years, priorities tend to shift.

The Bay-View Pizza   Makes four 16-inch pizzas

Unless you want to be prepping all day, you should purchase prepared pizza crust. Boboli crusts work for this, as do Tiseo's and Baker's Quality frozen pizza dough.

SAUCE

6 cups crushed tomatoes

2 tablespoons freshly squeezed lemon juice

1 tablespoon chopped fresh basil

2 tablespoons chopped fresh oregano

2 tablespoons chopped fresh Italian parsley

1 tablespoon chopped fresh thyme

1 tablespoon freshly ground black pepper

1$\frac{1}{2}$ teaspoons minced garlic

1 tablespoon minced onion

1 tablespoon salt

GROUND BEEF TOPPING

2 pounds ground sirloin

1 cup chopped onion

$\frac{1}{2}$ cup chopped tomatoes

$\frac{1}{2}$ teaspoon ground cumin

$\frac{1}{2}$ teaspoon dark chili powder

Salt and freshly ground black pepper

4 (16-inch) prepared pizza crusts

6 cups shredded mozzarella cheese

6 cups shredded Cheddar cheese

POTATO CHIPS

2 medium Idaho potatoes, peeled and sliced
$\frac{1}{8}$ inch thick

3 tablespoons olive oil

Salt and freshly ground black pepper

$\frac{1}{2}$ cup crumbled blue cheese

To make the sauce, combine all of the ingredients in a large stockpot and simmer over medium heat for about 15 minutes, stirring frequently. Remove the pot from the heat and blend using an immersion blender until the sauce is smooth.

To make the beef topping, heat a large sauté pan over medium heat, add the ground sirloin, and cook until browned throughout. Drain any grease, then add the onion, tomatoes, cumin, chili powder, and salt and pepper to taste. Simmer for 5 minutes.

Preheat the oven to 400°F. Spread one-fourth of the pizza sauce on each of the 4 pizza crusts. Top each pizza with one-fourth of the beef mixture and the mozzarella and Cheddar cheeses.

To make the potato chips, toss the potato slices in a bowl with the olive oil. Season lightly with salt and pepper and arrange them in a single layer on a baking sheet. Bake in the oven until golden brown, 12 to 15 minutes.

Meanwhile, bake the pizzas according to the instructions on the package of prepared dough. If it instructs you to cook the pizza at 400°F, you can cook the pizzas at the same time as the potato chips.

To assemble, place the baked potato chips on top of the cooked pizza. Sprinkle the blue cheese on top and serve.

LIBRARY MALL (State Street) Madison

Madison has two primary concentrations of food carts, the Capitol Square and the University's Library Mall. The Square has a handful of carts, typically only bustling on Saturdays during the Dane County Farmers' Market, but the Mall cart lineup is twenty-two strong, all open for business Monday through Friday, generally from about 10:30 a.m. until around 3 p.m.

1 The Bayou New Orleans Solid Cajun classics from gumbo to pecan pie.

2 Café Costa Rica Try the Jamaican iced coffee.

3 China Cottage Decent Chinese standards with plenty of vegetarian options.

4 King of Falafel Fine falafel and filling gyros.

5 The Dandelion Vegetarian and Vegan Sweet potato wraps and portobello reubens are signatures.

6 Ernie's Kettle Korn Not exactly a cart but exactly what the name implies.

7 Athens Gyros Tender and juicy gyros plus yummy honey-soaked walnut cake.

8 Surco Peruvian Food Traditional Peruvian dishes like grilled beef (*lomo saltado*) and braised lamb shank (*seco norteño*).

9 Buraka As popular as its parent restaurant, this African cart serves up hefty portions of peanutty chicken, curried beef, and lamb stew, with spongy *injera* bread to take it all in.

10 Hibachi Hut Basic grilled teriyaki steak, chicken, and veggies.

11 Mama Aurora's Cucina Meatball subs and decent thin-crust pizza.

12 Taste of Jamaica The spin-off of the Madison restaurant Jamerica, this brightly colored cart delivers Caribbean flavors via jerk chicken and pork heavy on the allspice with faint heat. Check for occasional multicultural specials like spicy jerk sausage jambalaya and coconut macaroons.

13 Loose Juice The smoothies at the oldest cart in town (it opened in 1976) are tasty and all, but owner Karleton Armstrong's story is more interesting. A political activist in the '60s, Armstrong was a member of the New Year's Gang, a group convicted of bombing UW–Madison's Sterling Hall in protest of the Vietnam War.

14 Yon Yonson The name of this sandwich and burger cart might evoke Vonnegut's *Slaughterhouse Five*, but the nod to the "My name is Yon Yonson, I come from Wisconsin . . ." chant has more irony: the owner is actually named John Johnson and he does actually come from Wisconsin. Clever, and the walnut burgers aren't bad either.

15 Fresh Cool Drinks Freshly squeezed juices and smoothies, plus a massive veggie spring roll for two bucks.

16 Caracas Empanadas Follow up a Venezuelan *empanada* with a freshly fried churro.

17 Natural Juice Nearly identical to Fresh Cool Drinks but smaller spring rolls.

18 Monty's Blue Plate Diner and Just Coffee Co-op Portable diner comfort foods and coffee from local gurus.

19 Electric Earth Sandwiches and salads with a healthy slant.

20 Kakilima Probably the most interesting cart on the Mall, Kakilima specializes in hard-to-find Indonesian food. Barbecue chicken doused in peanut sauce and tofu in candlenut curry come with crispy rice puffs (*krupuk*) and a bright and crunchy salad of pickled carrots and cucumbers (*acar*).

21 Zen Sushi Care is taken with each Japanese classic at this origami-adorned cart, from earthy homemade miso soup to the *futomaki*, a tightly wrapped assembly of seared salmon, shiitake mushroom, omelet, cooked spinach, and crunchy carrot.

22 Santa Fe Trailer New Mexico's famed Hatch green chiles in comforting dishes like pork stew.

Chef Shack

KEEP UP WITH IT: **www.chefshack.org**

Somebody had to go first.

In a city with a culinary scene that's spawned a James Beard winner (Tim McKee of La Belle Vie), a food writer with a national profile (bug eater Andrew Zimmern), and as many Ethiopian restaurants as natural foods co-ops, where are all the food trucks? That's what Carrie Summer asked herself when she returned to her native city after cooking in New York, working in the pastry departments of Jean-Georges Vongerichten's JoJo and *Iron Chef* Morimoto's eponymous restaurant. "It was 2006 and I was hearing about all of these food trucks, and thought, 'This is gonna be big,'" Carrie says. But Lisa Carlson, her longtime partner in cooking and in life, wasn't so sure. Lisa had a good-size ego and the resume to back it up—she'd held her own on hot lines at snooty spots around the globe, from Manhattan's Lespinasse under the legendary Gray Kunz to London's L'Escargot in its Michelin-starred hey-day. And now her girlfriend was trying to talk her into opening a doughnut truck. In Minneapolis. Land of September snow.

Love will make you do the damnedest things. Turns out, a little snow doesn't deter Minnesotans from fresh doughnuts. Chef Shack opened in 2007 for the St. Paul Winter Carnival, and the wait for Carrie's Indian-spiced doughnuts and hot chocolate was longer than either chef had seen in their careers. They knew they were on to something, but a tabletop fryer wasn't going to cut it for two experienced chefs, so Carrie and Lisa regrouped and outfitted their 9 by 12-foot trailer with a $6,000 "doughnut robot" that squirts perfect cylinders of dough into a vat of hot oil, as well as a refrigerator, freezer, griddle, and small prep counter. The new and improved Chef Shack set up shop the following spring in the Mill City Farmers Market. Lines formed immediately for the hand-cut fries and bacon ketchup, tongue tacos dressed with corn salsa, and all-natural beef hot dogs loaded with gourmet toppings. "We were raking in more in a day than a cook is really used to making in a week, and Carrie was like, 'Are you ready to be famous for hot dogs?'" Lisa says. "At first I was like, 'I went to New York and I cooked at all these really great places, and I'm finally getting known for french fries?' It was kinda hard for my ego, but I realized if you do one thing you just do it really well, no matter what it is."

Demand brought Chef Shack to four farmers' markets and drew plenty of requests for private events. In fact, business has been so good that Carrie and Lisa close up shop in winter and head for Asia, living off of $20 a day while getting Thai massages in Bangkok and eating their weight in street food in Singapore. "We've created exactly the lifestyle we want, and we've never lost the passion in our cooking," Lisa says. "And yeah, my ego is doing a whole lot better now that the cash box is full."

French Toast with Shaved Apples and Bacon Beer Brats Serves 4

If you really want to replicate the Chef Shack's most popular fall dish, go organic with the eggs and milk, try to get your hands on some bacon beer brats (they use Fischer Farms), and crisp up the bread in a deep fryer. If that sounds out of reach for you, your favorite pork sausage links will do, and a griddle or frying pan should work almost as well.

4 eggs

1 cup whole milk

3 tablespoons brown sugar

1 teaspoon freshly grated nutmeg

1 tablespoon ground cinnamon

1 teaspoon ground cardamom

1/4 teaspoon vanilla extract

Pinch of sea salt

12 slices multigrain bread, sliced 1/2 inch thick

4 pork sausage links

2 tart-sweet apples (Pink Lady or similar variety), cored and cut into matchsticks or small slivers

1/4 cup maple syrup

Beat the eggs in a large mixing bowl. Add the milk, brown sugar, nutmeg, cinnamon, cardamom, vanilla, and salt and stir well to combine. (If you have one, use an immersion blender to emulsify all the ingredients.)

Soak the bread slices in the egg mixture until saturated. Meanwhile, split each sausage link down the middle, almost cutting it in half but not severing it. Brown the sausages on a griddle or in a frying pan over medium-high heat. While the sausages are cooking, heat a deep fryer to high or a heat a lightly oiled griddle or frying pan over medium-high heat. Fry the bread until both sides are deep brown. Plate 3 slices of French toast with 1 sausage link, top with a pile of apple slivers, and drizzle the entire thing with 1 tablespoon of maple syrup. Repeat with the remaining ingredients.

SOUTH

YEAH, WE HAVE VEGGIE BURGERS, TOO

Austin, Texas

I f you've trademarked your city as the Live Music Capital of the World, you better have plenty of booze and the grub to soak it up. Austin has both. With nearly two hundred live music venues funneling what the city estimates as close to $700 million in revenue, the local music industry is massive. Downtown clubs have been booming since the 1970s (in 1973 my dad's band Headstone played the South Door, which he recalls as "the hip place to be"), prompting food vendors to set up on the sidewalks to offer cheap, quick eats to the partying masses.

These days, annual events like the Austin City Limits Music Festival draw close to sixty-five thousand people daily, all of them hungry and thirsty. Again the solution is simple: a kebab cart, a taco truck, a cupcake trailer . . . fast enough and affordable enough that their patrons can return their focus to the band onstage and the beer in hand. There's enough demand for street eats that, as of 2010, more than a thousand mobile food vendors were licensed in Travis County. Many are tiny one-man carts, either pushed to a preferred sidewalk spot or towed by hitch. A few years ago, though, hordes of newcomers hit the scene. The funky gleaming trailers, all retrofitted to deliver delicious food while maintaining that iconic Americana look of mid-century leisure, demonstrate the city's unofficial motto, "Keep Austin Weird." In true individualistic spirit, many find a spot under a shady tree, set up a few picnic tables, and hang out until people find them. Others band together in groups of three or more to take over a parking lot as a hybrid between trailer park and food court. And still others stick to dancing with the one that brought 'em, hitting the streets after dark and positioning their mobile kitchens right along the blurred sight line of those music lovers that keep this city afloat.

FOOD TRUCKS

East Side King

FIND IT: 1618 E 6th St. (back patio of the Liberty Bar), Austin, Texas
KEEP UP WITH IT: www.eastsidekingaustin.com

In pairs, sometimes threes, people duck into a little roadhouse on a fairly desolate street in East Austin, the first wave around dusk, another wave much later, right around the time the late-night munchies set in. Most are nailing the rockabilly daddy-o and rollergirl look (which is big here in Austin), so it's hard to tell if they're headed for the Liberty Bar or the tattoo shop upstairs. Surprisingly, some aren't aiming for either. They're snaking through the Liberty long enough to buy a bottle of Lone Star, then beelining for the back patio, where a tiny camping trailer sits at the edge of the fence. Covered in abstract bursts of Day-Glo-bright paint, the trailer looks like the spaceship that fell out of the sky to deliver George Clinton. It's not. It's actually the side project of two supremely talented local chefs who met at the famed contemporary Japanese restaurant Uchi. Paul Qui is a native of the Philippines but was raised in the States and has been in Austin since coming for culinary school in 2002. Moto Utsonomaya, who is Japanese, left his country just after his twenty-first birthday to join up with the Texas Eastside Kings, an electric blues band that's been gigging around the South for decades, backing legends that roll through town and cutting records here and there. The band of Southern African Americans in their sixties and seventies play like they're exorcising the blues in their blood, but Moto and his guitar were taken in nonetheless, a natural fit that looks odd only at first.

Something like that trailer, which Moto found about ten blocks from the Liberty, abandoned in an overgrown front yard like a broken toy. He and Paul tracked down the owner, bought it for next to nothing, and then went about installing a few essential pieces of kitchen equipment (convection oven, fryers, a sink), all while working their regular shifts at Uchi, Paul as chef de cuisine and Moto as sushi chef. In November of 2009 they towed the trailer behind the Liberty and opened for business under the name East Side King. When word got out that two Uchi chefs were doing late-night pan-Asian snacks like pork belly buns and fish sauce–marinated chicken wings, selling them from the patio of one of Austin's coolest bars until 2 a.m. on weekends, the chowhounds and fellow chefs came pouring in.

Paul credits Moto with putting in much of the work at East Side King, since his responsibilities at Uchi mean he's not at the trailer as much, but Moto hands credit right back by saying that Paul came up with most of the menu.

Here's his breakdown of the eats that give Austin's food scene a shot in the arm:

Thai Chicken Karaage: Deep-fried chicken thigh with sweet and spicy sauce, fresh basil, cilantro, mint, onion, and jalapeño.

> "It's kind of influenced by Pok Pok in Portland, even though I've never been there. I was looking at their menu after I saw a show on TV that featured them, and I was like, 'That sounds awesome.' I marinate the thighs in fish sauce, lime juice, garlic, and Thai chiles and it sits in that brine. Sometimes we do tongue, and I brine it in that as well. We tried dusting it in both cornstarch and rice starch, but I think the cornstarch comes out better. And we finish it up with a sauce that has chiles and garlic and shallots and fish sauce again."

Poor Qui's Buns: Roasted pork belly in steamed buns, with hoisin sauce, cucumber kimchi, and green onion.

> "So, yeah, the style is a little bit Momofuku. I staged there for ten days because I knew Tien Ho, who used to be the executive sous at the Driscoll here in Austin. He was very welcoming of me checking out his kitchen. Those guys are very open, really cool. But we use cucumber kimchi on ours instead of chilled cucumbers. We roast ten-pound pork bellies in the convection oven for two hours at around 300°F with salt and sugar on the outside, and we buy the steamed buns at an Asian supermarket

According to Mike Rypka, he didn't give his food truck **Torchy's Tacos** (1311 S 1st St.; see www.torchystacos.com for additional locations) its tagline– his customers did. "After we opened in 2006, people tried our tacos and were constantly saying, 'Damn, this is good.' So after a while we just added 'Damn Good Tacos' to the name because we believed them." Apparently those customers weren't just being nice, at least not if Torchy's growth is any indication. Since Mike left the world of corporate chefdom to start his little taco truck (in his past life he cooked for execs at World Bank, Dell, Enron, MTV, and Disney), Torchy's has blossomed into four brick-and-mortar taquerias, plus the humble trailer that started it all. These days it sits in what Mike dubbed the South Austin Trailer Park & Eatery, a nice-size lot with plenty of shade trees, a few picnic tables, a covered eating area, and two other food trailers: **Holy Cacao**, which specializes in cake balls, and **Man Bites Dog**, a sausage joint on wheels. Mike estimates that the trailer sells about two thousand tacos a day, most of them of the green chile pork carnitas variety, slow-roasted shoulder infused with the bright heat of New Mexico hatch chiles. The runner-up is a heat lover's ➜

up north. Moto named it. He's making fun of his own accent since it's hard for Japanese to make "r" sounds. So it's kind of how he pronounces 'Paul Qui,' but pronounced right it sounds like 'Porky.'"

Beet Home Fries: Deep-fried roasted beets, Kewpie mayo, *shichimi togarashi*, and green onion.

"We had some old beets we didn't want to serve at Uchi one day, and Moto fried them up. I just stored it in the back of my head, like, 'Ah, we're gonna make a million dollars off those beets someday.' They're basically like home fries, cut into triangles and fried. Then we just put *togarashi* (Japanese chili powder) into Kewpie mayo, then slice green onions really thin and put them on top."

Fried Brussels Sprout Salad: Fried Brussels sprouts, sweet and spicy sauce, fresh shredded cabbage, alfalfa sprouts, fresh basil, cilantro, mint, onion, and jalapeño.

"Honestly, this isn't really influenced by the Momofuku Brussels sprout salad. I've played with it at Uchi before, probably during the same time but without knowing it. Tyson Cole, executive chef at Uchi, was like, 'I want Brussels sprouts, but I want them crispy,' so basically this is what I did."

Ginger Garlic Jasmine Rice: Steamed jasmine rice, ginger and garlic oil, fresh basil, cilantro, mint, onion, and jalapeño.

"Coming from Filipino decent, garlic rice is an everyday breakfast thing. I wanted the fried flavor of rice without having fried rice. It's essentially a side, but you can put any of the food on top of it. We sell it as the combos below. We almost didn't do the rice, but Yoshi, one of our lead sushi chefs at Uchi, convinced us to keep it."

Curry Buns: Homemade peanut butter curry in a deep-fried bun, with fresh basil, cilantro, mint, onion, and jalapeño.

"I was working at the trailer one night and I was bored, so I threw a *bao* bun into the fryer and it came out good! Pre-opening I had made this peanut butter curry sauce from red and green Thai curry paste and peanut butter, but I decided that I didn't like the dish it was going on, so I shelved the sauce. Then I took the fried *bao* bun and slathered it with the curry sauce, kinda like a peanut butter sandwich, and to give it a fresh flavor I added the herbs, onion, and jalapeño. It's pretty much our trademark now, and I love it, too."

Homemade Cookies:

"The rootbeer snickerdoodles are made by the pastry chef at Uchi, Philip Speer. He and his wife Callie have a cake company called Cakemix and they came up with these cookies, plus they sometimes do curry–peanut butter and carrot cake sandwich cookies for us."

dream dubbed "Brushfire," jerk chicken revved up with grilled jalapeños and a "Diablo" sauce of fire-roasted habaneros, fully deserving of its name. Since they have upped their sales from about 150 tacos a day to a couple thousand, that tagline seems safe from scrutiny. ◉

Thai Chicken Karaage Serves 2 to 3

BRINE

1 cup fish sauce

1 cup white vinegar

1 cup sugar

1 head garlic, cloves separated and minced

4 Thai chiles, coarsely chopped

6 boneless, skinless chicken thighs, diced

Canola oil, for frying

1 cup cornstarch

1/4 onion, thinly sliced

2 jalapeños, thinly sliced

1 cup chile sauce, such as Mae Ploy brand

Salt

12 fresh cilantro leaves, torn

6 fresh mint leaves, torn

6 fresh basil leaves, torn

To make the brine, combine all of the ingredients. Set aside 1 cup of the brine for use later. Add the chicken thighs to the remaining brine, cover, and refrigerate for 24 hours.

Remove the chicken from the brine and place the pieces in a strainer or colander, letting the excess brine drain off. Discard the brine.

Pour enough oil into a deep pot or countertop fryer to cover the chicken and heat to 370°F.

Dust the chicken generously with cornstarch and fry until golden brown. Use tongs to turn the pieces for even browning. Remove the chicken from the fryer with tongs or a slotted spoon and transfer to a large mixing bowl. Add the onion, jalapeños, the reserved 1 cup brine, and the chile sauce, toss to coat, and season with salt to taste. Garnish with the cilantro, mint, and basil and serve.

Lulu B's

FIND IT: 2113 S Lamar Blvd., Austin, Texas
KEEP UP WITH IT: www.myspace.com/lulubssandwiches

When Laura Bayer told her Vietnamese relatives she was going to open a *banh mi* business out of a trailer parked along a busy road in Austin, Texas, the laughter could almost be heard from Saigon. "*Banh mi* are like hot dogs there," Laura says. "They just couldn't believe I would be here in America selling this Vietnamese snack food."

Selling street food seemed perfectly normal for Laura's fifty-five-year-old aunt, Long (pronounced Lum), who has peddled thick avocado smoothies from her front patio for years. But why would the younger generation, the one raised in Southern California and given every opportunity to be successful in the world, choose a profession common throughout Asia as a mode of survival? "I really, really needed a good Vietnamese sandwich," Laura says. "Every time I would crave one I just couldn't find one. In Southern California, where we have a huge Vietnamese population, they're all over, but there was really nothing here in Austin. So after a few years of teaching here and becoming emotionally drained from that, I just started thinking, 'I could do that, I could fill that void.'"

The idea floated around for a few years, during which Laura made countless versions of the crusty Vietnamese sandwich for her friends, many of them *banh mi* virgins. She spent hours on the phone with her Vietnamese-born mother Thao, gleaning tips on how to perfect the lemongrass pork and chicken her taste buds recalled from childhood. She even made the trek to South Vietnam, working alongside her aunt to master *sinh to bo*, a milkshake made from avocado and sweetened condensed milk that's so rich, you have to come up for gulps of fresh air between sips. Laura had no culinary training—had never even worked in a restaurant—but tradition was on her side. With family secrets as the backbone of her operation and a custom-built trailer kitchen (thanks to Visa) on its way from Florida via uShip, Laura's craving for a great *banh mi* was about to become a business.

Lulu B's opened in January 2008, parked just off of Austin's South Lamar Boulevard under a massive oak tree whose branches shoot out small bursts of Spanish moss. The lot is owned by the guy who runs the adjacent tire shop, which is far enough away from Laura's cute little white trailer that there's plenty of room for a peaceful eating area. Shaded by that giant oak, hungry workers on lunch break and preshift restaurant and bar folk fill up the handful of tables and chairs, digging into tightly wrapped summer rolls, bowls of vermicelli topped with Chinese-style barbecue pork (a Vietnamese staple), and, of course, sturdy *banh mi*, split French loaves filled with the perfect ratio of pickled daikon and carrots, Kewpie mayo (a Japanese brand preferred by most *banh mi* makers), raw jalapeño, fresh cilantro, and tender hunks of grilled meat or tofu. The lemongrass pork is the standout, with plenty of citrusy herbal punch and meat that's sweet, sour, and salty all at once, with the added benefit of slight char from the grill. The one classic that's missing? The favorite *banh mi* of most old-school Vietnamese, piled with ham, headcheese, and pork pâté. "I hate it, all that stuff," Laura laughs. "Biting into that was always disgusting to me. When my mom would make it I was always like, 'Ugh.' My whole thing was I wanted to make a Vietnamese sandwich the way *I* wanted to eat it. I wanted to do things that *I* loved because there would be love in it. And I focus on very particular things."

She's particular about lemongrass, insisting that her marinades include both fresh and prechopped (which is slightly mellower), and that the fresh stalks are diced so finely that they almost disappear. And she's particular that the cilantro is stemmed, to save customers from biting into bitter bits, and that there's a balance of vegetables to meat, "more like a burrito and not like a taco." She's also convinced that lunch is her bread and butter, so there's no reason to put night hours in the picture; she's fine with the fact that her younger sister Christina is "so over working the truck" and ready to move on; and she feels that even doing $1,000 a day in business, she'd eventually like to shift Lulu B's into a brick-and-mortar restaurant, where more space will mean customers won't have to wait forty-five minutes for a sandwich during a rush. In other words, the girl with no restaurant experience knows exactly how she wants hers to run, and that doesn't exactly jibe with a meddling mother.

"When I first opened, my mom came out to help us. She was here for three months, until she couldn't stand us anymore," Laura laughs. "Being my mom and being Asian, everything was, 'No, that's wrong. You should do this or that.' And she would try stuff and not tell me, like sneaking spring mix into the noodle bowls, or she'd be sitting outside under a tree peeling carrots and daikon, and I'm like, 'Uh, Mom, we have health codes here. This isn't Vietnam.' So she got mad and went home. But she taught me her fish sauce and her summer rolls, and she fixed our peanut sauce. She would walk around the lot asking people how they liked their food, and you could just see she was very proud. After all, she's the one who gave us the love of Vietnamese food and culture, so I wouldn't have this if it weren't for her."

Lemongrass Pork Banh Mi Serves 8

2 tablespoons fish sauce (preferably Phu Quoc brand)

1/4 cup low-sodium soy sauce

4 cloves garlic, minced

2 stalks lemongrass, finely chopped

1/4 cup canola oil

1 tablespoon freshly ground black pepper

Juice of 1/2 lime

1 pound pork butt, cut into 1/4-inch-thick slices as long as the butt is wide

2 cups water

2 cups cider vinegar

1/4 cup sugar

1/2 pound carrots, julienned using a mandoline

1/2 pound daikon, julienned using a mandoline

8 banh mi rolls or mini baguettes

1/4 cup Kewpie mayonnaise or regular mayonnaise

Handful fresh cilantro leaves

24 sliced rounds English (hothouse) cucumber

2 jalapeños, stemmed and sliced crosswise

Combine the fish sauce, soy sauce, garlic, lemongrass, canola oil, pepper, and lime juice in a bowl and whisk to blend. Pour the marinade over the pork butt slices in a large resealable bag and seal, or combine the pork and marinade in a nonreactive baking dish and cover with plastic wrap. Refrigerate overnight.

Combine the water and vinegar in a large mixing bowl and pour in the sugar, whisking to dissolve. Add the carrots and daikon, then cover and refrigerate overnight.

Prepare a grill for direct cooking over medium-high heat. Grill the pork until it is just pink in the center, with an internal temperature of 160°F. Remove from the grill and cut each of the slices again into small bite-size pieces.

Toss the rolls on the grill for just a minute to toast and then slather each with about 1 1/2 teaspoons of the mayo. Add a portion of the grilled pork, a few cilantro leaves, a portion of cucumber and jalapeño slices, and some of the pickled carrot and daikon mixture. Serve.

Gourdough's

FIND IT: 1219 S Lamar Blvd., Austin, Texas
KEEP UP WITH IT: twitter.com/gourdoughs

Ask Ryan Palmer and Paula Samford how the couple met and you'll get sheepish laughs, followed by, "Well, we were both jogging at Town Lake, which is kind of funny, since we're both fat now from Gourdough's."

They can blame their doughnut truck for their weight gain, but go one step further and the whole concept can be blamed on the housing slump. Paula and Ryan started their own realty company just after meeting in 2005 (she's a realtor and he's an attorney specializing in realty law), but when the recession hit, the couple were nursing their wounds by frying up batches of doughnuts in a wok on the stovetop. "I was using my grandmother's recipe, but she had always just made them plain," Paula says. "So I started taking ingredients from other family recipes, and just coming up with my own creations, and topping the plain doughnuts with all of this stuff."

People convinced Paula and Ryan that the results were good enough to sell, so after outfitting a 1978 Airstream with enough fryers to make South Austin good and fat, they opened Gourdough's in fall of 2009. They haven't quit the realty business, so combined with their new venture they each work around ninety hours a week. But they still have time when they get home for a little of the R&D that stole their svelteness, with Paula constantly tweaking the lineup of two dozen doughnuts, coming up with new concoctions, and brainstorming with Ryan for names as creative as the doughnuts themselves. Since the menu looks like something that came out of a meeting among a gourmet chef, a mad scientist, and a serious stoner, it's probably best to have Paula explain a few of the signature creations herself.

Granny's Pie: "My grandmother, whose dough recipe I use for all of the Gourdough's doughnuts, used to boil a can of sweetened condensed milk for hours and then pour it into a graham cracker crust with pecans and bananas. This doughnut recreates that, with caramel standing in for the caramelized condensed milk."

Baby Rattler: "I was trying to come up with something to entertain kids, so I looked for the largest gummy candy out there I could find, which is a giant three-foot rattlesnake. I wanted it to look like the snake was slithering on the ground, so I added the crushed Oreos, getting them to stick with a slather of fudge icing."

WELCOME TO

GOURDOUGH'

BIG. FAT. DONUTS.

Try one, they're delicious!

1219 S LAMAR BLVD, AUSTIN, TX 78704
GOURDOUGHS1219@GMAIL.COM
WWW.GOURDOUGHS.COM

Pick one of ours or make your own!
ALL DONUTS ARE $4.25. ADD $1 FOR ME
ADD A SCOOP OF ICE CREAM FOR $1.

(SIDE DISH)

Real estate developers have been threatening to turn the strip of food trucks at 1600 South Congress into a hotel for a couple of years now, but thanks to the recession (sorry, hoteliers), this mobile food court might be safe just where it is for a while. One or two of the vendors here seem to rotate quite frequently, with one barbecue trailer disappearing and another popping up in its place every few months. But three of the destinations in this lot seem cemented in place, despite their wheeled status. Jaynie Buckingham and her **Cutie Pie Wagon** (www.cutiepiewagon.com) are tough to miss–both she and ➡

Flying Pig: "This one, which is one of our best sellers, came from my love of crumbling bacon on top of pancakes and adding syrup to the whole thing, so this basically mirrors that by subbing the doughnut for pancakes and layering the bacon strips on top with maple syrup icing."

Mama's Cake: "When I was growing up I always used to lick the bowl when my mom or grandmother was baking, but the bowls with yellow cake batter and brownie batter were my favorites. My great-grandmother sort of combined the two flavors with her recipe for yellow cake with chocolate icing, which she always called "Mama's Cake," so I basically recreated that by filling the doughnut with yellow cake batter and finishing it with chocolate icing."

Black Out: "I wanted something for chocolate lovers, some sort of 'Death by Chocolate,' so I just went all out and stuffed my favorite brownie batter inside the donut, and then added chocolate-covered brownie bites and fudge icing on top."

Porkey's: "One of my favorite appetizers is a block of cream cheese topped with jalapeño jelly, with crackers for spreading. I also love Canadian bacon rolled up with cream cheese, so I decided to marry these all into a doughnut."

Slow Burn: "This is basically the Porkey's minus the bacon for those who aren't as adventurous or people who don't eat meat. I named it after the local company Austin Slow Burn, since I use their habanero jelly for this, combining it with the cream cheese and slathering it on the doughnut."

Miss Shortcake: "Really this is just a twist on classic strawberry shortcake, and I wanted something really light and airy to counter the doughnut. The tartness of the fresh strawberries and also the cream cheese in the frosting make it a perfect summery combination—no matter what time of year it is."

Dirty Berry: "I tried to fry strawberries but just couldn't perfect it, so I tried grilling them instead. They were delicious, but I wasn't done yet. I know people love chocolate-covered strawberries, so I added fudge icing and topped it off with some cinnamon and sugar so it would look a little 'dirty' but still be scrumptious."

Funky Monkey: "This is a play on bananas Foster, which I've always done at home by grilling bananas after they're coated in brown sugar. That basically evolved into this doughnut, which also adds cream cheese frosting to the mix."

her wooden hitch trailer are decked out in hot pink, with pink and purple feather boas for that little extra bling. From housewife to household name (well, in Austin at least), Jaynie got her start after taking first place in a 2008 pie competition hosted by the Driskill Hotel, bringing home the blue ribbon with her mother Betty Lou's buttermilk pie. This Southern staple is sweet and creamy, like buttery custard poured into an endlessly flaky crust–there's a reason it's the best seller.

Cutie Pie sits smack-dab in the middle of the strip, anchored on one end by **The Mighty Cone** (www.mightycone.com). Austin chef and restaurateur Jeff Blank opened his critically acclaimed restaurant Hudson's on the Bend twenty-five years ago, and he's been synonymous with Hill Country cuisine ever since. After selling twenty thousand of his "Hot & Crunchy Cones" over the three-day Austin City Limits Music Festival, Jeff decided his culinary invention needed its own year-round truck. He dropped a cool $70,000 on a state-of-the-art trailer outfitted with air-conditioning and a full kitchen with enough fryers to keep up with the demand for those cones. What's all the fuss about? Jeff concocted a signature coating of cornflakes, almonds, sesame seeds, arbol chile flakes,

CONTINUED ON PAGE 118 ➜

sugar, and sea salt, and he rolls just about anything that'll sit still in the mix, then deep-fries it in a bubbling vat of canola oil. Plump shrimp, boneless chicken, even ripe avocado aren't immune from the Hot & Crunchy treatment (although, honestly, you could put that stuff on tree bark and people would wait in line for it).

At the opposite end of the lot is the senior of the scene, impossible to miss and beloved by Austinites young and old. A gleaming silver Airstream sporting a giant frosted cupcake shooting out of its roof, the **Hey Cupcake!** (www.heycupcake.com) trailer is a beacon of nostalgia and relentless temptation at any time of day. Wes Hurt launched his sweet stop in early 2007, with a roster of cupcakes in classic flavors like red velvet, carrot cake, and simple yellow cake frosted with fudge. In the few years since, Wes has grown the business into four trailers (all identical Airstreams) and a brick-and-mortar cupcake shop. He's also invented the Whipper Snapper, a take on the Twinkie that injects the cupcake with a shot of whipped cream (think Hostess Cupcake, but better). These handheld habit formers will eventually have you looking at your reflection in the Airstream hoping that's a fun-house effect staring back at you. ◉

Naughty and Nice: "I wanted something that was really simple but still delicious, and this was it—a basic doughnut rolled in cinnamon and sugar. Even after coming up with all of these flavors, this is still probably my favorite, especially with warm honey butter (which you can add to it when you order, just like you can customize any doughnut using any of the ingredients on the menu)."

Blue Balls: "It must have been late at night and my mind was going in a bad direction, but I thought of filling doughnut holes with blueberry pie filling, and I couldn't help but call them Blue Balls. I love watching grown men at the window embarrassed to order the Blue Balls, but they still do!"

ODB: "After the Blue Balls my mind was really going in the ditch, and so somehow I arrived at the Old Dirty Bastard, doughnut holes I rolled in white icing and then shredded coconut. It tasted too plain, so I had to add the coconut cream filling, which completed the, uh, package."

Sailor Jerry: "Ryan lived in New Orleans and apparently ate rum cake quite a bit there, so he really wanted to incorporate that into a doughnut, so we soak the hot doughnut in a rum sauce, give it a rum glaze, and then top it with cinnamon and sugar. Beware: It definitely has its fair share of booze."

Mother Clucker: "Similar to the Flying Pig, the idea behind this is salty meat with something sweet. Since chicken and waffles is such a classic, I figured it wasn't too much of a stretch to sub a doughnut for the waffle, but instead of using syrup I came up with using honey butter for the icing and then laying the freshly fried chicken strip on top of that."

PB&J: "I could eat PB&J sandwiches every day if my clothes allowed it, so I thought why not do this combo with a doughnut, injecting it with grape jelly, icing it with peanut butter, and adding peanut butter morsels at the end."

Heavenly Hash: "When I was growing up my mom would top her homemade brownies with a layer of marshmallow crème, then pour chocolate icing on top and call it 'Heavenly Hash.' It was so amazing that I used the same flavors on this doughnut and dedicated it to her."

Odd Duck

FIND IT: 1219 S Lamar Blvd., Austin, Texas
KEEP UP WITH IT: www.oddduckfarmtotrailer.com

Pretty much every contemporary American small plates hot spot around the country is serving pork belly right now. They might be sealing it, then cooking it low and slow, using the sous vide method championed by culinary gods like Thomas Keller. They might also be serving it as a slider on a brioche bun, topped with pickled onions and fresh arugula. In fact, you could probably trip and fall into a dish like this in cities like San Francisco or New York. But only in Austin will you find sous vide pork belly on a 1980 Fleetwood Mallard travel trailer, finished to order on an oak-fired grill, sold for six bucks, and served under the stars in a gravel lot where BYOB is not only allowed but encouraged.

Odd Duck owes its name to the Mallard trailer, not to the fact that chef-owner Bryce Gilmore needs his head examined. He's not any more odd than any other twenty-seven-year-old chef working a hundred hours a week turning seasonal, organic, local products into delicious small plates—he's just doing it in a twenty-foot trailer. Painted tangerine orange, trimmed with white, and plastered with signs that announce the business's tagline and Gilmore's mission, "Farm to Trailer," Odd Duck is the new kid on the block in Austin's trailer scene. Bryce is from Austin, where his dad, Jack Gilmore, has been known for his chef skills for a couple of decades, earning himself a good rep first at Z'Tejas and now at his own restaurant, Jack Allen's Kitchen. Not surprisingly, Bryce joined his dad in the kitchen by the time he was fourteen, then headed west to San Francisco's California Culinary Academy, where he fell in love with farmers' markets and eventually landed a job cooking at Boulevard under James Beard–winner Nancy Oakes. "As much as I love San Francisco, I love Austin more," Bryce says. "Austin's my home, and really, as I was getting exposed to all this stuff in San Francisco, Austin was also getting into the local food movement and the farmers' markets were starting to get better. I felt like I wanted to be a part of the beginning of this and felt I had a lot to offer Austin. This trailer was the easiest way to do my own thing and cook some good food."

So that's what he's doing, cooking good food and keeping the same hours as most "real" restaurants of his caliber: dinner only, closed on Sundays and Mondays. On those two days, Bryce is usually heading out to farms to restock and then prepping for the week ahead. He'll buy a whole pig from Richardson Farms in Rockdale, then spend half a day breaking it down so that he can use every inch: belly for sliders, shoulder for braising in

Given the state's shared border with Mexico, it's no surprise to find plenty of Mexican food in Texas. But even the most jaded Tex-Mex diner would be awed by the wealth of options at **El Gran Mercado** (S Pleasant Valley Rd. and Elmont Dr.), a weekend-only daytime flea market where the food trucks and trailers are certainly more of a draw than the blingy belt buckles and "gold" jewelry. Since 2006, Spanish-speaking immigrants preparing all manner of culinary specialties have been setting up shop in this concrete lot, nearly twenty operations in all, the majority Mexican but with a few Salvadoran and Honduran choices sprinkled in (as well as one trailer hawking that ingenious Sonoran-Southwest hybrid, the bacon-wrapped hot dog). The abundance of tacos, fruit *cocteles*, and *elotes* can overwhelm, but be sure to stop at **Tacos Flor** for a *pambazo* (think torta dipped in guajillo chile sauce), **Mari Susi** for lamb barbacoa, and **Carnitas Santa Rosa** for the namesake fat-braised pork. And if you see something you like the looks of but can't muster the proper Spanish phrase to order, go for the universally understood request by pointing then pulling out cash. ◉

coffee, parts and pieces for sausage. He might also start to marinate quail that will eventually hit the grill to order, then get served up with roasted heirloom potatoes and garlicky aioli. There's also rabbit leg that needs to be cooked for hours until the meat just falls from the bone to wind up a beautiful mess with kale and carrot salad. And his signature "slow-cooked" duck egg lives up to its name; a crippled turtle could cross the street before it's ready, since it takes a more than hour-long water bath in an immersion circulator set to 145°F until the yolk takes on an amazing soft custard texture. That egg is always on the chalkboard menu, but the weather determines what you'll see alongside. It might be goat cheese polenta and spring ramps, or fall's finest grilled squash with sautéed wild mushrooms.

Odd Duck opened in early 2010, and most Austin diners seem like they're still trying to wrap their heads around the menu, surprised when they wander over the lot from Gourdough's and find slow-cooked rabbit leg for $6. But so far business is steady, especially when the sun sets, the lights strung up around the lot throw out a misty glow, and the beer and wine help folks endure the fifteen- to twenty-minute wait for trailer food. If a trailer like Odd Duck can make it anywhere, it's probably in a town with a slogan like "Keep Austin Weird."

Coffee-braised Pork Shoulder with Chiles and Sweet Potato Serves 20

Serve this braised pork over polenta, or make tacos with the tender meat.

2 dried ancho chiles

2 dried chipotle chiles

10 pounds pork shoulder, cut into
   1½-inch cubes

Salt and freshly ground black pepper

2 tablespoons vegetable oil

1 yellow onion, diced

3 large carrots, peeled and diced

3 large sweet potatoes, diced

8 cloves garlic, sliced

3 tablespoons cumin seeds

2 tablespoons Spanish sweet paprika

8 cups brewed coffee

¼ cup sherry vinegar

2 bay leaves

5 sprigs fresh thyme

1 sprig fresh rosemary

5 fresh sage leaves

Place the dried chiles in a large bowl, then pour over enough boiling water to cover them. Cover the bowl and let the chiles steep for about 1 hour, or until completely soft, turning halfway through to make sure they are completely submerged. Once the chiles are rehydrated, drain, reserving the water, and scrape the seeds and veins from the chiles using the back of a spoon or a paring knife.

Preheat the oven to 350°F.

Liberally season the pork with salt and pepper. Heat the oil in a large ovenproof Dutch oven or deep cast-iron pan over medium heat. Working in batches, lightly brown the pork shoulder, then remove from the pan and set aside.

Add the onion, carrots, sweet potatoes, garlic, cumin, and paprika to the Dutch oven and stir to scrape the bottom of the pan while the vegetables begin to brown. Once they've softened and are lightly brown, deglaze the pan with the coffee and vinegar.

Add the pork back to the pot, along with the herbs, soaked chiles, the soaking water from the chiles, and enough additional water to just cover the pork. Cut a piece of parchment paper to the shape of the pot and place it directly on top of the pork. Transfer to the oven and cook for 2 hours, until the meat falls apart easily when pierced with a fork. Remove the meat with tongs and serve.

Flip Happy Crêpes

FIND IT: **400 Jessie St., Austin, Texas**
KEEP UP WITH IT: **www.fliphappycrepes.com**

Meet Nessa Farrow and Andrea Day-Boykin. They're friends, their kids are friends, and most of their friends are friends, but Nessa and Andrea are also business partners. They're the brains and brawn behind Flip Happy Crêpes, one of the first of Austin's cool little vintage food trailers. Nessa and Andrea pretty much share a brain, and talking to them usually turns into listening to them, as they tend to go back and forth like two blue-haired ladies hopped up on decaf at the local bingo parlor. So rather than tell you more about them, let's let them tell you about them.

Andrea: I don't even know how it all started. When I was in Ireland, where my husband Patrick is from, I had a crepe that blew me away. It was in Galway, which is like Ireland's Austin, and it was this Irish hippie guy making crepes out of a teeny tiny trailer, and I never got over it. So it was twelve years later and I'm still talking about this crepe. And you were like, "Let's make them in a trailer."

Nessa: I know, and I had never worked at a restaurant. Well, once as a hostess. My mom's side of the family always had restaurants, and we would visit them when I was little. But I had no idea what we were doing.

Andrea: Because you're not that interested in food. My husband, a chef, passed off the food bug to me. We actually met in a restaurant. I was the bartender and he was a cook at the Levy in New York. We stayed there a couple years, then moved to New Orleans, where he worked for Emeril. Then I came to Austin for grad school.

Nessa: Which is so weird, because I was in New Orleans going to Loyola at the same time. . . .

Andrea: But when I met you I was teaching art out of my studio. . . . Both our kids were five, going to school together. You were in film production and getting certified to be a teacher but . . .

Nessa: But then we were like, "Let's do this," and I would just drive all over looking for trailers and putting notes on people's doors when I saw ones that were abandoned.

Andrea: We were driving around weird parts of town and the outskirts.

Nessa: Because we wanted a cheap one.

Andrea: Yeah, because Craigslist had these really fancy Airstreams that were expensive. We just wanted one in someone's yard for a couple grand, which is what you found from Crazy Cowboy Dan.

Nessa: Then Patrick and this other guy gutted everything, did all the electricity, put the windows in, the plumbing, eventually the air-conditioning. We started with two grills, you making savories and I made sweets.

Andrea: Patrick and I looked at French cookbooks and we used a classic French crepe batter. That crepe in Galway, I just wanted to taste it again. You know how things build up in your memory? I called him, the crepe guy, to ask him for advice. I just searched on the Internet for "crepes" and "Galway." Like when I was in New Orleans and we got obsessed with the Cubano sandwich at this little divey place and just knew we were going to put a Cubano crepe on the menu. And I was always obsessed with one that Patrick made when he used to work at a café, one with spinach, feta, and roasted garlic. There was another one with roasted vegetables, sun-dried peppers, balsamic, harissa sauce, and cumin. And we always had the caramelized onions because we knew they'd be delicious on anything.

Nessa: Then we hit it hard. We just got everything up and running.

Andrea: We got really lucky. We were mentioned in *Texas Monthly*. We won Best Crepes in the *Chronicle*. It grew pretty quickly.

Nessa: Back then we would make a few hundred a day and the trailer would look like a tornado hit it. Now on Saturdays we'll sell between four hundred and five hundred crepes in a six-hour shift. After the Bobby Flay thing aired the business quadrupled. We had no preparation. We got one extra cook and a few extra folding chairs.

Andrea: Yeah, because the Food Network told us, "In our experience, your business will quadruple after *Bobby Flay's Throwdown* airs."

Nessa: My family was out of town, Patrick was out of town. It was the worst time. People were coming from every state. The line would be like down the . . .

Andrea: That first shift was unbelievable. Nessa went in the middle of the shift to find another cook.

Nessa: I didn't even know who Bobby Flay was. People were telling us about this *Throwdown* but we never heard of it. So then I watched the show and you kept saying "no" and I was saying "yes."

Andrea: He made a duck chanterelle crepe, and his filling was totally delicious, but remember the problem was his crepe? His crepe was so rubbery. He pulls up in this $100,000 Airstream, brand new, so sharp and slick, and they pull out their awnings and his cooks storm out. It was so very exciting. But he was just working with pans, and the crepe iron gets so much hotter. So we had this really crisp thing going on.

Nessa: It's not easy. It takes a while to get the hang of it.

Andrea: But after the show so many people wanted the Cuban and the bananas and we just couldn't get the bananas the way we wanted them anymore because we were making such huge batches. So we took it off the menu because we weren't happy with the quality. Then people started asking about a restaurant, but I just couldn't even entertain the idea.

Nessa: In the beginning we never talked about eventually doing a store-front because we had no idea it would even work. I don't even remember what I was thinking.

Andrea: You weren't. We never thought past opening a trailer.

Flip Happy Crêpes Makes about twenty 12-inch crepes

6 large eggs

3 cups whole milk

1 cup water

3 1/2 cups all-purpose flour

3/4 cup unsalted butter, melted, plus more
    for cooking the crepes

2 (16-ounce) jars Nutella, for serving

Fresh sliced strawberries, for serving

1 cup heavy cream (optional)

1 teaspoon vanilla extract (optional)

1 tablespoon powdered sugar (optional)

In a large bowl, whisk together the eggs, milk, and water. Whisk in the flour until blended. Add the melted butter and mix again just until combined, being careful not to overmix.

Heat a 12-inch nonstick skillet over medium-high heat. Coat with about 1 table-spoon melted butter. Pour in 1/3 cup of the crepe batter, swirling the pan to spread it evenly over the bottom. Cook for about 2 minutes, until the underside has golden brown spots all over, then flip and cook until speckled on the second side, about 1 minute more. Transfer the crepe to a plate and cover with a kitchen towel while you repeat the process to make the remaining crepes.

To assemble, spread about 1 1/2 tablespoons Nutella inside each warm crepe. Fold in half, then fold in half again to form a triangle. Top with the strawberries. If you want to finish it with a dollop of whipped cream, in a large bowl, whip the cream until it thickens slightly. Add the vanilla and powdered sugar and continue whipping until it forms soft peaks. Spoon the cream on top of the crepes and serve.

The Best Wurst

FIND IT: **6th and San Jacinto Sts. or 6th and Red River Sts., Austin, Texas**
KEEP UP WITH IT: **www.thebestwurst.com**

If you can remember eating a brat at the Best Wurst, you weren't doing it right. Since the cart served its first sausage in Austin's downtown district in the early '90s, it's been the savior of drunkards from far and wide, offering up a little bit of sustenance to help wobbly revelers make it from the show they just saw back to their hotel or into a cab home. Live music venues have been Austin's draw for decades, and in fact, that's what brought Jon Notarthomas to town from Seattle almost twenty years ago. His band, Kaz Murphy & the Pony Mob, played a rowdy house show that sold Jon on Austin, and he quickly relocated, took over his friend's coney stand Flaming Hots, and rebranded it the Best Wurst. That was "probably around 1995," Jon says, dusting off his memory, and since then the little "New York-German-Texas-style" sausage cart has sold over 720,000 encased meats, all grilled on a tiny flattop on wheels next to deep brown, caramelized onions and steaming sauerkraut. Working at lightning speed to satisfy the line that stretches for blocks come last call, Jon and his pit crew have seen their fair share of pukers, flashers, spitters, screamers, kissers, and fighters (Jon even took a sucker punch from a *Real World: Austin* cast member who was promptly cuffed and hauled off by the cops).

"There's been hundreds of arrests here, mainly because there's always some drunk guy who thinks he can cut in front of people and tries to push his way to the front of the line," Jon says. "But we're sort of like the doughnut shop of Sixth Street. The cops are always coming by to check in and they know we're something of a community lookout. We don't want any trouble, but when there's a lot of drunken testosterone, sometimes trouble just happens."

Standing next to his 5 by 6-foot cart as he talks, Jon fields a generous mix of "Hey, Jon!" and "Wooooooo, Best Wurst!" from passersby. A longtime staffer is prepping the three-foot grill for a busy weekend night, coaxing a mountain of sliced onions to caramelize and lining up locally made Smokey Denmark brats next to Italian links from Texas Sausage Company. The crew will sell around 600 sandwiches tonight, with two guys crowded into the cart working with assembly-line precision, another handling the cash, and Jon running "interference," the position responsible for keeping some semblance of order when the bars let out and the line triples in size. "That's when the craziness starts," Jon says. "And it's when we do more than half of our business, between 1:30 and 2:30 a.m. But it wasn't always like this. To be honest, the beginning was brutal."

When Jon bought the cart in the mid-'90s from a fellow Syracuse native attempting to get a true coney and frank operation going, he decided he'd rather take advantage of the Texas Hill Country sausagemakers nearby and quickly switched up the menu. German-style brats, smoked pork Italians, an all-beef dog, and the jalapeño sausage synonymous with Texas became the signature roster, one that hasn't changed to this day. "At the time there was only one guy doing a late-night cart downtown, and that was Johnny Johnson," he recalls. "Johnny was set up in the witness protection program and he liked to brag about it. And he was *extremely* territorial. Early on, he kind of succeeded in pushing us out, but he pushed so hard he actually irritated cops down here and they were like, 'We'd like to see you on Sixth Street, and don't worry about Johnny Johnson.' At one point, he finally disappeared, and as time went on the brats, the name, the signs . . . it all just caught on. But for a while there we were, borrowing money from friends just to buy product every week."

The signs he refers to are a nod to the snarky East Coast sensibilities Jon has long associated with hot dog carts: one barks, "If you can read this, you're in the wrong place! Order from the other side!" and another warns, "Courtesy Counts! . . . and NO bribes, EVER!" Nearly every night the cart is open (Wednesday through Sunday to catch the bar crowd), at least one impatient fool feeling loose with his money can be found wagging a hundred dollar bill in the direction of the grill guy, begging to bypass the twenty-minute line for a sizzling-hot brat *right now* (Jon swears they've never accepted a single one). The urgency, the loyalty, and the lore surrounding the Best Wurst grows each year, compounded by appearances on shows like *Insomniac with Dave Attell* and visits from touring celebs, including Willie Nelson, David Cross, and Guy Fieri. "It's kinda crazy that it went from 'Oh my God, this is what my life's become, a hot dog salesman' to making perfect sense," Jon says. "I've always loved the food, stood behind the quality, and it became freedom for me, being my own boss, using Old World ideals—in that we try to treat people fairly and we don't take credit cards, but if people we know don't have cash we'll extend credit the old way. Still, I wouldn't say the customer is always right, because if a drunk asshole is being a drunk asshole, we don't have to take it. After all, we *are* the Best Wurst."

Food Shark

FIND IT: Highland Ave. between Marfa Book Co. and the railroad tracks under the big pavilion, Marfa, Texas
KEEP UP WITH IT: www.foodsharkmarfa.com

If Austin's motto is "Keep Austin Weird," then the dusty old town of Marfa, an eight-hour drive due west, should be "Keep Marfa Weirder." In the late 1800s, Marfa was little more than a stop for trains to take on water before chugging along to something bigger and better, but when iconic minimalist artist Donald Judd took root there in the early '70s, Marfa started its journey toward outsider artist retreat.

Today, the town of just over two thousand is known for a few things, including a cluster of buildings and open-air spaces known as the Chinati Foundation, conceived by Judd to showcase permanent large-scale art installations. More of a draw to the kind of believers who tune in faithfully to George Noory's *Coast to Coast* radio show are the Marfa Lights, an unexplained phenomenon of glowing spheres occasionally spotted in the sky near Route 67. Perhaps celestial beings are attracted to hip art communities, the kind that span age groups and where everyone somehow resembles either a young Bob Dylan or an old Beck. And nowhere in Marfa do the masses mingle as freely with the occasional gawking tourist or just-passing-through outlaw than at Food Shark, a 1974 Ford Brothers bread delivery truck, wrapped snug in hammered aluminum and given little more than a barn-red door and matching hubcaps for glam. Inside you'll find Adam Bork, an Austin transplant with a mess of hair and Buddy Holly frames, possibly tinkering with one of his many eight-track players taking up space on the truck's dashboard. His girlfriend, Krista Steinhauer, also an Austinite, carved herself the position of Food Shark chef, with little more than two years as a cheese and chocolate buyer for experience. Her crispy chickpea "Marfalafels" have earned plenty of rave reviews (they're packed with fresh herbs and tucked into a flour tortilla with hummus, harissa, tahini, and the usual vegetables), but as popular as they are, Krista gets bored with the standards, gets to tinkering, and whips up daily specials the likes of spiced chicken *banh mi*, *carne guisada* (Tex-Mex meat stew) tacos, maple-glazed ham on rye, and shrimp salad with saffron mayo—a lineup as random as, well, Marfa.

"In Marfa, your neighborhood is your whole town, so you're much more connected," Krista says. "We both grew up in Austin, and the thing that really bugged me is that it's really smug, just so pleased with itself, relentlessly hip and just not very interesting. Here the landscape is extraordinary, and it's a better quality of life. Many . . . people are drawn out by that and by the art, and some of those people stay."

Krista and Adam are now among them, counting themselves as locals since 2004, when they followed their boss, Liz Lambert, from Austin's uber-hip, bungalow-style Hotel San Jose to Lambert's newer project, which was reclaiming a classic mid-century motel in Marfa and reopening it as the ultra-stylish Thunderbird. Two years in, Krista and Adam got antsy and came across the Butter-Krust bread truck, plopped down $1,900, and found themselves in business. Folks in town were looking to turn an abandoned lot near the railroad tracks into a community hub, so they encouraged the couple to park their newly christened Food Shark there. In the six years since, the space has evolved into the site of a weekend farmers' market, a vintage school bus has been added as a dining car for winter months, and chunky wooden Judd-designed picnic tables and benches were added to the lot.

Food Shark is only open from 11:30 a.m. to 3 p.m. Tuesday through Friday, but Krista and Adam still put in twelve-hour days, from prepping the specials from scratch daily to changing out the water on the truck and swapping out fuel tanks. Still, they find time to pursue their passions—her photography, his electronic media–based art—plus they put together quirky YouTube videos, including a Food Shark commercial of the truck tooling down a desert road, leading a pack of vintage cars in a Blue Angels–style V formation, set to an Asian-accented theme song just made for viral video. Only in Marfa.

Krista's Lamb Kebabs Serves 12

4- to 5-pound boneless leg of lamb

MARINADE

2 tablespoons minced garlic

1 tablespoon freshly ground cumin

1 teaspoon paprika

1 teaspoon ground coriander

1/2 teaspoon cayenne

1 teaspoon dried mint

1/2 teaspoon ground ginger

1/2 teaspoon cinnamon

Juice of 2 lemons

2 tablespoons pomegranate molasses

1/2 teaspoon freshly ground black pepper

1 teaspoon salt

1/4 cup olive oil

TOMATO-CUCUMBER SALSA

2 tomatoes, diced

1 cucumber, diced

8 mint leaves, chopped

Salt and freshly ground black pepper

1 tablespoon sumac

2 bunches green onions

12 Anaheim chiles

Olive oil, for tossing

Salt and freshly ground black pepper

12 pieces flatbread or pita

2 cups Greek yogurt or labne

1 tablespoon freshly squeezed lemon juice

1/2 teaspoon freshly ground cumin

Trim the excess fat from the leg of lamb and cut into 1-inch cubes.

To make the marinade, place all of the marinade ingredients in a bowl, whisking to combine, then pour over the lamb, massaging the marinade into the meat. Seal in a large resealable bag and refrigerate for at least 4 hours or up to 24 hours.

To make the tomato-cucumber salsa, combine the tomatoes, cucumber, and mint in a bowl and gently stir together. Season with salt and pepper and set aside.

Thread the lamb cubes onto metal or wooden skewers (if using wooden skewers, soak them in water for 20 minutes first). You should have 12 to 15 skewers, depending on their size.

Toss the whole green onions and chiles with a bit of olive oil and season with salt and pepper.

Prepare a grill for direct cooking over medium-high heat. Grill the lamb to medium-rare, turning as you grill to get a nice char. Grill the chiles and green onions until charred and blistered. Add the flatbread to the grill for just a minute, turning once, to warm through.

In a bowl, stir together the yogurt, lemon juice, 1/2 teaspoon salt, and cumin. Sprinkle the sumac onto the tomato-cucumber salsa. Set out both as toppings and serve everything family-style.

The Que Crawl

FIND IT: twitter.com/thepurpletruck

You can thank young love for New Orleans's best food truck. When Nathaniel Zimet was in his twenties, he cared about cooking, a girl, and little else. So after that girl stuck by him during culinary school in London and Sydney, he returned the favor by following her to New Orleans, where she was heading for college. But when the young chef got to Emeril's city, he wasn't that impressed with the cooking he was seeing: "My mentor, Shane Ingram from Four Square Restaurant in Durham, was rockin', with a menu that changed 100 percent every month, and now I was in a place where the cuisine was very stagnant," Nathaniel says. "I worked and staged at every place I'd ever read about that I thought would be worth anything—all of Emeril's restaurants, Commander's Palace, Stella, Upperline—but I always quit because I wasn't learning anything."

Right around the time that Nathaniel was getting antsy, trying to figure out how to make his mark and where to make it, Hurricane Katrina hit. He and his girlfriend evacuated to North Carolina, but he returned a few weeks later to assess the damage. He didn't expect their place to be in that bad of shape—it was a third-floor apartment in the Uptown neighborhood, an area that didn't see the worst of it—but the building's roof was destroyed, and so was their apartment underneath it. Nathaniel thought he was returning to New Orleans to collect what was left of his things before hightailing it back to North Carolina, but in the wake of the storm, he finally found some pride in his adopted city. "I really just came to clear everything out and figure out what was going on," Nathaniel says. "But the storm just really renewed the community, and all of a sudden I felt a tie there."

As New Orleans started to get back on its feet, Nathaniel was still weighing his cooking options, not exactly excited about the opportunities around him. So he went to Florida for a few weeks to help out at his dad's roofing company, and as the pale redhead was getting scorched in the summer sun, talking over his issues with his dad up on the roofs, he confessed that what he really wanted to do was open a Carolina barbecue joint in New Orleans and use that as a moneymaker to finance his fine dining dream. "My dad said, 'Well, why not do it in a truck?' and that was pretty much that. I was like, 'Uh, yeah, why didn't I think of that?'" With a bit of start-up help from Dad, Nathaniel ordered up a custom mobile kitchen from a manufacturing company, requesting a purple exterior, mainly because "all the white ones I had seen looked dingy to me, and, coming from fine dining, cleanliness is not an option, it's mandatory." The color of a grape juice stain, the Que Crawl

was up and running almost one year to the day after Katrina rolled through town. The hefty box truck has a standard kitchen setup, but no barbecue joint, mobile or not, is complete without a smoker the pit master feels at one with. Nathaniel looked at plenty of options, but in the end he and a friend decided to Dr. Frankenstein it and turn a refrigerator into a giant smoker, pulling out all the rubber gaskets and installing a smoke box on one side to hold the fire and a chimney that sticks out through the top like a straw on a juice box. "It's frickin' awesome," Nathaniel says, his Southern drawl deepening as he gets excited. "In about a year I'm gonna start entering barbecue competitions where they have all their high-tech smokers, and I'll pull up and roll out this fridge on casters and just frickin' destroy 'em all."

He's confident because his barbecue can back it up. It's Low Country know-how with highbrow ingredients: his slow-smoked brisket is made from Wagyu beef, he knows the name of the pig farmer behind his Carolina-style pulled pork, his signature "Boudin Balls" combine Cajun dirty rice with smoked pork and duck liver, and his collard greens get cooked down overnight with a rich duck stock potlikker before they're teamed up with thick fries made from cheesy grits.

The Que Crawl's reception was huge from its inception, with local and national press jumping all over this talented young chef on wheels and catering requests flying in daily. Soon Nathaniel was rolling his purple truck onto movie sets to cater for the day, and he was turning down jobs because he could only be in one place at one time. The success came at a price—the girl got tired of playing second fiddle to that refrigerator smoker, and the restaurant the truck was supposed to finance just couldn't get going because there weren't enough hours in the day. "At one point I said to my dad, 'I'm gonna either sell everything and go run away somewhere or I'm gonna open a restaurant,' and he said, 'You gotta do what you gotta do, boy,' and I knew what I had to do was open the restaurant."

And so the truck took a bit of a back seat for a while until Nathaniel was able to realize his dream. In 2008 he opened Boucherie, a forty-one-seat contemporary Southern spot in a charming Creole cottage. There are tablecloths, but they're topped with brown butcher paper; there are scallops and duck on the menu, but they're priced around $15. Nathaniel calls it "fine dining for the people." It's critically acclaimed, and it's packed. And, luckily, since it has opened Nathaniel has built up a good support team, strong enough that he can turn some of his attention back to the truck that started it all. "I have a retirement plan in mind, a family plan, a three-pronged attack involving the restaurant, the truck, and the next project, which I'm hoping to get off the ground by 2012 at the latest." And as for getting the girl back? "I'm an optimist," Nathaniel says. "Anything's possible."

Que Crawl's Boudin Balls Makes about 40 meatballs

2 pounds pork butt or shoulder

Salt

Spice rub (purchased or made from chili
    powder, paprika, cumin, coriander,
    mustard seed, garlic powder, onion
    powder, and black pepper, to taste)

5 cloves garlic, 1 minced

1/2 sweet onion, such as Walla Walla or
    Vidalia

1 stalk celery, coarsely chopped

3 green bell peppers, coarsely chopped

2 tablespoons unsalted butter

2 1/2 cups chicken stock

1 teaspoon cayenne pepper

2 bay leaves

1/2 bunch fresh thyme

1 sprig fresh sage

1 cup Louisiana popcorn rice or long-grain
    white rice

6 ounces duck livers, finely chopped

3 green onions

Canola oil, for brushing and frying

Freshly ground black pepper

2 cups all-purpose flour

6 eggs, beaten

2 cups fine dry bread crumbs

Dipping sauce (preferably garlic aioli)

Heat a smoker to 180° to 200°F, preferably using a mixture of oak, hickory, and pecan.

Season the pork butt liberally with salt and the rub, place in a large pan, and transfer to the smoker. Cook for about 6 hours. Remove the pork from the smoker, cover the pan with a lid or tented foil, and transfer to a 250°F oven. Cook until you can pull the meat apart with a gentle tug, about 2 additional hours. Remove from the oven, let cool, and shred the pork. Set aside. Reserve the pan juices.

While the pork is cooking, purée 4 cloves of garlic, the onion, celery, and bell peppers in a food processor. Heat 1 tablespoon of the butter in a sauté pan over medium heat and sauté the onion mixture until all of the moisture has evaporated.

Add the chicken stock, 3/4 cup of the reserved stock, the cayenne, bay leaves, thyme, and sage and bring to a boil. Add the popcorn rice, reduce the heat to low, cover, and simmer for 20 minutes. Remove the bay leaves and set aside.

Heat the remaining 1 tablespoon butter in a sauté pan over medium-high heat. Add the minced garlic and duck livers and sauté until browned, about 7 minutes. Set aside.

Brush the green onions with canola oil and season with salt and pepper. Either grill them until they are lightly charred, about 2 minutes, or sauté until the edges brown, about 4 minutes. Chop finely.

In a large bowl, using your hands, mix together the pulled pork, cooked rice, duck livers, and green onions, then form the mixture into golf ball-size balls.

Heat the oil in a deep fryer or large heavy-bottomed pan to 350°F. (The oil should be at least 3 inches deep.) Meanwhile, spread the flour on a plate, put the beaten eggs in a shallow bowl, and spread the bread crumbs on a separate plate. Dredge the boudin balls in the flour, then the beaten eggs, and then the bread crumbs and carefully drop into the hot oil. Working in batches, fry them until brown, 4 to 5 minutes. Using a slotted spoon, transfer to a paper towel-lined plate. Serve immediately with dipping sauce.

Only Burger

KEEP UP WITH IT: twitter.com/onlyburger

There's no way to determine exactly how many trips to Disney World the NFL has inspired since the signature Super Bowl quip started in the late '80s. But we can definitely thank the Dallas Cowboys for the sales of around two hundred burgers a day in Durham, North Carolina. "I'm a big Cowboys fan," explains Tom Ferguson. "So one year I was watching this interview from Thousand Oaks, California, where the Cowboys have spring training, and the guys were talking about loving the In-N-Out Burger truck. That was it. I decided then and there to do a burger truck in Durham."

Luckily, Tom knew a thing or two about food. The CIA grad had two decades of cooking experience under his belt, with time spent at kitchens around the country, from Seattle to Austin, Nashville to D.C. But it was what he calls "L.A.'s burger culture" that made him a patty connoisseur and pushed him to concoct a burger "not quite as big as Fat Burger but not as thin as In-N-Out." Tom secured a grass-fed beef source to supply him with hormone- and antibiotic-free meat and an 80/20 meat-to-fat ratio; lined up a local butcher to coarsely grind the meat daily; and developed a double-fry Belgian-style method for his hand-cut Idaho potatoes, first frying the pinkie-thick, skin-on sticks, resting them, then frying once again to order before sprinkling on salt and pepper. He also purchased a hefty twenty-four-foot workhorse truck fully converted by a Jersey company specializing in mobile kitchens, and since he had already been running Durham Catering Company for nearly a decade, licensing the burger truck through that commissary kitchen was a cinch. In line with his desire to keep things simple—burgers, fries, and drinks are it—he and his team christened their rig exactly what it was, Only Burger, as in "What is that?" "Durham's Only Burger truck."

The start-up was simple enough, but operations weren't as smooth. Tom set up as a campus vendor at Duke when Only Burger launched in fall of 2008, but his catering responsibilities meant he wasn't always on the truck flipping burgers. The concept was popular initially, but inconsistencies, such as oversalting fries and overcooking burgers, made their way onto the local blogs and didn't do much to help business. Almost by divine intervention, an accident put the truck in the shop for a good three months, just around the time Brian Bottger got wind of the project. Brian had worked for Tom in the past, had plenty of restaurant experience, and was actually looking to start up his own truck, so he offered to buy Only Burger, damaged or not. Tom wasn't ready to let go, so he brought Brian on as a partner, and they got the truck back on the streets in March of 2009.

"This time around we first perfected the product, and while we did go to Duke, we also found street corners with high traffic throughout all of Durham," Brian says. "We were putting out a consistent product, and it didn't take long of us sitting parked in lots waiting before people started discovering us and the buzz started building."

"Brian is really the face of the company," Tom says. "What he brought to it was what we were missing: a working partner, running the truck and working the crew. And he really worked on developing the clientele, hitting the neighborhood parks and pulling up to people's parties for an hour before moving on, just engaging the community. You can have a great burger, but until the community latches on to you, you don't really have anything."

The Only Market Burger Serves 4

1 quart vegetable oil	1/2 cup panko (Japanese bread crumbs)
1/2 cup all-purpose flour	2 green tomatoes, ends removed and
1/2 teaspoon salt, or to taste	thickly sliced
1/2 teaspoon freshly ground black pepper,	4 hamburger buns
or to taste	3 tablespoons unsalted butter, melted
6 eggs	1/2 pound grass-fed beef (80/20 ratio)
1/4 cup water	4 ounces pimiento cheese

Heat the vegetable oil to 375°F in a deep fryer or a deep, heavy pan.

In a bowl, season the flour with the salt and pepper.

In another bowl, whisk 2 of the eggs with water to make an egg wash. Spread the panko on a plate. Dip the tomato slices, one at a time, in to the seasoned flour, transfer to the egg wash, and then toss in the panko until coated. Carefully place them in the hot oil and fry until golden brown. Using a slotted spoon, transfer to a paper towel-lined plate to drain.

Heat a large griddle over medium heat, brush the buns with 1 tablespoon of the melted butter, and toast on the griddle until golden brown. Set aside.

Form the beef into 4 patties of equal size. Liberally season with salt and pepper. Heat a large griddle pan or stovetop grill pan over medium-high heat and add the burgers to the pan. Cook, turning once, until medium-rare, 2 to 3 minutes, or longer if desired.

While the burgers are cooking, heat a large nonstick pan over high heat, add the remaining 2 tablespoons butter, and crack the remaining 4 eggs into the pan, frying until cooked over easy, or over medium if preferred.

To assemble, spread 1 ounce of the pimento cheese on the top half of each bun, then layer 1 burger, 1 egg, and 2 slices of the fried green tomatoes on the bottom of the bun. Assemble the two halves and serve immediately.

(SIDE DISH)

Out-of-towners might breeze past **Sam's Quik Shop** (1605 Erwin Rd., www.samsquikshop .com), a squat mid-century-era convenience store, and think it's nothing more than an indie, old-time 7-Eleven. And it is. But it happens to have the best beer selection in Durham, and thanks to the chutzpah of Only Burger's Brian Bottger, it also plays host to the **Bull City Street Vendors Rodeo**, an occasional event of a half-dozen food trucks and trailers that turn the parking lot into a mobile food court. Aside from grass-fed patties from Only Burger, the lineup includes sweets from **Daisy Cakes** Airstream (www.eatdaisycakes .com), Korean tacos by **Bulkogi Korean BBQ to Go** (twitter.com/ NCBulkogi), the made-to-order namesake at **Parlez-Vous Crepe** cart (www.parlezvouscrepe.com), comfort food from **Mom's Delicious Dishes** (www.moms deliciousdishes.com), fresh-squeezed drinks out of a mini-bus dubbed **Liberación Juice Station** (www.liberacionjuice station.com), and South Indian fare from a red school bus named simply **Indian Food on Wheels** (parked at Sam's daily). Tables and chairs lend a picniclike atmosphere, and many take advantage of Sam's beer selec-tion, washing down their truck lunch with a cold one. ◉

It's natural to think that the Gateway to the Americas would have some serious ethnic food options. It does, but not so much in the way of mobile eats. The city with the largest Cuban population in the country is known more for cafeterias sporting walk-up windows, where tanned and toned locals make their daily stops for *café con leche*, guava empanadas, and, of course, the king of pressed sandwiches, the Cuban. So while grab-and-go eating is still very much a part of Miami life—as much if not more so than the glitzy South Beach spots with pulsating music and tropical cocktails—food trucks have yet to make their mark.

The city began recording mobile food vending licenses in 1979, and although the numbers for Miami-Dade County reached an impressive 650 in 2003, they've been dropping like flies ever since. The majority of street vendors remaining in Miami peddle hot dogs, bottled water, and soda, with the number of food trucks actually cooking fresh food somewhere in the teens. Perhaps because of that, innovative truck chefs like GastroPod's Jeremiah Bullfrog aren't just creating a stir when they roll into a spot and start cooking pork belly sliders and *banh mi* tacos—they're helping keep Miami on the culinary map, one mobile meal at a time.

Miami, Florida

GastroPod

KEEP UP WITH IT: twitter.com/gastropodmiami

Cooking on private yachts and beachside hotels in exotic locales like St. Thomas and Belize sounds like every chef's dream, but Jeremiah Bullfrog left it all for a 1962 Airstream. The Miami native took his Johnson & Wales culinary education about as far as any chef could hope to, parlaying an internship at Spain's famed house of molecular gastronomy, El Bulli, into opportunities to cook with the Stateside titans of the movement, New York's WD-50 and Chicago's Moto. For those who've been living under a comfort-food rock, these are the freak-geeks your science teacher threw out of class for nearly burning down the lab, only now they've become chefs and they're tinkering with chemicals and equipment that equates to hard-to-snag reservations and tasting menus starting at $100 a head. Jeremiah's time at El Bulli was his gateway drug, and after more tutelage in the realm of foams, Cryovac machines, and liquid nitrogen tanks, he settled into his own style of cooking: part gadget cookery obsession, part Caribbean influence via Miami, a foundation of classic techniques from his culinary education, and that dash of Asian flair almost impossible to avoid when coming of age as a chef during the 1990s. He rolled it all into a package perfect for island resorts and their well-fed clientele, but the only trouble was, those island riddims are tough to hear from inside the kitchen. "You're living in paradise, but the work is hell," Jeremiah says. "The conditions are extremely difficult, with this third-world setup where 80 percent of the stuff you need coming in from outside the island, so you're spending so much time sourcing product, plus trying to assemble a quality staff is tough. It's always a ninety-hour workweek, and after doing it for a while, I was done."

So he returned to Miami in 2005 and turned a warehouse into a trial venue for his vision of a nontraditional restaurant, which Jeremiah describes as "more of a hangout than a restaurant." There was no set menu, fluctuating hours, periodic events with local artists and bands—essentially a business model that makes no sense to the kind of businessmen with the money to make such ventures work. And so after two years of some interesting food and a lot of fun, Bullfrog Eatz morphed into a catering company, a natural fit for a chef with a resort-padded Rolodex. Around this time, Jeremiah got his hands on a forty-foot-long fire engine–red trailer emblazoned with a giant pig and the words "Mmm mmm barbecue," and he used the rig for catering gigs. "It was kinda cool that we had this obnoxious trailer and were doing gourmet food out of it, but it was too big and too bulky and just wasn't set up right," he says. Still, the seed was planted.

After Jeremiah unloaded the pig-mobile, he bought a vintage Airstream off eBay and immediately started drawing up plans for turning the iconic RV into a state-of-the-art kitchen on wheels. The equipment you'd find on the GastroPod is the same stuff you'd find in the best kitchens in the country, from Alinea to the French Laundry. A CVap "Cook and Hold" oven cooks food to a precise temperature, then holds it there using what's called "controlled vapor technology," essentially surrounding the food with moisture and creating a pressure chamber that keeps it in a holding pattern. GastroPod is also outfitted with three five-gallon water baths with thermal immersion circulators, the devices behind a method of cooking known as sous vide, a technique so popular that chef Thomas Keller published a whole book on it in 2008. A flattop griddle is the most recognizable device in the Airstream, used by Jeremiah to "pick up" (finish) orders that are about 90 percent completed using the other equipment on board.

With a setup that could make any young chef drool, Jeremiah launched GastroPod in late 2009, taking his old-school trailer and new-school ideas to music festivals, beachside bonfires, and backyard cocktail parties throughout the Miami area. His triple-decker slider was an instant hit: three patties formed from a special blend of brisket and short rib meat, stacked one on top of the other with a shaving of pork belly between each layer. Yep, you heard right. Jeremiah first cooks the belly sous vide, then freezes it and uses a microplane grater to create a snowlike dusting of pork flavor. The tower is held together using Activa (a.k.a. meat glue), then grilled on the flattop to order. For equal flavor but a little less Frankenfood style, the Sloppy Jose is it: beef brisket soaked in espresso-spiked barbecue sauce and cooked until spoon-tender in the CVap, served on toasted potato bread with "Stupid Slaw," a vinegar-based cabbage slaw revved up with Sriracha. Pulled pork gets a similar treatment, braised in *nuoc cham* (the chile–garlic–fish sauce nectar of the Vietnamese gods) and tossed into a corn tortilla along with pickled breakfast radishes, fresh cilantro, and more of that Stupid Slaw (which, in case you're wondering, gets its name because Jeremiah deemed it "stupid good").

On paper, the menu sounds fairly straightforward (with, of course, the occasional exception of a liquid nitrogen shake or deconstructed gazpacho). But remember that while the end result might resemble a normal hot dog or hamburger, no freezer or factory-produced package was opened in the making of them. On the contrary, hours of prep go into each seemingly simple menu item, with both Jeremiah and his state-of-the-art equipment responsible for the execution, important whether serving Miami's movers and shakers poolside or six hundred drunk and sunburned music festival–goers. Gastropod's success among those with an eye for details and with local and national media alike has spawned private event requests throughout

(SIDE DISH)

When **Latin Burger & Taco** (twitter.com/latinburger) first launched in early 2010, much of the opening buzz centered around the Food Network's Ingrid Hoffman, billed as the consulting chef for the impressive eighteen-foot kitchen on wheels. Soon enough, though, the truck became better known for their burger, a flavor-packed blend of chorizo, chuck, and sirloin, topped with wisps of Oaxacan string cheese, caramelized onions, blistered jalapeños, and a lime-packed avocado sauce. And it's a good thing the focus shifted, too, because, as it turns out, Hoffman is no longer involved with the business. Her former boyfriend Jim Heins is plugging along as the truck's owner/operator regardless, building up quite a reputation for the burger that started out as the focus of a friendly cook-off between the couple. Heins says the winning recipe is an amalgam of both his and Hoffman's signature burgers, but from the looks of his booming lunch business, no one seems to care much who's behind the food–they're more concerned with eating it. ◉

the region, even prompting an East Coast tour last summer with stops in Charleston, Asheville, Brooklyn, Long Island, and Connecticut—exactly the kind of road trip this kitchen was built for.

GastroPod's Sloppy Jose Makes about 12 sandwiches

4 pounds beef brisket

1/4 cup smoked paprika

1 tablespoon ground cumin

1 tablespoon ground coriander

1 tablespoon garlic powder

Kosher salt

2 cups packed brown sugar, plus more
    as needed

1 cup malt vinegar, plus more as needed

1 cup ketchup

1 shot espresso or 1 cup coffee, plus more
    as needed

24 slices potato bread

Melted unsalted butter, for brushing

Cut the brisket into 4 equal pieces. In a bowl, stir together the paprika, cumin, coriander, and garlic powder to make a rub. Season the brisket generously with salt and the dry rub, massaging the seasonings into the meat. Allow the meat to rest until it starts to moisten, about 10 minutes.

Preheat the oven to 350°F. Heat a large sauté pan over medium-high heat and, working one at a time, sear each piece of the brisket until it is evenly browned on all sides. Transfer the brisket to a baking dish with high sides in which the brisket fits snugly in a single layer.

In a bowl, whisk the sugar into the vinegar until it dissolves. Add the ketchup and espresso and stir to blend. Pour the liquid over the brisket and add enough water so that the liquid just covers the meat. Cover the pan with foil and transfer to the oven. Cook until the meat reaches an internal temperature of 185°F, which should take around 3 1/2 hours. Remove the foil during the last 45 minutes of cooking time.

Remove the brisket from the oven and allow it to cool to room temperature. Carefully remove the brisket from the pan. Chill the liquid in the refrigerator until the fat hardens on top. Scrape off the fat, add the remaining liquid to a saucepan, and bring to a simmer over medium heat. Simmer until the liquid has thickened and reduced by half, about 30 minutes. Taste and adjust the flavor, adding more vinegar, sugar, salt, or coffee as needed; you want the sauce to taste earthy, sweet, and sour.

Chop or shred the brisket into small pieces and toss with the sauce. Brush the potato bread with the butter and toast in the oven. Pile the brisket between slices of bread and serve.

Yellow Submarine

FIND IT: weekday lunches, at 137 Ave. and 128th St.; nights except Monday, at 147 Ave. and Kendall Dr., Miami, Florida
KEEP UP WITH IT: twitter.com/yellowtwiter [sic]

Flavio Alarcon wishes he got laid off a long time ago. After spending seven years as an accounts manager for a distributor of Dietz & Watson deli meats, his company merged with the cold-cut giant, essentially eliminating his position. Flavio decided to make good on a decade-old idea to launch a food truck, putting his deli meat savvy to good use with a menu of hoagies and putting his Colombian family to work as the staff. "I always wanted to do something in a truck, really since I moved to Miami from Colombia in 1998 and started seeing them around," Flavio says. "I did look for a retail space for a sandwich shop, but in Miami it's impossible to a get good location for a good price, so I said, 'Okay, this is it. This is the time. Let's do it on wheels.'"

A music fanatic and guitarist for a band that bangs out '80s covers, Flavio tapped into a Beatles vibe by dubbing his new business Yellow Submarine, painting a former postal truck happy face–yellow, and slapping it with a cartoonish logo depicting a periscope cruising through the waters. Sub sandwiches with names like Lady Madonna, Killer Queen, and New Sensation are built from classic hoagie rolls, standard toppings, and, of course, high-quality cold cuts. But it's when Flavio's mother Myriam dips her hands into the menu that things get interesting. Apparently, in Colombia, a burger without pineapple sauce and crushed potato chips ceases to be a burger—it's simply a waste of time. Yellow Submarine pays homage to this tradition, adding the toppings to Myriam's blend of ground chuck, cumin, garlic, and onions. She's also behind the homemade mustard, the pesto, the pineapple sauce, and the *salsa rosada*, a salmon-colored condiment that could simply be called tomato-mayo, but that wouldn't have quite the same ring to it.

Flavio and his younger brother Andres work the truck, parking near their commissary warehouse by day and in a shopping mall lot by night. They take turns manning the window and grilling mom's hand-formed burgers on the truck's flattop, smashing the edges down with a spatula as they sizzle to lacy perfection. Like the Colombian-style hot dog the truck sells, the burger gets shredded lettuce, tomato, provolone, and that homemade mustard. But clearly it's the marriage of tart, sweet, and crunchy that happens when the *salsa rosada* meets the pineapple and crushed chips that make this patty memorable. Couple the Yellow Burger with home-style

The last thing you'd expect to see among the mansions and sprawling condo developments on the swank island village of Key Biscayne is a Peruvian guy dishing up ceviche out of a van. But that's precisely why Marcelo Florindez does such good business–he's impossible to miss. Parked near the entrance to Calusa Park, just off the Rickenbacker Causeway, **Marcelo's Ceviche** (Crandon Blvd. near the entrance to Calusa Park) is a mobile taste of the sea, dished up Peruvian style from noon to 3 p.m. daily. Locals ride up to Marcelo's white van by bike and then fork over a few bucks for impeccably fresh *ceviche de corvina*, bite-size hunks of firm fish soaked in lime juice before being tossed in a Styrofoam cup along with red onion slivers, corn kernels, diced potato, and a squirt of *aji amarillo*, a fruity hot sauce made from Peruvian yellow chile peppers. Order it "*mixto*" and get just-shucked shellfish tossed in; order it "*tiradito*" and your fish is sliced in razor-thin strips. Marcelo assembles each ceviche to order, giving this coastal classic a custom treatment, and does nothing else out of his setup other than *chicha morada*, a fermented purple corn drink, spiced like Christmas and refreshing enough to send those cyclists on their way fully fueled. ◉

desserts (like ambrosia and chocolate pudding pie) courtesy of Flavio's sister, Angela, and you just about feel like you're in the Alarcon dining room, eating simply, leaving satisfied. "By myself, I couldn't do it, but with the help of my family, I know this is going to work," Flavio says. "Before, I was getting by, doing fine in my job, and when you are okay in a job, you don't look forward. But when you are forced to make a change, you realize anything is possible. For me, it was the best decision I ever was forced to make."

Myriam's Yellow Burger Serves 4

1 teaspoon ground cumin
1 teaspoon pepper
1 teaspoon salt
1 teaspoon chopped garlic
1 onion, coarsely chopped
4 teaspoons bread crumbs
2 pounds chuck ground beef
1/2 tablespoon olive oil

PINEAPPLE SAUCE
1 cup canned pineapple
Juice of 1/2 lime
1 tablespoon sugar

SALSA ROSADA
2 Roma tomatoes
2 tablespoons chopped sun-dried tomatoes
1/2 cup mayonnaise

4 teaspoons butter
4 hamburger buns
4 butter lettuce leaves
4 tomato slices
4 onion slices
4 handfuls potato chips (kettle style preferred), crushed

Combine the cumin, pepper, salt, garlic, onion, and bread crumbs in a food processor until all ingredients are well chopped. Add this mixture to the ground beef and incorporate well with your hands. Form the meat into 4 round balls and flatten into patties 1-inch thick.

Heat a griddle or skillet over medium-high heat, add the olive oil, then add the beef patties and cook for 5 minutes on each side, or as desired.

To make the pineapple sauce, purée all of the ingredients in a blender.

To make the salsa rosada, purée all of the ingredients in a blender.

While the burgers are cooking, lightly butter and toast the buns on a separate griddle or pan on the stovetop. Slather the top bun with the pineapple sauce and the bottom bun with the salsa rosada. When the burgers are ready, transfer to the buns and top with lettuce, tomato, onion, and potato chips. Store any unused sauce covered in the refrigerator for up to 3 days.

Angela's Chocolate Pudding and Cookies Serves 8 to 12

2 (3.5-ounce) boxes chocolate pudding
   ("cook and serve")
4 cups cold milk
1 can Nestlé table cream

1 can condensed milk
2 (3.15-ounce) packages Goya Maria cookies
   (Mexican butter cookies)

Make the chocolate pudding with the milk following the package instructions. Let the pudding rest for 2 to 3 minutes, then add the table cream and condensed milk, mixing well.

Into a large, round glass bowl, pour enough of the chocolate mixture to cover the bottom of the container. Add a layer of the Maria cookies, then top with a layer of the pudding; repeat this procedure until the cookies and chocolate mixture are used up. Let the dessert rest in the refrigerator for 2 hours, then slice into portions, spoon out onto plates, and serve.

(SIDE DISH)

For the most part, the clientele frequenting strip clubs aren't expecting much in the way of, uh, sustenance. And that's exactly why Benjamin Nelson rigged his smoker up to his truck and brought his **Fat Man's Barbecue** (333 NE 79th St.) to the parking lot of a roughneck gentlemen's club in Miami. With hip-hop booming out of the bar and a steady stream of smoke pouring out of the Fat Man's hickory-fired cooker, there's a definite block party vibe at Take One Lounge come weekend nights. Benjamin sells fried chicken, burgers, a rotating lineup of grilled seafood, and moist lemon cake, but it's the slabs of spareribs cooking low and slow that brings the fellas out of the club and into the lot, cash in hand. The pole girls normally aren't too happy about watching clients walk out the door to spend money some-where else, but as long as the guys return with an extra rib or two to spare, that's the only tip they need. ◉

EAST COAST

Follow Us on Twitter
jamaicandutchy

H ot dog carts are as firmly associated with New York City as the Empire State Building (just try and watch a *Law & Order* episode without seeing a cop ordering at one). The city can't claim the frankfurter as its own, but there are accounts of hot dogs showing up at Coney Island as far back as the 1860s, cooked over coal and sold from a cart. Soon after, these pushcarts made their way to Manhattan, becoming a staple in areas thick with pubs. By the 1920s, mobile hot dog businesses were popping up around the country, but New York owned the game, with pushcarts, wagons, and even horse-drawn carts hawking hot dogs throughout the state. The affordable, portable snack continued to dominate New York's street food options through the 1970s, a decade that saw the city's color palette change considerably, thanks to a 1965 immigration law that did away with quotas. Those quotas had meant the majority of immigrants hitting New York City from about the 1920s on hailed from different parts of Europe. Most of the street food businesses up until that point were run by Greek immigrants, who jumped on the hot dog (band)wagon and were considered flashy if they added souvlaki to their lineup. But by 1970, Jamaicans, Cubans, and the Dominicans got in on the game, although they largely catered to their own communities, meaning unless you were a part of it, you were not a part of it. *Village Voice* food critic Robert Sietsema recalls the street food scene in 1977—the scene accessible

to the average American-born New Yorker, anyway—as "dismal." He recounts: "When I first came to New York, 90 percent of the street food I saw was hot dog carts, which people had derisory names for like 'floaters' and 'dirty water dogs.' And you ate those out of both love and hatred. Love because it was so New York, but hatred because it was all you could get. You just knew there was more."

"By 1990 there were illegal carts in Chinatown and carts in Astoria nobody ever bothered to chase down," Sietsema recalls. "Around that time, the halal carts in Midtown arose out of necessity for Muslim taxi drivers, traders, and delivery drivers from the Middle East, Malaysia, and Africa. It turned into this cart-specific pan-Muslim world of food, from kebabs to curries to biryani."

As the immigrant population continued to swell through the end of the last century, so did New York's street food options. According to the Population Division at New York's Department of City Planning, 18.2 percent of the city's population was foreign-born in 1970. By 2000, the number had doubled to 36.6 percent. A food cart is much easier to start than a restaurant, especially for someone new to this country, its laws, and its language. On the other side of New York's street food coin is the gourmand with social media savvy and a flush audience of followers at his or her fingertips. The range could lazily be defined as low-end to high-end, but

Muhammad Rahman is the kind of character who makes the Midtown halal cart scene more enticing than any soap opera. The Bangladeshi chef and entrepreneur has taken his Russian Tea Room pedigree (plus his chef's coat and toque) and combined it with his mother's tutelage at **Kwik Meal** (W 45th St. at 6th Ave.; www.kwikmeal.net). Devotees include Ruth Reichl and Jane and Michael Stern, and everyone raves about the lamb. In a genre where "lamb on rice" usually means "gyro meat on rice," Muhammad stands out for using actual leg of lamb, which he marinates in a mashup of cumin, ginger, garlic, coriander, and green papaya before sizzling it to order on the tiny cart's white-hot flattop. (Interestingly enough, the tiny globes of bright green falafel are even better, the sleeper hit indeed.) But more interesting is keeping up with Muhammad: in the ten years since opening his original cart, he has built an empire of four carts, branched out with an Italian cart called Kwik Pasta, and taken over a Harlem pizzeria called Presidential Pizza. After Obama took office, Muhammad unveiled a cart by the name of "Meal O'Bama," whose sign he later changed to "Kwik Meal IV" after enough people asked him 1) Why the Irish-ish apostrophe? and 2) Wasn't he worried ➜

it's more than that. On one end of the spectrum it's cooks catering to their community by creating a menu of what they know, and selling it from a cart that's generally parked in one place. At the other end, it's cooks coming up with a concept, developing a brand, and investing a good amount of money on a truck, giving themselves the mobility to chase the crowds.

When it comes to the latter, just about every big-name chef in New York has likely tossed around the idea of taking his or her food to the streets. The only problem? The city has a cap on permits, and no amount of pressure has been able to raise it. There are 2,800 permits available for citywide operation, and an additional 50 per borough (Bronx, Brooklyn, Queens, and Staten Island). In a city of eight million, there's a permit waiting list that's longer than the Brooklyn Bridge. Cruising Craigslist on any given day will deliver "turnkey" (ready to roll) mobile kitchens sans permits in the neighborhood of $20,000 to $30,000. A truck with a two-year citywide permit? Try $80,000. In the cart community, it's not uncommon for family members to swap permits from one cart to another, and there's definitely a black market for fake permits. But as Sietsema says, "I don't even care about legalities. The city just wants to stick their fat fingers in so they can collect money . . . I say, the more the merrier."

NY Dosas

FIND IT: **West 4th St. at Sullivan St., New York, New York**
KEEP UP WITH IT: **twitter.com/nydosas**

"I'm listed in forty-two countries in tour guidebooks as a landmark. People wear my T-shirts. I have fan clubs in Japan, Canada, and San Francisco. I have a Facebook page under 'The Dosa Man' that someone started for me. I won the Vendy Award in 2007 and *New York Magazine*'s 'Best Cart' in 2003. I have a following so big now I can't stop even if I wanted to."

Thiru Kumar isn't bragging; he's just proud. And he has every right to be. In the mid-1990s he came to New York from Jaffna, Sri Lanka. Twenty-seven years old, he had nothing to call his own but a wife and young daughter. He started out in construction and wound up in the *New York Times*. What happened in between is not that different from the stories of many immigrant food vendors: get a job in a fellow countryman's restaurant, gain experience, scrape together some money, buy or build a tiny cart, get a green card (if you're lucky) and a vending permit (if you're even luckier), and open for business. Except Thiru didn't want to blend in with the hot dog and halal carts cluttering New York's city streets. His own personal eating habits and those of his friends inspired him to plaster "PURELY VEGETARIAN" along his tiny grill on wheels, and he set about bringing dosas to the masses. In Sri Lanka, a stone's skip across the water from Southern Indian, these lacy lentil and rice crepes are common. But, as Thiru is quick to point out, "Ours are different. You won't get the Jaffna dosa in India, and you won't get my dosa, my grandmother's recipe, anywhere else. Nowhere."

The NYU students he knows by name seem to agree; they've been forming lines that resemble concert queues since the day NY Dosas opened on the edge of Washington Square Park in 2002. Grinning through his thick moustache while calling out to regulars—"Kristen, Pondicherry dosa today, yeah? Michael, samosa, green chutney, and Jaffna dosa, yeah?"—Thiru works the scorching griddle like he could do this blindfolded, drunk, with one hand tied behind his back. A mountain of potatoes the color of sunflowers, dotted with tiny black mustard seeds and peas, stays warm in a corner of the griddle. Dunking his ladle into one of three fat containers of batter, Thiru comes out with the perfect amount for one dosa, pouring it onto the grill in one continuous circle that grows bigger from the center until the pancake is almost two feet across. "I make three different batters: the *uttapam* is real rice and lentils, and the dosa batter is rice and lentil *flour*, plus wheat flour. And the Jaffna dosa also has a lot of natural herbs, like *methi*, and onions in the batter. Plus I don't use any yeast," Thiru says

about legalities? Shortly after that, his disgruntled brother Fahima opened a cart only a few feet from the original Kwik Meal, posting a sign that read, "Why pay more money? Fahima-Halal food much better than Kwik Meal." Fahima alleged his brother hadn't been paying him for his work, so he decided to retaliate with some, uh, healthy competition. Eventually, Fahima moved his cart a few blocks away, but the family feud went down in the books among the many in the street food world. ◉

Word among New York's culinary cognoscenti is that at one time Chinatown was lousy with street food, most of it about as regulated as backyard wrestling. These days, most of the eating has moved indoors, not that you won't find a few sit-down storefronts where the sidewalk out front might actually be cleaner. Still, a handful of carts manage to do good business, likely because they've each carved out their own niche, getting tongues wagging for one or two particular specialties. Of these, the standouts include an unmarked cart on the southeast corner of Mott and Canal where **The Wus**, a mother-father-son team, have a way with fried chicken. Hoisin and garlic salt do half of the work, mixed into the cornstarch that clings to each piece, but the matriarch handles the other half, deftly dunking the drumsticks in vegetable oil to the most perfect shade of brown. Over at Grand Street and Bowery, at **Huan Ji Rice Noodles**, scissors fly with each order of *cheung fun*. The ribbons of silky rolled rice noodles are snipped with precision over a seemingly bottomless takeout container, topped with spongy curried fish balls, and finished with a hat trick of oyster sauce, peanut sauce, and sesame seeds. Save room for dessert; a few steps away ➔

proudly. "It ferments naturally. The rice soaks for six hours, then sits for another six hours outside to ferment, to give it that flavor, that tang."

After spooning some of the curried potatoes onto a nearly finished Pondicherry dosa, Thiru scatters a tricolor mix of raw julienned bell peppers and carrots, slides his spatula under a crispy edge, and folds the dosa over onto itself. He starts in on an order of *uttapam*, forming tiny white pancakes the size of silver dollars, then turns his attention back to the dosa, gently transferring it to a Styrofoam cradle and crowning it with shavings of toasted coconut and a dollop of ginger-coconut chutney, faintly orange-red from chili powder. He hands the order over to the salivating customer, a fresh-faced Indian-American kid sporting an NYU backpack and gripping a Gatorade, then turns back to his orders sizzling away on the grill. He never needs to handle money, and he likes it that way. A guy in his early twenties wearing a "NY Dosa" T-shirt dips in and out of his fanny pack making transactions; his female counterpart sports a shirt that reads "Team Vegan," and her primary task is keeping the line moving while checking in with Thiru to make sure the orders are on track. "They are my friends, volunteers, they do this for me because they have been coming here to eat and they like me, so they want to help out," Thiru says. "They are vegan like me because it's the more peaceful way. In my life, at my cart, I'm not hurting animals, I feel very healthy, and I can go to sleep at night. I'm free."

NY Dosas' Special Rava Masala Dosa Serves 12

All of the optional condiments for serving are available at most Indian grocery stores.

2 cups rava/sooji (or semolina or Cream of
    Wheat, if you can't find it)

3 cups rice flour

1/4 cup *maida* (fine wheat flour)

1/2 cup cumin seeds

1 tablespoon *ajwain* (also called *carom*)

1 tablespoon salt

6 cups water

2 pounds potatoes, peeled

1 cup olive oil

1 tablespoon mustard seeds

1/2 white onion, finely diced

2 teaspoons ground turmeric

5 curry leaves, minced

Handful cilantro, minced

1 carrot, julienned or finely diced

3 red bell peppers, julienned or finely diced

Coconut chutney, for serving (optional)

Mint-cilantro chutney, for serving (optional)

Sambar, for serving (optional)

Combine the rava/sooji, rice flour, maida, cumin seeds, ajwain, 2 teaspoons of the salt, and the water in a large stockpot and mix well until it forms a thin batter. Cover the pot and leave it outside in a warm place for 2 hours to ferment.

While the batter is fermenting, boil the potatoes in a saucepan with enough water to cover them until they are soft. Using a fork, crush them lightly, but don't mash or purée them; leave some cubed chunks.

Heat 2 tablespoons of the olive oil in a large, deep sauté pan over medium heat. Add the mustard seeds and cook for 2 minutes. Add the onion and sauté until translucent. Add the potato chunks, the turmeric, curry leaves, and the remaining 1 teaspoon salt and stir to combine. Taste and readjust seasonings with more salt, if needed, and turn down the heat to low.

Heat 1 tablespoon of the remaining olive oil in a large nonstick pan or griddle over medium heat for about 3 minutes. Using a ladle, transfer a small circle of batter to the middle of the pan. Use the bottom of the ladle to gently spread the batter into a larger circle, swirling it in a clockwise circle. Add a second ladleful of batter around the first circle and spread the batter once more so that you have a crepelike round the size of the pan. After 3 minutes, the crepe should become crispy and lightly golden in color on the bottom. At this point, scrape off the top, uncooked layer of the batter with a spatula, leaving only the crispy part on the pan. (You can transfer the uncooked layer to the bowl of batter.) Working quickly, so that the dosa doesn't overcook, add a pile of the crispy potatoes just to one side of the center of the dosa, and top with a sprinkle of the cilantro, a bit of carrot, and a bit of red bell pepper. Use a long spatula, or two spatulas, one on each side, to fold the dosa in a half-moon shape and transfer it to a plate. Repeat the same process with the remaining batter and fillings, adding more oil to the pan before cooking each dosa. Serve with the chutneys and sambar.

toward Christie Street you'll find **All Natural Hot Mini Cakes**, where Shao Chen, an adorable seventy-something Hong Kong native, methodically works to classical tunes piped out of a small stereo lassoed to the cart, churning out tiny pancake puffs on a waffle iron pocked with round divots for browning batter. Similar to Dutch *poffertjes*, these mini cakes are nothing more than flour, sugar, eggs, and a little milk. They're slightly sweet, completely perfect with a cup of coffee, and, at only a buck for twenty, truly a vestige of old Chinatown. ◉

The Arepa Lady

FIND HER: Roosevelt Ave. between 78th and 79th Sts., Queens, New York
KEEP UP WITH HER: www.myspace.com/arepalady

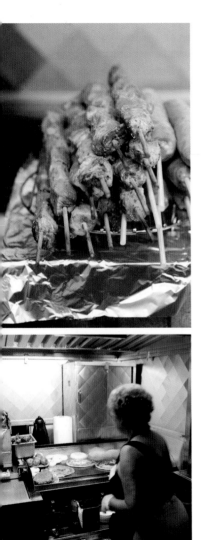

In Manhattan, foodie yuppies (fuppies?) talk about her in hushed tones, as if she were some mythical creature like the Loch Ness monster: "The Sainted Arepa Lady, she's under the 7 train in Jackson Heights grilling up the most amazing arepas you've ever had—cash only, Fridays and Saturdays until four or five in the morning."

In Queens, no one really talks about her, and if they do they don't call her the Arepa Lady. They call her by her name, Maria Piedad Cano. They speak to her in Spanish, usually ordering along the lines of, "*Dos arepas de queso, una arepa de choclo, y dos chorizo.*" They don't blink at seeing a sixty-five-year-old woman working a food cart until 5 a.m., patting arepas with a spatula as they brown on the grill, waving away neighborhood drunks with the other hand, waiting until the train rumbling overhead passes before telling customers what they owe. She's done this for twenty years, in this same spot, during these same hours, selling the same food: Colombian arepas, small discs of cornmeal dough that are tossed onto a flattop to brown on both sides. The smallest of the three Maria sells are plain arepas, only a little bigger than a silver dollar, almost eggshell white, and somewhat dry, the common starch served with grilled meats and most other meals throughout Colombia. When Maria folds shredded mozzarella into the cornmeal, it becomes an *arepa de queso*, taking on an almost spongy quality, puffing up a bit as it cooks. These she slathers with margarine and tops with a second cheese, crumbly *queso blanco*. But it's her *arepa de choclo* that is surely the Arepa Lady's holy grail. The most labor-intensive of the lineup, the *choclo* are made from fresh sweet corn that Maria slices from the cob, soaks overnight to loosen the seed germ, grinds by hand in a large stone mortar known as a *pilón*, then cooks and kneads into a dough. The dough sets up over a day or so before she pats it out into pancakelike rounds with a true yellow color. Griddled to golden brown and then folded in half with a spoonful of white farmer's cheese tucked inside, the *arepas de choclo* are slightly sweet, with a nutty texture from the fresh kernels.

With her thirty-one-year-old son Alejandro translating by her side and stoking the grill's fire while scored chorizo links sizzle away, Maria recounts how her legendary cart came to be. "I came to America in 1984 with my husband and four sons, right here to Jackson Heights," she says. "I started working at the cart of a Colombian man, selling shish kebabs, but after a year I decided I wanted my own cart, so I got one. At first I was only selling chorizo and pork kebabs, simple, just marinated in onion and garlic and sold with baby potatoes."

But after a couple of years, Maria explains, she noticed that although Jackson Heights was becoming the unofficial entry point for New York's Colombian immigrants, no one was selling arepas on the street, a common sight in her country. She started making the plain arepas and the *arepas de queso*. When, soon after, a couple of other arepa spots popped up, Maria set her cart apart by grinding the corn herself to offer *arepas de choclo*.

Over the years, she developed a routine, preparing the arepas throughout the week from her home while raising her four boys, loading up her cart on Friday before wheeling over to her spot, working 9 p.m. to 5 a.m. Fridays and Saturdays, attending church on Sunday, and starting the whole thing over come Monday. Winters she flees the cold to visit family that remains in Colombia, but her travels don't always line up with the dates of her six-month vending permit, which she has to apply for annually. When she's working without a permit, Maria usually works her "old cart" so that if the police hassle her and end up seizing her cart, they won't get the shinier, newer model she upgraded to a few years back. "I've been here so long they don't bother me that much, but sometimes they decide to, maybe since the arepas got famous," she says. "When I first started this was a bad, bad area, but the neighborhood has changed so much since, and now it's safer for people to come and business is better."

She's become a street vendor legend, raised a family, and makes a decent living, but she admits that although the late hours are wearing on her, she's in no place to retire yet. "When I win the lottery, that's when I stop selling my arepas."

(SIDE DISH)

Williamsburg, Brooklyn, measures an eleven on the hipster meter. The boutiques are great, bars are plentiful, and, yes, there are food trucks. Occasionally, the **Van Leeuwen** truck pulls up in the 'hood to scoop its artisan ice cream, but you can score their pints at Whole Foods throughout New York. What you can't get at the grocer are fish tacos from **Endless Summer** (Bedford Ave. between 6th and 7th Sts.). The brainchild of two musicians–Bad Wizard's Curtis Brown and The Jewish's Jeffrey Jensen–this boxy white truck has taken flack as gringo Mexican, has been under fire from local businesses looking to squash the competition, and is staffed by dudes who seem stoned half the time and hung over the other half. Still, when it's parked on Williamsburg's main vein Bedford Avenue, the line is never less than a dozen deep with people waiting on the very popular fish taco: crispy-edged tilapia tucked into tortillas with purple cabbage, white onion, cilantro, and crumbly cotija cheese. Sure, you can get pork, beef, or chicken, but in this part of town, the buzz is the thing. ◉

(SIDE DISH)

In Queens you'll find two cousins operating different Italian sausage trucks only a bun's toss away from each other on Woodhaven Boulevard (one marked **D'Angelo's**, the other **Dominick's**). In Manhattan's Financial District, John Braun slaves away in his own sausage rig, joking that, as a relative by marriage, he's the Cinderella of the family. Still, his stepfather, Dominic Felico, trained him well before his passing in 1995, setting him up with a hundred-year-old supplier, Continental Capri in Jersey, and the truck John has now operated for sixteen years as **Dominic's** (Whitehall and Bridge Sts.). Suits from Wall Street stand next to construction workers wolfing down juicy fennel-flecked sausages, either crimson from chili powder or deep brown, sweet, and mild. Caramelized onions and peppers top John's best sellers, but the one menu item that sets this truck apart from its kin is piping hot cheesesteaks, streaked with fat and smothered in liquefied American, "the thing I got that they don't," as John says. ◉

Arepas de Queso Serves 6

2 cups masarepa (arepa flour)

2 cups hot water

1/2 teaspoon salt

1 cup shredded mozzarella cheese

3 tablespoons margarine

1 cup queso blanco (crumbly white
    farmer's cheese)

Mix the *masarepa,* hot water, and salt in a large mixing bowl and let rest for about 10 minutes. Knead the dough until it starts to take on a sheen, kneading in the shredded mozzarella as you work. Form 6 round patties about 1/2 inch thick and set aside.

Heat a large nonstick pan or griddle over medium heat. You'll use about 1 1/2 teaspoons of margarine per arepa, so add the margarine to the pan according to how many will fit at a time without crowding. After each arepa browns on one side, flip it and immediately baste the top with a little of the margarine from the pan. Continue to cook until both sides are browned and lightly crispy.

Transfer each arepa to a plate and top with a sprinkle of the *queso blanco* before serving.

Jamaican Dutchy

FIND IT: W 51st St. between 6th and 7th Aves., New York, New York
KEEP UP WITH IT: www.thejamaicandutchy.net

Square white guys in suits and ties queuing up for Midtown lunch carts is not an unfamiliar sight. But you do tend to notice when one of them is bobbing his head to Marley tunes floating out of a cart marked by a waving Jamaican flag, especially when he's shouting to anyone who will listen, "This jerk chicken is the bomb!"

O'Neil Reid has seen it before, so he nods in appreciation without looking up from the Styrofoam container he's loading up with rice and peas, fiery chicken thighs, and caramelized plantains. It's just another Friday, and Jamaican Dutchy is just another Midtown lunch cart, handing over plastic bags of the day's meal to nine-to-fivers who'll head back to the office and wolf it down in ten minutes, trying not to slop hot sauce on their computer keyboard. But O'Neil's cart stands out as one of only a couple of Jamaican operations in the area, and it's the leader for intense flavors and daily specials like braised cow foot, peanut porridge, and goat stew. Granted, most of the customers ordering from that lineup hail from the Caribbean like O'Neil, but the fact that they're even offered is impressive.

"I've been in New York for ten years, and when I was working security downtown I would go to different carts for lunch," he says. "But then I said, 'You know what? I could do better.' So I got a cart and I asked my mom about recipes. We live together, so she helped with taste testing, giving me opinions, especially with the breakfast porridges. My mom makes the best porridge in the whole wide world. Trust me."

I do. I've had O'Neil's version, and it pretty much flips the bird to American oatmeal. The porridge rotates daily: cornmeal on Mondays, banana and oats Tuesdays, plantains Wednesdays, hominy Thursdays, and peanuts Fridays. No matter the base, the key is Mother Reid's secret of adding four different kinds of milk to the starch as it cooks: fresh milk, sweet milk, condensed milk, and coconut milk. Ridiculously rich and filling, it could fortify someone enough to head out into the wilderness and slay a wild beast, or at least make it from the subway station to the office on a cold winter morning.

"Mostly, though, the Midtown crowd, they come for my jerk chicken," O'Neil says. "And I don't soften it up . . . it's got some heat." Ginger, garlic, allspice, Scotch bonnet chiles, and a couple of "secret spices" go into the jerk rub, which gets massaged into the chicken to soak overnight before the thighs and legs hit the grill. Slow-cooked stew peas and braised oxtails are equally time-intensive, but worth the effort: O'Neil packs up most

(SIDE DISH)

Okay, so I know I said I wasn't going to include anyone in this book that doesn't actually cook on his or her truck, but rules were made to be broken. Two trucks in NYC who do all of their production in a real brick-and-mortar kitchen are **Treats Truck** (twitter.com/thetreatstruck) and **Rickshaw Dumpling** (twitter.com/rickshawtruck), and both are worth a stop if you see them on the road. Kim Ima left the theater world to start up the bakery case on wheels she dubbed Treats Truck, and now she starts her days at the crack of dawn, pulling classic cookies and bars hot from her oven in Red Hook. She then loads them onto a streamlined silver step van, tools over to Manhattan, vies for a parking spot in Midtown, and opens the window for business. Sandwich cookies in combos like brown sugar with vanilla crème and oatmeal with seasonal jam are big sellers, but it's the pecan-topped butterscotch bar that has otherwise civilized suits cutting in line. Likewise, the goods on the Rickshaw truck aren't actually made in a mobile kitchen; dumplings the likes of chicken–Thai basil and pork–Chinese chive are assembled back at the company's Dumpling Bar in Manhattan's Flatiron District, under the guidance of award-winning chef Anita Lo.

CONTINUED ON PAGE 156 ➡

Still, massive steamers keep the puffy pouches warm on the run, until they're tossed into a carton by the half dozen and paired up with dips like soy-sesame and lemon-sansho. Don't miss the calamansi-ade, a super refreshing drink made from Filipino citrus fruit—you'll need it by the time you get to the front of the line. ◉

nights with an empty cart. "The cart life is what you make it. If you're just going to sell hot dogs, everyone else is already doing it," O'Neil says. "I'm here to do some real business, so I give them a full menu of Jamaican cuisine. I know if the food is good, people will continue to find me. I'm here for longevity."

O'Neil's Jerk Chicken   Serves 5

1 bunch green onions, chopped
1 bunch fresh thyme, chopped
1/2 cup ground allspice
8 Scotch bonnet chiles

1 tablespoon salt
1 onion, chopped
10 pieces bone-in dark-meat chicken

Combine the green onions, thyme, allspice, chiles, salt, and onion in a blender and purée.

Rinse the chicken and pat it dry. Massage the jerk rub into each piece of chicken and let marinate in the refrigerator for at least 24 hours.

Prepare a grill for indirect cooking over medium heat or preheat the oven to 350°F.

Place the chicken on the grill over indirect heat or in a casserole dish in the oven. Cook until the skin is nicely charred and the juices run clear (about 45 minutes on a grill, 1 hour 15 minutes in the oven). Serve hot.

Big Gay Ice Cream Truck

KEEP UP WITH IT: www.biggayicecreamtruck.com or twitter.com/biggayicecream

A classically trained bassoonist, with degrees from the Manhattan School of Music and Juilliard, is finishing up his doctorate in musical arts while shuffling back and forth between Manhattan and Boston to perform with the Pro Arte Chamber Orchestra of Boston, the Boston Pops, and so on. So what does he decide to add to his résumé? Ice cream man.

"My flutist friend from Julliard was driving an ice cream truck for a few summers, and I was sort of following her adventures, living vicariously through her, thinking it was such a funny thing for a conservatory person to hop into this blue-collar job," Doug Quint explains. "Then, in late winter of 2008, I see on her Facebook page something like, 'If you ever want to drive an ice cream truck, contact me because I'm selling it.' I just turned to my boyfriend Bryan on the couch and said, 'I should probably get in touch with her, right?' and he nodded, like, 'Naturally.'"

And so it was. The ice cream truck exchanged hands, and by summer of 2009 Doug had added weekday truck outings to his ridiculously full plate. But this wasn't work. It was playing ice cream man, and hanging out in the kitchen with his partner coming up with fun toppings like wasabi pea dust and olive oil with sea salt, and it was, ultimately, a way to put the LGBT in rainbow sprinkles. "It really wasn't premeditated, but when we were getting started and were talking about setting up a Facebook page, I was telling friends, 'Oh, it's for me and my big gay ice cream truck,' and we realized we had just named it," Doug says. "We felt that even if it wasn't successful, if people just walked by and laughed, that's something positive right there. And we like the idea of people having to realize that if they had a problem with a big gay ice cream truck, if that can actually bother them, they would learn a lesson in a way. Some will actually stop and you see this look like they're trying to figure out a reason to walk away, and then they realize how silly that is, so they just order ice cream."

What they order is half the fun. The truck is still very much an old-school Mister Softee–style truck, from the soft-serve machine doling out vanilla, chocolate, and twists to the faded menus advertising glorious dipped cones, shakes, and sundaes, all of which Doug happily makes. But alongside the traditional lineup are handwritten signs under photos of his signature creations, sporting names like the Bea Arthur and the Salty Pimp, with add-ons including dulce de leche, Sriracha hot sauce, saba (a thick and concentrated liquid similar to balsamic vinegar), and pumpkin butter. Doug says getting to experiment with tradition is what drew him in to

You could eat at the **Heavenly Delights** (161st St. and Concourse Village West) cart in the Bronx every day for a month and never repeat a dish. Like any contemporary American tablecloth spot over in Manhattan, the chef here crafts the day's menu according to her mood. Fauzia Abdur-Rahman is in her fifties, good at what she does, and beloved by loyal customers who will wait in the rain for her home-style food. Fauzia is from Kingston, Jamaica, so occasionally her hand-scrawled list of daily specials will lean toward the Caribbean: jerk chicken, crispy codfish, curried vegetables. But usually it's tough to put a finger on the origin of dishes, as honey mustard might mingle with tofu, fresh basil finds its way into a sautéed heap of whiting, and desserts lean Southern, with red velvet cake popular. Fauzia opened her cart in 1995, and little has changed since, although she did upgrade to a deluxe model sporting a six-burner stove. That hasn't done much to speed up production, but it's given Fauzia more room for her one-woman show. ◉

begin with, so here's his take on the top sellers that took the Big Gay Ice Cream Truck from formulaic to fabulous:

The Bea Arthur: Vanilla ice cream on a cone drizzled with dulce de leche and rolled in crushed Nilla wafers.

> "I just knew the caramel and vanilla were classic and that the Nilla wafers would add that texture it needed, but the name came from someone on Twitter. The cone has this great golden color from top to bottom, and it became our little Golden Girl. Plus it turns out that in her will, Bea Arthur left a huge sum of money to a shelter for homeless LGBT teens, so the idea of naming something after her was a nice tribute."

The Choinkwich: Caramelized bacon and chocolate soft serve between two chocolate wafer cookies.

> "A couple years ago Bryan and I had this chocolate bar with bacon from Vosges, and we really liked the idea, but our initial experiments with this were horrible. We tried making bacon bits as a topping and it was absolutely disgusting, soaking wet and cold and hopeless. Then it occurred to me that a sandwich was the way to go, and Bryan played

around with caramelizing bacon, found a nice lean cut since fat doesn't chew well once it's cold, and found the right sugar, and voilà! Someone on Twitter suggested naming it Pig Cream, but that was a bit much."

The Salty Pimp: Vanilla ice cream drizzled with dulce de leche, sprinkled with sea salt, and dipped in dark chocolate.

"Again, you have the salt and the chocolate, which is so good, with a bit of the dulce de leche for that caramel savoriness. And the name actually came from this strange altercation on the street with a pimp who was at the truck with his girls. I had to ask them to leave and he got a bit salty. That kind of thing happens: school kids one second, junkies the next, then German tourists, then undercover cops. What can I say? It's New York."

The Gobbler: Vanilla ice cream sundae drizzled with pumpkin butter and topped with crushed graham crackers, dried cranberries, and whipped cream.

"This is essentially a mock pumpkin pie, bringing in the cranberries for color and the fall thing. It was called 'Thanksgiving' originally, and I was only doing it on Thursdays, but people were gobbling it up, so I put it on the menu and switched the name."

Trini Paki Boys Cart

FIND IT: 43rd St. and 6th Ave., New York, New York

"My husband, Abdul Sami Khan, was the first person to do curry chicken on rice at a cart in New York, and he was the very, very first person to have a halal cart," claims Fatima Khan proudly. In the New York City cart game, just about every vendor you meet alleges he or she was the first to do this or that, but something about Fatima makes her boasts believable. Her confidence is much bigger than her five-foot frame, and she works in molasses-slow movements, gathering up her flowing sarilike wrap to squat on a milk crate while counting out change. "How much does he owe, boy?" she calls out to her son Muhammed, who works the grill like nobody's business while his face shows boredom beyond belief.

"My husband started it, but we run it because he got lazy," Fatima explains with a laugh. "Plus he runs a 99-cent discount store in Brooklyn, so maybe fifteen years ago we took over. I have six sons, and everybody used to help, but now they all branched out, so it's just me and this boy."

This "boy" is actually in his early thirties, but when you've been making chicken and rice on a street corner in Midtown for half of your life, you tend to get that glazed-over look of a weathered assembly-line worker. Fatima smiles enough for the both of them, telling her story to anyone who will listen, explaining the handwriting on the menu board ("I'm from Trinidad, my husband from Pakistan, this cart is run by my boys"), and soaking up the compliments for the Caribbean specialties she added to the menu just a couple years ago. Her "doubles" are similar to Indian poori, fried puffs of white flour colored from a little yellow curry powder and topped with curried chickpeas. *Palourie* are spongier, smaller balls of fried chickpea flour that soak up the sweet-and-sour tamarind chutney Muhammed ladles over them before sealing the foil package like a stuffed purse. Fatima snuck these two Trinidadian specialties onto the menu to spice things up for regulars who might be tiring of chicken and rice—although if you ask any of the dozen or so people in line about their chicken and rice habit, the words "crack" and "addicted" inevitably come up.

Spiced hunks of chicken or lamb over rice are served at just about every halal cart in existence, so ubiquitous in this part of the country that it's earned its own nickname: street meat. The phrase might turn the stomachs of the uninitiated, but it's almost a term of endearment among Manhattan's nine-to-fivers. (In fact, Zach Brooks, founder of the exhaustive blog Midtown Lunch, has conducted a "Street-Meat-Palooza" for three years running in which he and a crew of iron stomachs sample around a dozen different chicken and lamb on rice dishes.) Linger near any of the Midtown halal carts for a few minutes and you'll overhear regulars sticking to their usual, ordering as nonchalantly as mumbling a "bless you" to a sneeze. "Chicken on rice, lotta hot, lotta white," is the mantra at Trini Paki Boys, the "hot" referring to the blazing orange sauce of puréed Scotch bonnet peppers, vinegar, and water; the "white" a request for a thinned yogurt and mayo blend; and the chicken, well, Fatima isn't exactly the kind to cook and tell.

"It's just regular seasoning, you know? Nothing special," she says. "The most important thing in food is salt and pepper. If you don't have salt and pepper there, forget it. You can put a million seasonings and you have no taste."

Pulling a recipe out of a fifty-five-year-old career cook who has never owned a measuring spoon and has no use for one takes a bit of time. Eventually though, Fatima warms up and lets on that she marinates the whole chicken thighs in an oil-based rub spiked with garam masala, curry powder, and, of course, salt and pepper. After Muhammed greases up the cart's flattop, the thighs hit the surface with a sizzle. Stained yellow-brown by now, the chicken is ready to be chopped into hunks with the sharp edge of a metal spatula as it cooks. Once the edges crisp and each bite cooks through, a towering mound is transferred to a container waiting with a warm pillow of rice. Curried chickpeas and potatoes are sloshed on, one ladle each; a tiny green salad brings color; and generous squirts of the hot and white sauces finish the dish—the signature in the corner of a masterpiece.

(SIDE DISH)

Thomas Yang learned the food truck biz with two of the busiest operations in town: Endless Summer and Rickshaw Dumpling. Firsthand experience of running a mobile kitchen is valuable–an uncle's authentic Taiwanese recipes are priceless. Before launching **NYC Cravings** (www.nyccravings.com or twitter .com/nyccravings), Thomas and his sister Diana talked their uncle Steven into giving New Yorkers the one truck it hadn't seen: true Taiwanese. Steven, a native of Hualien, turns standard meats into home-style succulence with a marinade that's at once sweet, salty, and slightly sour. Both the chicken and the pork chop are fried after being brined, then plated over fluffy rice with tart pickled greens and what's cryptically described as "pork sauce." The Yangs know better than to divulge its ingredients ("uh, soy and herbs and spices" was the repeated description), as their bamboo-decaled truck depends on those flavors for survival. Looks like Thomas also learned Trade Secrets 101. ◉

ROOSEVELT AVENUE (Jackson Heights/Elmhurst) Queens

Most carts and trucks operate in the evenings, often staying open very late if not 24 hours on weekends. This list is by no means exhaustive, but it is selective.

❶ Sammy's Halal NYC's ubiquitous cart dish chicken-and-rice is the name of the game here, but Sammy's stands out for über tender chicken, nicely spiced rice, and fierce hot sauce. Order "chicken with hot and white" to get both the red hot sauce and the thinned mayo-yogurt, but tack on "green" to that request for the secret sauce with punchy brightness.

❷ Potala Fresh Food For an Eastern escape from the plethora of Latin American eats in this neck of the woods, make a quick pit stop at this Tibetan cart, which sits just a few feet from the Roosevelt Avenue subway station. Stacked silver steamers hold freshly formed *momo*, plump dumplings filled with oniony ground beef that come in orders of eight.

❸ Quesadilla Sabrosa Taqueria The cart operators might hail from El Salvador, but they have a way with Mexican-style quesadillas nonetheless, using just enough margarine to soften the tortilla while crisping the edges. As usual, the *huitlacoche* (a.k.a. corn smut, prized black corn fungus) is canned, but combined with fresh farmer's cheese and pickled onions, this quesadilla stands out.

❹ The Arepa Lady (see page 152).

❺ Guayaco's Comida Ecuatoriana One of a handful of Ecuadorian trucks along the strip, Guayaco's is known for its supremely fresh shrimp ceviche, chock-full of raw red onions and steeped in a slightly sweet and tart mix of orange and lime juices. It goes fast on weekends, but the braised goat stew is a respectable replacement.

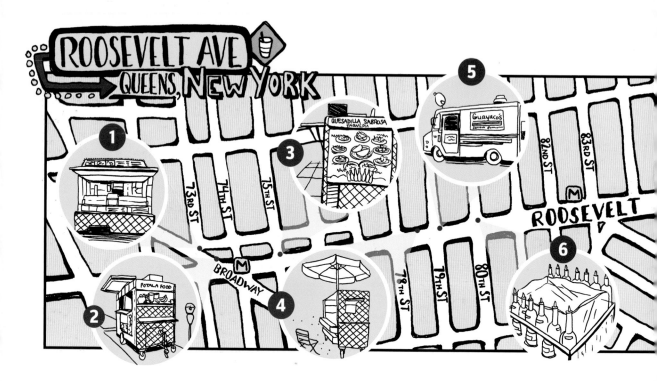

6 Raspado Lady (seasonal) Come summer you'll spot wide-eyed kids forming a line at this tiny cart, waiting and watching as the *raspado* (snow cone) lady methodically shaves down a block of ice to yield the base for a dozen flavored syrups. Many flavors (bubble gum, blue raspberry) are clearly synthetic and ultra-sweet, so stick with the few she makes herself, like coconut, tamarind, and mango.

7 Delicias Isabel As reliable as a 7-11, this cart is always open. Standard Mexican fare is advertised, but the cart owners are actually Salvadoran. Order a *pupusa* and the *masa* is hand-formed to order, filled with a layer of beans, cheese, and (by request) a few crunchy *chicharrones*, or pork rinds, before it's tossed onto the griddle.

8 Antojitos Mexicanos la Tia Julia *Barbacoa de chivo* is the specialty of this massive truck, goat tacos confusingly listed on the menu yet only offered as a special but on no particular days. If you luck out, order a couple to start (you pay at the end of your grazing) and pile on a few sprigs of *papalo* offered near the window; the peppery herb is perfect for the ultra-rich and tender goat.

9 La Caserita Don't be scared off by the whole roasted pig sprawled across the many platters crowding this rickety cart's griddle. It's the signifier of Ecuadorian authenticity, intended to be hacked to pieces and dished up over corn cakes, an indulgence only outdone by the *chicharrones*, wide strips of deep-fried pig fat.

10 El Guayaquileño With a handful of stools and a flatscreen showing Ecuadorian videos mounted to its exterior, this truck intends on its customers staying a while. Regulars make a meal of standout specialties like conch ceviche topped with crunchy corn kernels, pork sausage soup (*caldo de salchicha*), and hen stew (*seco de gallina*).

11 Pique y Pase El Pepin Sporting a nearly identical lineup to its fellow Ecuadorian competitors parked nearby, this truck seems to do a better business in roast and fried pork (*hornado* and *fritada*, respectively), as well as tamales steamed in banana leaves and thick links of blood sausage known as *morcilla*. When the truck is open for breakfast, try the *morocho con pan y nata*, a warm corn drink sold with a thick slice of bread drizzled with cream.

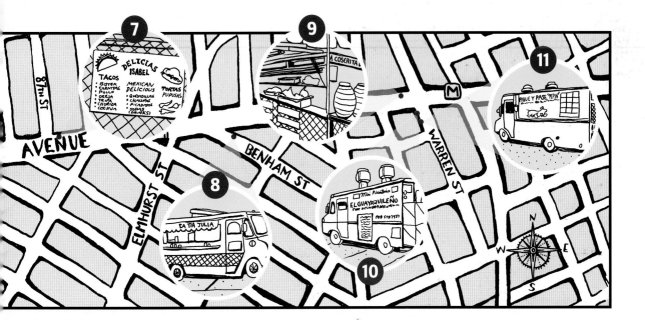

Philadelphia, Pennsylvania

I f Portland is the ever-evolving hipster of the mobile food scene, Philly is the grizzly old man, content with its standbys, a bit battered and bruised, and far from concerned about perpetual motion, let alone Tweeting any movement. Parked in clusters in two main areas of Philadelphia—City Center, a.k.a. downtown, and University City, home to Penn, Temple, and Drexel—boxy, white, warhorse Grumman trucks have served sustenance to hungry nine-to-fivers and students alike for decades, under regulation since 1975. Grumman, a military aircraft manufacturer based across the state line in New York, also churns out UPS-style step vans, plenty of which were converted into mobile kitchens throughout the 1970s and '80s. Second-generation Greek and Italian immigrants set their trucks up like roving delis, the fridge stocked with all the usual cold cuts and sliced cheeses, warmers holding thin shavings of "steak," all to be piled onto split buns for hoagies and the city's namesake cheesesteaks. Scrapple, that Pennsylvania specialty of spiced pork scraps and cornmeal seared to a crispy puck, anchored the trucks' breakfast offerings, joined by pepper-and-egg sandwiches, sold with or without a couple of thick rounds of sagey sausage. Likewise, hot coffee, shot out of the same insulated urn that brewed it, carried no pretension, just good and strong, and as cheap as the plain white Styrofoam cup it was served in.

FOOD TRUCKS

Fast-forward to the present day, and not much about Philly's food truck landscape has changed. Walk the streets in the city's "special vending districts" and it's tough to differentiate truck from truck, the impossibly lengthy menus blurring together into one big hoagie-chef's salad-gyro affair. Chinese trucks, most of which arrived in the '80s, are just as indistinguishable, each plastered with a roll call of chop suey classics at least forty dishes deep. Egg foo young, lo mein, fried rice, beef with broccoli, cashew chicken . . . all as gloopy and oddly satisfying as ever, handed over in Styrofoam squares nearly buckling from the weight of thick white rice. The '90s brought similarly stout portions of Caribbean soul food to the streets, with a handful of Jamaican and African American proprietors outfitting their Grummans with steam tables, each slot a natural extension for the day's menu at their brick-and-mortar restaurants. Double batches of stew chicken, braised oxtails, and collard greens heavy with potlikker meant half would be loaded onto the truck, the other half staying behind for a carryout lunch crowd. Mexican arrived next, along with a couple of Indian options, the random Korean and Southeast Asian truck, and plenty of small carts hawking freshly cut fruit, the operations nearly camouflaged by bushels of produce stacked high in crates on all sides.

Both the name and the concept of **KoJa** (University Ave. between Sansom and Walnut Sts.) are an amalgamation of Korean and Japanese, with *bulgogi* and *mandoo* sharing menu space with soba noodles and teriyaki dishes. The truck itself has been serving both Korean and Japanese food for two decades, but the current owner, Soo Lee, and her brother Douglas have been operating under the name KoJa since 2006. Teriyaki chicken over soba noodles and *bulgogi* on rice are the most popular standards, but it's the *jigae*, Korean stews, that are criminally overlooked. Lee's *sundubu*, a traditional spicy tofu soup, is dotted with shrimp, squid, and clams and packs plenty of heat via *gochujang* (chile paste) for a steaming and sinus-clearing solution to a cold Philly day. ◉

What Philly has lacked in creativity it's made up for in volume and value, with many trucks (around 165 at last count in 2010) strategizing to compete by offering the exact same thing, but a bit more for a bit less. "We're not a trendsetting town generally," says Craig LaBan, the *Philadelphia Inquirer*'s restaurant critic for more than a decade. "Food trucks have long been a part of our culture, but it's just that the selections haven't been that inspired. I find that most aren't especially good, and I really wouldn't go out of my way to eat at most, but they serve the purpose of serving hearty food at a good price. I've been waiting for somebody to bust out and do something high-grade, and that's really just starting to now. I believe our revolution is going to happen this year."

LaBan points to Honest Tom's as "one of the first sort of twenty-first century hipster food trucks where people were checking Twitter and giving reviews with texting emoticons," and he's particularly excited about the impending arrival of Guapo's Tacos, an upscale taco truck from *Iron Chef* Jose Garces, whose army of restaurants—including Tinto, Amada, and Village Whiskey—are far and away the city's strongest concepts. The city has designated three hundred as the magic number to limit the amount of food trucks parked on Philly's streets, so if the trend does catch fire as LaBan hopes, there's still plenty of room out there. But whether or not the new guard can tap into the average Philadelphian's wallet and stomach remains to be seen, as they've long been quite practical with both.

La Dominique

FIND IT: Market St. at 33rd St., Philadelphia, Pennsylvania

The ridiculously long line snaking up the sidewalk to La Dominique isn't because Zbigniew Chojnacki makes a crepe unlike any other. It's because "Ziggy" (as he's known to friends and regulars) makes a crepe slower than any other. Calmly spreading the batter with the back of a ladle until it reaches the edges of the hot crepe iron, reaching into his tiny cooler to pull out whole strawberries to slice to order, cutting strips of red bell pepper over his three-foot flattop grill—everything Ziggy does is methodical, graceful, and done with care. But it's enough to drive a short-order cook (or an impatient and hungry customer) mad.

In his fifties, with a full head of silver hair, wire-rimmed glasses, and the lanky frame of a European who likes red wine and cigarettes, Ziggy is not concerned with the speed of his creations, but only with the process and the final work of art. A trained metal sculptor, Ziggy has been making and selling his jewelry and large-scale works in this country since the mid-1980s. He and his wife Krystyna fled the political upheaval of Dansk, Poland, in 1984, settling in Los Angeles with help of a Catholic refugee organization. Ziggy sculpted, Krystyna painted, and the couple eventually found considerable success with their art in the States. Moves to Colorado and then Michigan were dictated by their oldest daughter's figure-skating career; she was training to qualify for the Olympics when she suffered a concussion at fifteen and had to retire. Soon after, a fellow artist lured Ziggy to the East Coast, and in 2000 the family settled in Philadelphia, where Ziggy wasted little time getting his work into the Philadelphia Museum of Art. "But then so many art shows where I used to go for many years disappeared. The buyers stopped buying," Ziggy recalls. "This was the time of the war and all of this spending by Bush and the economic downturn. The first victim of the war is always culture, and I saw that there was no way to stay in art. At that time, a guy here in Philadelphia told me, 'You're never going to make money with jewelry. You can only make money selling guns or food.' He was very right. And I chose the food."

When Ziggy showed up in the driveway with a food cart in tow, Krystyna was "furious," as Ziggy puts it. "She told me I was losing my mind." But a fellow artist had recently made the same move and was not only supporting herself but also having fun doing it. Eventually Krystyna came around, helping Ziggy concoct the menu of fillings and toppings for the crepes he channeled via memories of his mother's weekend treats back in Poland. His plan from the outset was to keep it simple (the six by three-foot cart doesn't allow for the complex), to use hormone- and antibiotic-free chicken, free-range eggs, organic produce, and a classic batter. Now that she's on board, Krystyna helps out by preparing a few fillings: a creamed spinach, chicken stewed in coconut milk, fresh hummus, and a spreadable sweet cheese flecked with orange zest. These are the only items on the cart prepared before Ziggy sets up for the day, the savory fillings taking their place in two small warmers alongside the pair of crepe irons. Only one of the irons is in constant use; the other Ziggy uses to keep nearly finished crepes warm while he fusses with the container, the toppings, a napkin, a fork, waving hello to a passing friend . . . any of the myriad things that make the process of ordering a test of wills.

Still, the people come. They wait, they order, they leave with a savory crepe bigger than an ironworker's forearm, and they fire back to first-timer friends with, "Yeah, but it's worth it." The most basic crepe on the menu might also be the best: a simple squeeze of lemon and a dusting of powdered sugar leave room to focus on the wafer-crisp edges and perfectly spongy center. It's worth every cent of the three-dollar price tag, and it's probably the only moneymaker on the menu. Ziggy insists on stuffing his savory crepes until they look like a fat man's button-down after Sunday supper. He claims the customers have come to expect value from his cart, even while he admits he's not making much money in his new career. His business-minded daughter, now in college, tries to help Dad with the basics of profit and loss. Ziggy shows little patience for the topic, waving away money talk and focusing instead on adding just one more swirl of sauce or dollop of whipped cream to the towering crepes before closing their containers and handing them through the window. Occasionally he winces, smacks his forehead, and asks for it back, taking a moment to pop open the lid and add a final touch. "I am working with my hands, so it is familiar," Ziggy says. "But sometimes I'm not happy with the design."

FOOD TRUCKS

Pear Crepes   Makes about 16 crepes

1¹/₂ cups unbleached flour

1¹/₄ cups milk

1¹/₄ cups water

3 eggs

1 tablespoon unsalted butter, melted

¹/₂ teaspoon salt

1 cup white farmer's cheese

1 cup sour cream

1 tablespoon sugar

1 teaspoon vanilla extract

Zest of 1 orange

4 d'Anjou pears, cored and thinly sliced

1 cup dark chocolate sauce (preferably
   Trader Joe's brand)

1 cup sliced almonds, toasted

In a large bowl, whisk together the flour, milk, water, eggs, butter, and salt until free of lumps. Set aside.

In a separate bowl, combine the farmer's cheese, sour cream, sugar, vanilla, and orange zest. Beat with a hand mixer or blend with a spatula until creamy.

Heat an 8-inch nonstick pan over medium heat (use a 10-inch pan if you want larger crepes). Pour enough of the batter into the center of the pan so that when you pick up the pan and swirl the batter it reaches the edges but is no thicker than ¹/₄ inch in the center.

As the edges begin to turn light golden brown, use a spatula to lift up the crepe at the edge to check the bottom. Once it is golden brown, flip the crepe. Continue to cook until the other side is equally golden brown, then transfer to a plate. Slather some of the cheese mixture on top, arrange a few pear slices on top, and fold the crepe in half, then in half again. Drizzle with the chocolate sauce and garnish with the almond slices before serving. Repeat to make 15 more crepes.

the city's Mural Arts Program gave his truck a psychedelic paint job using every color on the wheel, business picked up and so did the requests. McCusker's repertoire now extends to lunch with sweet potato tacos, a grilled chicken version, and, on Fridays only, limey tilapia tacos topped with pineapple salsa. But for breakfast, he remains faithful to the meatless potato-egg-and-cheese tacos that started it all. ◉

Mr. C's "Sweetmeat" Bar-B-Que

FIND IT: N Broad St. between Jefferson and Oxford Sts. (Thursday and Friday noon–4 p.m.) or N Broad St. at Germantown Ave. (Thursday, Friday, and Saturday 4 p.m.–1 a.m.; Sundays 12:30 p.m.–8 p.m.), Philadelphia, Pennsylvania

You can smell the smoke before you can see the menu, sweet and pungent with a trace of hickory and the tang that makes your mouth water before you even know what it's watering for. Inside the hulking aluminum truck parked along Philly's busy Broad Street is Clifton Moore, part trucker, part pit master, every bit the gentle Southerner, and not at all resembling his seventy-two years of age. As a boy on his grandparents' farm in Orange, Virginia, Clifton helped raise hogs and chicken, pulled vegetables from the field, and tended to the cow. But when he came to Philadelphia in high school, he left the farm life behind for the open road, getting work at a trucking company hauling produce, a job he kept for nearly twenty years before quitting once he had enough money for his own rig. "Refrigerated," Clifton recalls. "I was running produce, a little meat, up the West Coast. I branched out and moved a little bit too fast, got up to fifteen trucks, but they started breaking down and then they deregulated everything, which put a damper on what you could make because a lot of people would haul for a lot cheaper. I went out of business in 1986, but, well, I went out and bought four more. I just couldn't stay away from those trucks. In the mean-

time I saw this fellow doing barbecue out of a truck. Now, I'm a pretty good cook, and if he had all these people lined up for what he was cooking? Well, I did the arithmetic."

And it added up to a new business. At first Clifton set up an old-school oil drum smoker and sold his "Sweetmeat" barbecue right on the street ("I call it sweetmeat 'cause it's so good"). The health department didn't like that too much, and after a couple of threats from an inspector to shut down the operation, Clifton decided demand for his ribs and chopped brisket was enough to take the plunge and go legit. He sold all his trucks but one and went to work installing a double-decker charcoal grill wide enough for a couple dozen slabs of ribs. He got his permit and hit the streets in 1988, selling his barbecue alongside his wife Beverly's Southern sides and pies. His spareribs are slow-cooked pork at its finest, rubbed with seasoning salt and pepper, then smoked over a fire that starts with hickory and progresses into lump charcoal. Those ribs share space with whole chickens sprinkled with lemon pepper and poultry seasoning, beef brisket in a garlicky salt-and-pepper rub, and pork shoulder, liberally salted and lightly sweetened. All are cooked slow and low in true barbecue fashion, emerging from behind the grill's heavy metal door with a caramelized crust of seasonings and showing just a touch of pink smoke ring when cut into.

As impressive as the "sweetmeat" is on its own, it rises to can-I-get-a-witness-inspirational when plated up with Beverly's creamy cinnamon-scented yams, collard greens soaked in turkey neck potlikker, and bubbly crusted mac and cheese, thick with Cheddar. Clifton brags that Beverly's sweet potato pie and peach cobbler are the best around, but he also gets his hands into the flour a bit, turning out a "five-flavor pound cake" typical of a Southern church bake sale. He doesn't keep track of which is the better seller, plus he eats too much of the cake himself for an honest count, but his customers love the lineup enough to support two trucks and a small storefront, all of which are closed Monday through Wednesday so that the couple can regroup, restock, and be grandparents for a few days. Beverly is ready to retire to their twenty acres in Virginia, and Clifton says he'd be ready himself after a few more years of work if he could sell the business to an aspiring pit master—but he stops short of promising to give up *both* trucks.

(SIDE DISH)

Ludlow Street (around 31st St.) is only about a block long, with one end fizzling out into the maze of Drexel University sidewalks and the other end forming a T that pushes most pedestrians left to the 30th Street subway station. Still, students have found their way to this concrete food court for almost thirty years, lured by the cheap eats slung out of eight battered and bruised food trucks showing their age and not giving a damn. Near the western end, **T&S Lunch Truck** is the patriarch of the bunch, opened by a family of Greek-Americans, the Stephanos, in 1983, while the Syrian-run **A&M Lunch Truck** that anchors the eastern end of the strip is the newcomer at only four years. All of the trucks' menus are nearly identical—hoagies, salads, burgers—but still the students and faculty seem to develop a taste for their favorites, from the fried rice at **Mai's Oriental Food** to the egg sandwiches at **Sue's**. You could choose blindfolded and still do okay in a pinch, but I'm guessing most of this stuff tastes better when you're broke and cramming for finals. ◉

Mr. C's Pulled Pork Serves 12 to 20

1/4 cup seasoning salt (such as Lawry's)

1/4 cup freshly ground black pepper

3 tablespoons salt

2 tablespoons granulated garlic

1 teaspoon cayenne pepper

1 tablespoon sugar

4 cups water

1 cup hot sauce (such as Louisiana)

5 to 6 pounds pork shoulder

Preheat a smoker or grill set up for indirect cooking until the temperature reaches 225°F.

In a bowl, combine the seasoning salt, pepper, salt, granulated garlic, cayenne, and sugar to make the dry rub.

Combine the water and the hot sauce in a deep pan large enough to hold the pork shoulder. Rub the spice mixture into the pork shoulder, then place it into the pan and transfer to the smoker. Cook for 12 to 15 hours, or until it is so tender it pulls apart with ease. (You will have to keep an eye on the fire, adding more wood every few hours, to keep it at a constant 225°F. Another option is to use a smoker with an automatic wood-pellet feeder.)

Serve chopped or sliced across the grain.

Mrs. C's Sweet Potato Pie Serves 8

1 store-bought pie crust

1 1/2 pounds sweet potatoes

1/2 teaspoon cinnamon

1/2 teaspoon nutmeg

1 teaspoon vanilla extract

1 egg

1/2 cup whole milk

2 1/2 tablespoons sugar

1/2 cup unsalted butter, melted

Preheat the oven to 300°F. Bake the pie crust for 15 minutes and set aside to cool.

Place the unpeeled sweet potatoes in a large pot of water. Bring to a boil, then cover, reduce the heat to a simmer, and cook until the peels slide off when pulled with a spoon, about 1 hour.

Drain the sweet potatoes. When they're cool enough to handle, remove the skins. Transfer them back to the pot and mash until smooth. Add the cinnamon, nutmeg, and vanilla, then beat with a handheld electric mixer until thoroughly blended.

In a separate bowl, beat the egg and the milk together. Add the egg mixture, sugar, and melted butter to the sweet potato mixture and continue to beat with the mixer until very smooth.

Preheat the oven to 400°F.

Spoon the mixture into the prebaked pie crust and bake for 10 minutes, then lower the temperature to 375°F and continue baking until golden brown, 30 to 45 minutes. Let cool for at least 30 minutes, then serve at room temperature.

Magic Carpet

FIND IT: 36th and Spruce Sts. or 34th and Walnut Sts., Philadelphia, Pennsylvania

Dean Varvoutis started serving '70s food in the '80s, hoping to combat the decade of New Coke and Nacho Cheese Doritos with hummus, falafel, and marinated tofu. Okay, so technically those aren't foods indigenous to the '70s, but that's when flower-powered healthy eating took hold in America—it just took baby boomer Dean a few years to get with the program. Once he did, he towed a horse-drawn cart to a sidewalk on the Penn campus, put out a sandwich board announcing the Magic Carpet specialties, and waited for the Birkenstocks to come clomping his way. "I made $7," Dean recalls. "I was driving all the way from Phoenixville, thirty miles, truckin' on down here in my Volvo pulling this cart, and the food ended up everywhere. I spent the first hour cleaning up because of all the bumping around. I was in the middle of the block because I didn't know where to go, and I made $7. The next day, this Asian man came up to me and said, 'Very nice cart. You should come down by me tomorrow.' So I did. I went down to his corner a half block down the street and that day I made $150. A week later, this other Asian man comes up and starts yelling at me that he was going to take that spot. Turns out the other guy I thought was being nice was just trying to block his competition. And that was just the beginning."

It was 1984 and Philly's vending regulations, or lack thereof, created lawlessness something like the Wild West. With no assigned locations for carts or trucks, owners would rise at the crack of dawn to race to their preferred spot, and if someone else had already set up camp, yelling matches or even knock-down, drag-outs weren't uncommon. Dean is a beefy guy who looks more like a short-order cook at a Greek diner than a pescatarian who sells tabouli for a living, but his Zen nature prevailed and eventually even became his calling card. His cart became popular with the kind of liberal college kids likely to backpack Europe and volunteer for Greenpeace, and they supported his venture as it grew to two carts, each with a steady stream of health-conscious customers. The falafel has been a big seller since day one (well, technically day three). The crispy little chickpea fritters have a good dose of onion and cumin, plus fresh parsley, and they're made from a recipe Dean's brother got off a Lebanese guy who ran a falafel shop in Manhattan. They're neck and neck with the tofu meatballs, baked rounds of extra-firm tofu bound with egg and packed with plenty of basil, garlic, and oregano. You won't fool a Soprano with these, but they're surprisingly flavorful, even for a devout meat eater.

After Drew Crockett got himself a history degree from Penn, he sold his dusty books and followed the scent of money to New York, where he somehow wound up in banking. There, inspired by the Mudd Truck, he hatched a plan for a gourmet coffee truck and started pestering Philly's powers-that-be for a spot in University City. After a couple of years of getting put on hold, being told he was either on a waiting list or just out of luck, Crockett hopped a train to his alma mater, found an empty spot along University Avenue (in the shadow of a Starbucks, no less), and marched down to city hall with permit applications and money in hand. His **HubBub Coffee Company** (University Ave. between Walnut and Spruce Sts.) opened in fall of 2009, a fire engine–red truck blaring music that'll wake you up almost as much as the Stumptown coffee, sold either as potent cups of drip or shots, or as a cappuccino or latte pulled from a fancy La Marzocco espresso machine. Flaky croissants and killer cinnamon rolls are trucked in from suburban Narbeth's Au Fournil bakery, the standard-bearer for Philly-area pastries and proof that Crockett studied up. ◉

With mellow music piped through tiny speakers, a counter of vegan baked goods, and an ice chest packed with organic sodas and green teas, Dean has transferred the vibe of a blue-state co-op to a little wooden box on wheels. He's been known to ask customers how their "energy" is after they've finished their lunch and admits to doing yoga and meditation, but he's loath to call himself a hippie. "I would say that I'm an earthling," Dean says. "A lot of folks assume I'm of a certain political persuasion and I always say, 'First of all, I'm a businessman, and I personally tend to want to support a smaller business rather than a bigger one. But at the same time I do want to grow, I want to see if I can take this beyond Philly. I'm fifty, and I have a five-year goal of not having to be here to run the cart every day. Still, I'm sure I'd miss it.'"

Ode to Magic Carpet's Tofu Meatballs Serves 4

The cart's owner wants to keep his recipes under wraps, so the following is an approximation of one of his signature dishes.

1 (14-ounce) package firm tofu	1/2 teaspoon freshly ground black pepper
1 egg, lightly beaten	1/2 teaspoon red pepper flakes
1/3 cup bread crumbs	1/2 teaspoon granulated garlic
1/2 small onion, minced	2 cups favorite tomato sauce, store-bought
1 1/2 teaspoons chopped fresh Italian parsley	or homemade
1 1/2 teaspoons chopped fresh oregano	1/2 cup freshly grated Parmesan cheese
1 teaspoon salt	4 cups cooked rice or pasta

Remove the tofu from its package and discard the liquid. Wrap the tofu in a few paper towels, place on a plate, and rest a heavy pan or cast iron skillet on top for 30 minutes. Unwrap the tofu and set aside.

Preheat the oven to 350°F.

In a large mixing bowl, combine the drained and pressed tofu, egg, bread crumbs, onion, herbs, and spices, mixing well with your hands until thoroughly combined. Form the tofu into balls the size of golf balls and arrange in a single layer in a baking dish. Transfer to the oven and bake for 20 minutes.

Remove the dish from the oven and increase the heat to 450°F (or preheat the broiler, if you have one). Spoon the tomato sauce over the top of the meatballs and sprinkle with the Parmesan. Place the dish back in the oven and continue to cook until the cheese has just melted and is lightly browned, 3 minutes. Remove from the oven and serve with the rice or pasta.

Irie Food

FIND IT: W Montgomery Ave. just east of N Broad St., Philadelphia, Pennsylvania

As an undergrad at Temple in the early 1980s, Marcella Folkes and her fellow Jamaican friends hit up the food trucks along 13th and Montgomery like the rest of the student body, scarfing down egg-and-cheese sandwiches in the morning, sometimes stopping for a cheesesteak or hoagie at the end of the day. But they craved the tongue-tingling spices of their own foods and were getting pretty sick of greasy pepperoni slices. "We had this group called SOCA, Student Organization for Caribbean Affairs, and we did cultural events and of course parties, but we really wanted to have a truck," Marcella recalls. "It was always pizzas. We wanted our own cultural food."

They didn't get it. Regardless, Marcella graduated with a business degree and went on to open a trucking company with her brother, who had come to America from Kingston along with their parents so that Marcella could attend Temple. The business was enough to sustain the family over the past twenty years, but periodically Marcella and her West Indian friends would stroll Temple's campus, scanning the food trucks for something, anything, Caribbean. What they saw were the same old trucks—literally, many of the exact same trucks—selling cut fruit, hoagies, and, yes, pizza. Finally, the lightbulb went off for the *Jamaican* who wanted a *Jamaican truck* . . . and just so happened to own a *trucking* company. But it turned out that running a food truck on campus was a job not unlike the vice presidency—you only get the coveted gig if someone dies. One man's heart attack is another man's . . . food truck? "There was a truck here for over twenty years, like many of the trucks," Marcella explains. "It was called Campus Grub, and the owner was tired of the business. He was getting old, and then he had a couple of heart attacks, so he decided he wanted to retire. We went to the university with a proposal, went to city hall to get our menu approved and get our license, set up the truck, and opened Irie Food in October 2009. Finally, we have a West Indian truck at Temple."

As lucky as Marcella was to find her spot, she's not going to complain about its location. At the far west end of Montgomery's cluster of trucks, it doesn't get nearly as much foot traffic as the main drag near 12th and 13th. Plus, surrounded on both sides by tall buildings, the strip where Irie Food sits is nicknamed "the wind tunnel," and it's noticeably a few degrees cooler than its neighboring blocks. So Marcella isn't taking any chances on being overlooked: the spic-and-span step van glows like an electric orange stabbed with a massive Jamaican flag, the unmistakable trinity of green, black, and yellow that calls out "get your jerk here" from a block away. Luckily for

Marcella, Temple's West Indian student body, which has tripled in size since her days, aren't big on pizza either. With SOCA still going strong (now with Twitter!), word traveled fast and support for Irie Food has been widespread. It helps that Marcella can cook.

Splashes of vinegar turn her jerk rub into a paste, and she massages those chicken legs and thighs like a Swede looking for a tip, infusing the meat with the bright heat of Scotch bonnets, woodsy thyme, and fragrant allspice. Like the oxtails, the chicken marinates overnight, but the nubby hunks of tail take on a full dose of clove and garlic. Marcella's stew chicken falls from the bone into a pool of brown gravy similar to the oxtail's slurry, and her curry chicken is stained marigold from turmeric and fully flavored with toasted cumin. All are piled onto red beans and rice that hide a hint of coconut milk in the grain, and all are memorable. The Jamaican patties and the coco bread are the only things not made on the truck (and, unfortunately, it shows), but the clusters of West Indian students and locals who find their way to the truck don't seem to mind; they gobble them up anyway, just happy to have them. A separate American breakfast touts bacon-and-egg sandwiches, and, yes, you can get a hot dog for a dollar here, but no one seems to pay Marcella's safety net menu any mind. And why would they? They've been seeing that stuff for years.

Irie Food's Oxtail Stew Serves 4

2 pounds oxtails

1 teaspoon garlic powder

1 teaspoon onion powder

1 teaspoon soy sauce

1/4 teaspoon Goya adobo seasoning

1/4 teaspoon Lawry's Seasoned Salt

2 sprigs fresh thyme

1 onion, chopped

1 carrot, coarsely chopped

Salt and freshly ground black pepper

Cooked rice, for serving

Clean the oxtail pieces thoroughly by rinsing them under cold water and trimming away the excess fat.

In a bowl, stir together the garlic powder, onion powder, soy sauce, adobo seasoning, and seasoned salt to make a paste. Rub the paste into the oxtails. Place in a covered container and let marinate in the refrigerator overnight.

Heat a Dutch oven or large pot with a lid over medium-high heat until nearly smoking. Remove the oxtail pieces from the marinade and brown them on all sides. Carefully add enough water to the Dutch oven to just cover the meat, add the thyme, cover, and lower the heat to medium-low. Add the onion, carrot, and salt and pepper to taste. Cook, stirring occasionally to prevent the meat from sticking to the bottom, until the oxtails are tender and the meat begins to separate from the bone, 1 1/2 to 2 hours. Serve over the rice.

Yue Kee

FIND IT: S 38th St. between Walnut and Spruce Sts., Philadelphia, Pennsylvania

Bi Pang has been compared to the Soup Nazi for her gruff demeanor. Prying more than a mumble or grunt out of her husband, Tsz Pong, is like getting a pearl from an oyster. But none of the Chinese college kids milling around the couple's battered old food truck seem to care, or even to notice. They're here to get full on cheap, home-style Chinese cooking, and they're happy to fork over four bucks for massive Styrofoam containers of steaming *mapo* tofu, Beijing hot noodles, or rib tips in black bean sauce. These kids know what's up, and Yue Kee is for them.

The wheezing Grumman step van the couple has operated for more than twenty years is a quintessential Philly food truck, a hardworking clunker that endures long hours, stands up to year-round weather, and gives its owners just enough room to somehow pull off a massive menu of anything customers might want. Yue Kee offers nearly a hundred dishes, mainly Cantonese but veering into Szechuan, Hunan, and, occasionally, into Tsz's Dandong upbringing via dishes like his father's steamed pork belly and ginger chicken. And while the menu reads like the typical, overwhelmingly dense roster required of '80s-era chop suey houses (beef with broccoli, chicken with broccoli, pork with broccoli), somehow Tsz pulls from his arsenal of pastes, oils, sauces, and herbs to give most of the dishes a subtle distinctiveness. Pity the uninitiated who write off the truck as another campus roach coach, or worse yet, order within their comfort zone and wind up with egg rolls and fried rice that are pedestrian at best.

Getting Tsz to come clean on how certain dishes can be complex revelations while others taste like a joke played on dumb Americans is like asking a magician what's under the hat. "Most customers are students and most of them are Chinese," Tsz says. "So this not American, only Chinese food. But Chinese know Chinese food and Americans know my truck for cheap. No Chinese truck is better than me in this way." As he talks, Bi stands over a sink near the rear of the truck, keeping one suspicious eye on this silly woman asking questions and the other on the snow peas she's cleaning. A customer approaches the window and Bi saunters over, yelling out, "Yeah? Okay. Yeah? What you want?" Earlier this morning when Yue-Kee rattled into the parking spot for which Tsz pays $3,000 a year, the same spot he's held for twenty-one years, some rube had unknowingly stolen their space. Tsz had a tow truck there within minutes, and the only smile he cracked all day spread across his face as he said, "This spot only for me."

The stretch of Spruce Street between 36th and 38th Streets is home to nearly a dozen food trucks, spaced out along both sides of Spruce and offering more global variety than the strip of trucks along Ludlow. Mexican, Chinese, Middle Eastern, Indian, and American eats are all represented here, but the trucks that stand out for character alone include the aptly named **Fresh Fruit Salad**–nearly hidden by crates of mangos and melons that are constantly plucked from to produce three-dollar mixed fruit plates–and **The Real Le Anh Chinese Food**, owned and operated by smiling Le Anh To, a wisecracking Vietnamese-born Chinese woman who ➜

Now that lunch is in full swing, Bi hollers out orders in Chinese to Tsz, who works his stove like an octopus, seemingly doing eight things at once. Spareribs that have been hacked into inch-long pieces get browned in a giant wok showing years of battle scars. A spoonful of fermented black beans is followed by brown sugar and dark soy sauce, all clinging to the bony hunks of pork with a few flicks of the wrist. Tsz slides the sauced rib tips onto a mound of white rice waiting in a container and immediately turns back to the stove, where ground pork is browning with ginger and garlic on another burner. He dips a spoon into a massive can filled with the secret weapon of stir-fry cooks: ground bean sauce, a gloopy paste of fermented soybeans, salt, sugar, and sesame oil that carries the rich umami flavor the Japanese find in miso. Crimson chile oil and cubes of firm tofu get tossed in next, a little sesame oil and white pepper last. Poured over a tangle of lo mein, the Beijing hot noodles are ready. Bi hands them over to a chubby-cheeked student waiting patiently with his friends, all of them Chinese-American, all of them holding Styrofoam containers from Yue Kee. They walk a few feet toward a student commons before deciding to squat on a few stairs and dig in. Chopsticks fly, food gets shoveled in less time than it took Tsz to cook it, containers get tossed in the bin in front of the truck, and each of the boys gives a quick nod and a "*xiexie*" of thanks to Bi as they move on. "Yeah, yeah, okay," she barks, her attention on the next customer. "Okay, hi, yeah. What you want?"

APPETIZERS
Fried Wonton (5)......................1.25
Shrimp Egg Roll (1)..............1.15
Pork ● Vegetable Dumplings (6)
    Steamed........................3.00
    Pan Fried.....................3.25

We open sundays
12 m- 8 py

SOUPS
Wonton Soup......(Pt.)1.25 (Qt.)2.25
♪Hot & Sour Soup
    ......(Pt.)1.25 (Qt.)2.25
Mock Shark Fin Soup (碗仔翅)
    ......(Pt.)1.25 (Qt.)2.25
Chicken Veg. Soup
    ......(Pt.)1.50 (Qt.)2.50
House Special Wonton Soup
    ....(Qt.)3.75

NOODLES
Veg, Chicken, Shrimp, Pork, or
    Beef Lo Mein...(Pt.)3.75 (Qt.)6.25
Subgum Lo Mein(Pt.)4.75 (Qt.)7.00
♪Beijing Hot Noodles
    ......(Pt.)2.75 (Qt.)4.00
Chicken, Pork, Beef, or Shrimp Yat
    Mein...............................2.75
♪Singapore Rice Noodles.......4.00

DISHES
(Includes Steamed or Fried Rice)
Bean Sprouts w. Shrimp, Chicken,
    Pork or Beef.....................3.50
Sweet & Sour Chicken 4.00
Mushrooms w. Chicken, Beef, or
    Pork.................................4.00
Tofu w. Chicken, Beef, Pork, or
    Shrimp.............................4.00
Chicken, Beef, Pork, or Shrimp
    Chow Mein 4.00
Pepper Steak.........................4.00
Vegetable Egg Foo Young......4.00
Tomato Beef.........................4.00
Cucumber Beef.....................4.00
Shrimp w. Lobster Sauce........4.00
Ginger Chicken or Beef..........4.00
Moo Goo Gai Pan.................4.00

Chicken, I
Bean Sa
Chicken,
    Foo You
Broccoli
    Shrimp.
Mix Veg.
    or Shrin
Chinese V
    Pork. or
♪Szechua
    Shrimp.
Snow Pea
    or Shrin
Beef w. C
♪Eggplan
    or Shrin

Beijing Hot Noodles Serves 4

You can find ground bean sauce, a gloopy paste of fermented soybeans, salt, sugar, and sesame oil, in Asian grocery stores or order a jar online.

2 tablespoons peanut or vegetable oil

2 tablespoons minced garlic

1 tablespoon minced ginger

2 green onions, minced

1 pound ground pork

1/4 cup ground bean sauce

1 (12-ounce) package firm tofu, drained
    and cubed

1 tablespoon chile oil

1 teaspoon salt

2 teaspoons sugar

1 1/2 teaspoons sesame oil

1/2 teaspoon ground white or black pepper

1 pound lo mein noodles, cooked

1/2 cucumber, peeled and diced

Heat the oil in a wok or heavy, deep sauté pan over high heat for 1 minute. Add the garlic and ginger and sauté for 2 minutes. Add the green onions and ground pork and cook until the pork is browned, about 5 minutes.

Add the ground bean sauce, tofu, chile oil, salt, and sugar and toss to coat, cooking for 2 to 3 minutes more. Add the sesame oil and pepper, stir, and turn off the heat.

Divide the lo mein noodles among individual plates, place the cucumber alongside, and top the noodles with the pork and tofu mixture. Serve immediately.

emigrated to America in the late '70s and opened this pan-Asian truck in 1981. Her stir-fries are good if a bit greasy, quick and cheap evolutions of Chinese classics. To's truck is the oldest on Spruce, but it's not the only one that has adapted over the years: **Mexi Philly** caters to Penn's vegans with tofu tacos and decidedly Anglo-aimed crunchy shells à la Taco Bell, while **Lucky's Mexican** has met popular demand by supplementing its taco and burrito lineup with *channa masala*, a holdover from when the cart was run by an India native. ◉

Washington, D.C.

It should come as little surprise that our nation's capital, the epicenter of ideas becoming law, enacted the earliest regulations on mobile food vending, with rules first appearing on the city books in 1890. In the century that followed the industry boomed, with peddlers setting up carts nearly side by side to cater to the steady stream of tourists looking for sustenance between a stroll through the Smithsonian and a stop at the Lincoln Memorial. By the mid-1990s there were close to three thousand vendors citywide, and the lack of laws assigning them to specific sites had created competition that regularly fueled physical violence. "It was first-come, first-serve, so naturally vendors were fighting for prime locations, bringing friends with baseball bats, carrying guns. . . . There were serious altercations with numerous people going to jail as a result," says Sam Williams, vending and special events coordinator for the District's Department of Consumer and Regulatory Affairs. Williams could be considered the Eliot Ness of D.C.'s street vending, using his position to restore order. A previous regime decided to deal with the increasing lawlessness by issuing a moratorium on vending licenses in 1998, and although that effectively reduced the number of vendors to about six hundred, it didn't solve what Williams and others later identified as the three main problems: the lack of assigned spaces, the monopoly of cart depots (where vendors are required by law to park overnight), and the homogeneity of the food being sold on the streets.

FOOD TRUCKS

"With the moratorium, they were essentially shutting everything down until they could come up with a new process, but for whatever reason, a lot of pieces within the legislation weren't done, so it languished for several years," Williams says. "It was picked back up again in 2005, just before I started, when a demonstration zone program started up that allowed for a study to begin as to how to create site agreements."

The result was that the city decided to grandfather in existing vendors, giving them first crack at a site-specific permit for spots that had been mapped out throughout the city. Most chose to remain where they had been for twenty, thirty, or, in some cases, forty years, but some took advantage of information the city disseminated through ongoing vendor orientations, shifting to areas with less competition and growing need. There's still a moratorium on curbside vending, meaning no new cart licenses, but food truck licenses are available to anyone who can get an operation up and running, a feat made just a bit easier through the city's zero-asset loan program aimed at would-be vendors. There are still very particular laws regarding truck size (related to parking space dimensions), and an old ice cream truck law that says that there must be a queue of customers waiting in order for a truck to make a stop. But thanks to a change in the food code since the days when trucks were almost all limited to selling hot dogs, vendors can now sell just about any kind of food they'd like, as long as they pass their health inspection.

As messy as the regulation overhaul has been (and this is just the abbreviated version), the issue of what's actually being served on D.C.'s streets seems to the hardest obstacle to tackle. Even a person with only a vague interest in food couldn't help but be disappointed to discover cart after cart selling nothing but chips, soda, hot dogs, and that D.C. signature, the half-smoke (a chili-slopped dog of debatable origin that could best be described as a Polish sausage). "The irony . . . isn't just that it's vegetarians selling hot dogs, but it's that the majority of these people would never conceive of eating the product they're selling," Williams says. "Many of our vendors are Ethiopian, some Eritrean, and a lot are living hand to mouth, with a tremendous amount of fear of trying something new. Plus they have these decade-long relationships with the cart depots, of which there are now only three that run everything, and those three have a stranglehold on the community."

To attempt to dismantle this monopoly, the city is encouraging new vendors to start their own depots, and at the same time keeping a closer eye on the Big Three, doing what they can to prevent strong-arming. And to give the vendors a little push to start serving their native cuisine, Williams and the Department of Health even held a course called "You Don't Have to Serve Hot Dogs" as part of a recent vendor orientation fair, which nearly five hundred people attended. "I would—and I know residents would—love to see injera and curries and all different types of food being sold from carts, not just to add a cultural element to the city, but the vendors might take more pride in their business if it's a product they grew up with," Williams says. "But so far, aside from a few new trucks embracing social media like Fojol Brothers, I haven't seen anybody do it. I can't think of one Ethiopian-owned cart selling Ethiopian food, but as long as we continue to improve our hand-holding, it *will* happen."

Fojol Bros. of Merlindia

KEEP UP WITH IT: www.fojol.com or twitter.com/fojolbros

Once upon a time, in the fantastical faraway land of Merlindia, four friends set out to change the landscape of D.C.'s street food scene. Inspired by the new leader elected in the land of America, Kipoto, Dingo, Gewpee, and Ababa-Du carefully dressed in their turban and neon-jumpsuit best, waxed up their moustaches, and loaded up their traveling culinary carnival with all the traditional Merlindian foods: Ababa-Du's spicy cyclones, mango lassipops, palakpaneer, chicken masala, and more. As millions filled the nation's capital on Barack Obama's inaugural day, the Fojol Bros. of Merlindia took their first lap around the city to a marching band soundtrack blasting out of their 1965 Chevy step van, selling their foods and spreading their message that it was indeed a time for change.

Nearly two years later, the Fojol Bros. are beloved by Washingtonians, probably more than the man they shared their own inauguration with. Now operated primarily by Kipoto (Peter Korbel) and Dingo (Justin Vitarello), the whimsical Indian-inspired food truck is welcomed with a line of loyalists every time it pulls over to set up shop. In fact, D.C.'s laws mandate that the truck *must* have a queue in order to park, so the Fojol Bros. have made something of an interactive game out of the regulation, encouraging customers who want to purchase food to stand on the corner and twirl like whirling dervishes, and giving a free meal to the first one to start the party. Don't laugh; it works. The sight of a bunch of suits and ladies rocking the business skirt–pantyhose–sneakers combo spinning like blindfolded kids at a piñata party is something, but then again, folks will do anything for free food.

It helps when the food is good. While the Fojol Bros. are ambitious twentysomething guys with good business sense, oodles of creativity, and a million-dollar (okay, maybe a couple-thousand-dollar) idea, they also realize they're a bunch of white guys looking to serve Indian food out of a truck while wearing turbans. Peter, er, "Kipoto," points to his theater background as the culprit for some of the shtick, and he defends the getups as being "the farthest thing from racially insensitive," pointing out that the guys have always been greeted with smiles and understanding that their headdress, like their Crayola-colored jumpsuits, gloves, and fake moustaches, is all part of a costume. What is authentic is the food, created by a consulting chef of Indian descent who wishes to remain anonymous—Peter simply calls their business partner "Suku" and says he has been in the Indian food business in the D.C. area for years.

If you see a crowd of suits clustered around Arlington, Virginia's, Ballston Metro station just past quitting time, it's not a sale on ties—it's resourceful locals stopping to bring home the best pizza in the area. Under the guidance of Naples native Enzo Algarme and his partner Anastasiya Laufenberg, **Pupatella** (twitter .com/pupatella) uses all of the ingredients required by Neapolitan pizza snobs: Caputo 00 flour kneaded with water, yeast, and a touch of salt; San Marzano tomatoes; fresh mozzarella; perfect basil leaves; and a drizzle of Italian olive oil. The only difference between this and a pizzeria in Naples? Pupatella is on wheels. The candy-red cart was a way for Enzo and Anastasiya to get their business up and running with little cash, and it's been a hit since they pulled the first pizza out of the propane-fired oven in the fall of 2007. So much so that investors stepped up to put Pupatella in a brick-and-mortar restaurant in May 2010, complete with an imported wood-burning oven that fires up pies at over 800°F. Still, the cart remains, with the duo splitting time between spots while keeping customers on their toes by topping the bubbly crusted pizzas with ribbons of bresaola, roasted eggplant, or wild mushrooms under gobs of Brie. No one ever makes it home without a missing slice. ◉

Suku's Indian standards are perfectly designed to be prepared ahead of time in a commissary kitchen, then loaded onto the truck for finishing (after all, it's the same principle behind the success of Indian buffets, perhaps the only buffets worth eating from). The cinnamon-tinged dark meat chicken in turmeric-yellow gravy is a hot commodity, right up there with the silky spinach dotted with cubes of paneer cheese. The truck always travels with two vegetarian and two meat options, assembling combo plates on fluffy basmati rice steamed on the truck. Crunchy, salty snack mixes made from an assortment of potato sticks, puffed rice, toasted nuts, and traditional Indian spices are sold under names like Wingo's Sweet Sticks, Gewpee's Garlic Ribbons, and Kipoto's Fortune Curls. But perhaps the cleverest concoction is the lassipop, a frozen take on the classic yogurt lassi, and flavored with fresh ginger, rose water, or mango pulp. The snacks, the lassipops, and even the bottled water are all packaged with the Fojol Bros. trademark carnivalesque logo, primed for placement in a supermarket near you—assuming the FDA accepts "Product of Merlindia" as sufficient labeling.

Fojol Bros. Butter Chicken Serves 4

1 pound boneless chicken breast

1 pound chicken thighs

1 tablespoon lemon juice

1 teaspoon red chile powder (Kashmiri preferred)

1 teaspoon salt

2 tablespoons unsalted butter, melted, plus extra for basting

MARINADE

1 cup yogurt

1 teaspoon salt

1/2 teaspoon minced garlic, smashed into a paste with the back of a spoon

1/2 teaspoon garam masala

1 teaspoon red chile powder (Kashmiri preferred)

2 tablespoons minced ginger, smashed into a paste with the back of a spoon

2 tablespoons lemon juice

2 tablespoons mustard oil

MAKHNI "GRAVY"

3 1/2 tablespoons unsalted butter

1 teaspoon whole green cardamom pods

1/2 teaspoon whole cloves

1 teaspoon whole black peppercorns

1 (2- to 3-inch) cinnamon stick

1 tablespoon minced ginger, smashed into a paste with the back of a spoon

1 tablespoon minced garlic, smashed into a paste with the back of a spoon

4 or 5 green chiles, chopped

14 ounces tomato purée

1 tablespoon red chile powder (Kashmiri preferred)

1 teaspoon garam masala

2 teaspoons salt

1 cup water

1/2 teaspoon ground fenugreek

2 tablespoons honey

1 cup cream

Rice and naan or paratha, for serving

Cut the chicken breast and thigh meat into equal-size hunks suitable to skewering and grilling. In a small bowl, combine the lemon juice, red chile powder, salt, and 2 tablespoons butter to make a paste. Rub the paste into the chicken pieces. Place the chicken pieces in a bowl, cover, and refrigerate for 30 minutes.

Meanwhile, make the marinade. Line a colander with muslin cheesecloth and drain the yogurt for 15 to 20 minutes to remove the excess water. Transfer the drained yogurt to a bowl and add the remaining marinade ingredients. Apply this marinade to the chicken pieces and refrigerate for 3 to 4 hours.

Prepare a moderately hot fire in a grill (Fojol uses a tandoor) or preheat the oven to 400°F.

Thread the chicken pieces onto skewers and grill them just until the juices run clear, about 4 to 5 minutes, being careful not to overcook. Baste the chicken with butter during the last couple of minutes of cooking. Remove from the heat and set aside.

To prepare the gravy, melt the butter over medium heat in a medium to large sauté pan. Add the cardamom pods, cloves, peppercorns, and cinnamon. Sauté for 2 minutes, then add the ginger paste, garlic paste, and chopped green chiles and stir to combine. Cook for 2 minutes. Add the tomato purée, red chile powder, garam masala, salt, and water. Bring the mixture to a boil, then reduce the heat and simmer for 10 minutes. Add the fenugreek and honey, then add the cooked chicken to the gravy. Simmer for 5 minutes, then add the cream. Stir and let simmer for just a couple of minutes, then serve hot with the rice and naan or paratha.

Food Chain

KEEP UP WITH IT: www.foodchaindc.com or twitter.com/foodchaindc

For the suits and ties walking on autopilot from the subway station to the office each morning, the battered battalion of aluminum food carts lining their route become a blur of monotony and coronary-inducing junk: chips, candy, soda, hot dogs . . . chips, candy, soda, hot dogs . . . chips, candy, soda . . . jerk chicken wrap with coconut rice and mango salsa? What the . . . ? That's the reaction Coite Manuel is counting on to make his Food Chain project a success.

When D.C. started reevaluating its street vending rules in 2007 and loosening restrictions on what could be sold from these decades-old carts, Coite took that as an opportunity to approach a few weathered vendors with a plan to help them invigorate their businesses. "My model is I operate like a small catering operation, looking at how I can work with existing vendors to do something different," Coite says. "These are longtime, first-generation immigrant hot dog vendors that don't have the financial means or restaurant savvy, and they've been selling all prepackaged food because for years that's all D.C. allowed."

Coite approaches vendors like Asefash Gebre, an Ethiopian immigrant who has spent every day for twenty years at her spot on 17th and M, selling the exact same lineup as every cart within a coin toss, purchased from the same mega-facility where the carts are stored for the night and restocked in the morning. If they agree to it, as Asefash did, Coite helps the vendors retrofit their carts, installing steam trays that will hold the food he prepares in his commissary kitchen, and offers training on what exactly a jerk chicken wrap or a Caribbean taco is and how to assemble it. He affixes new signage to their metal warhorses, stocks the coolers with Honest Teas, and gets on his Twitter account to let followers know the location of the newly Food Chain–ized cart. And in return, Coite takes a minimal fee, just enough to cover food costs, labor, and the kitchen space. So why does he do it? You could say he just came up with a smart business idea at the right time, or you could say the thirty-three-year-old Georgia boy just has a kind heart—after all, he volunteered in Guatemala for a couple of years before working at a D.C. nonprofit encouraging economic development in lower-income areas. "I'm glad to find him. He's a nice guy and I only like honest people," Asefash says. "I did hot dogs for twenty years, but we need money to pay the bills, and everywhere there are hot dog vendors, so I say to Coite, 'Okay, let's try your jerk chicken.'"

And how's business? "I get people who say, 'Oh this is great,' but they don't come every day. Still, I give it a chance. It's better than hot dogs."

Food Chain Chimichurri Makes 1½ cups

This classic Argentine condiment gets a bit of a Southwestern spin, making it ideal for brisket barbacoa tacos.

½ pound ripe tomatillos, husked and chopped

½ cup chopped Italian parsley, stemmed

¼ cup chopped cilantro, stemmed

2 cloves garlic, minced

Juice of 1 lime

1 tablespoon ground cumin

2 teaspoons dried oregano

1 tablespoon kosher salt

¼ cup extra-virgin olive oil

In a food processor, pulse the tomatillos, parsley, cilantro, garlic, and lime juice until finely blended. Add the cumin, oregano, and salt. Turn the food processor onto its slowest speed and slowly add the olive oil until the mixture is emulsified and a uniform consistency.

Sâuçá

KEEP UP WITH IT: www.eatsauca.com or twitter.com/wheresauca

When Farhad Assari is standing at the Sâuçá truck, there is no doubt he is the owner. Not only is he the most well-heeled guy around—sporting designer shades, a custom-tailored suit, buffed wingtips, and slicked-back salt-and-pepper locks—but he walks around like, well, like he owns the place. With his sunflower-yellow food truck parked on the George Washington University campus, Farhad is examining every element of his creation, as well as the students' reaction to it. "Why aren't all of the sauces out?" he asks a worker inside the truck.

"We have twenty-two, you know," he continues, turning to me to explain. "And we plan to sell them eventually, but I'm in the process of figuring out how I'm going to display them. We're going to have a sauce mixology thing where you can mix and match. And we have this amazing music system. That's a satellite TV antenna up there," he says, pointing to the roof of the truck. "We're going to show the World Cup, images from around the world. And we do karaoke with four microphones. And we have a phone that sits right here," he says, patting the silver counter jutting out from the truck's side. "It's called Token Time. And we give a token after the purchase of each Sâuçá, and every two tokens gives you a minute anywhere in the world to talk on the phone. It's for people to connect to the world."

He says this last part with a dramatic flourish, waving his arm to suggest "the world" before he goes on to explain that one of the four cameras mounted to the truck is a live webcam, inspired by a juice stand in Iran where people would line up to see themselves broadcast on the video screen mounted to the cart. Farhad is Iranian himself, but with a father who worked as a diplomat for the Iranian embassy, Farhad came about his wanderlust moving around from place to place before heading to Switzerland for boarding school. It was NYU for college, Wharton for business school, then two decades of investment banking that bounced him around to London, Kuwait, Geneva, Dubai, and Hong Kong while making him plenty of money doing it. He wound up back in D.C. when his mother became ill, moving in to care for her, and it became clear "that the sexy life as an investment banker wasn't going to work anymore," he says. "I had to think to myself, what do I really love? Other than making a lot of money, investment banking is not that gratifying. So my criteria were four things: whatever I do has to fit in my time schedule, it has to be something new and exciting, it has to be in the food world, and it has to do some good. And what is it about food that's interesting? It brings cultures together. All of us are the same other than our sauces. The protein, the carbohydrates are the same. It's the sauces that make the difference. And that is how I came up with Sâuçá." Originally, Farhad wanted to name his business Sauce, but his lawyer told him he couldn't trademark a common English word. "And I thought, so what? I'll just change the last letter and make it international. It's nothing language. It's nothingness. I wanted to put the two dots on the 'u' as well, but that was just too much."

The karaoke machine, the international phone, the webcam, the Putumayo world music CDs for sale: none of that is too much for Farhad. In fact, it's just the beginning. It's all part of his definition of Sâuçá: "a global lifestyle brand that combines food, travel, music, design, technology, and fun into the most interesting new concept to hit the streets." But to any normal college kid walking between classes, Sâuçá is a food truck, one with a menu of flatbread wraps ("Sâuçás"), Belgian waffles with sweet toppings ("Toffles"), and minty lemonade ("Limunad"). The Indian-inspired Mumbai butter chicken Sâuçá is the best seller, with hunks of curried chicken and toasted cashews tucked into Lebanese-ish flatbread. The ginger- and soy-marinated pork "banh mi" is a close runner-up, the lamb and beef merguez trailing just behind that. True to its tagline, "Eat the World," Sâuçá's menu is clearly globally influenced, designed by a consulting company Farhad worked with to execute his ideas. The sauces—white miso soy, Thai coconut, passion fruit mayo—are in the process of being set up to be bottled, branded, and sold as far as Farhad can reach. Ditto for his "Limunad." But first the busy businessman is getting a second round of trucks added to his fleet, which grew to four step vans only six months after Sâuçá launched in February 2010. Farhad is looking to put Sâuçás throughout the region within a year, throughout the country in two. "In my investment banking experience, the businesses that had the most value were those that created a brand, and a brand means expansion. "This," he says, waving his arm toward his multimedia boom box/global restaurant on wheels, "is only the beginning."

(SIDE DISH)

There's no Pedro and there's no Vinny at **Pedro & Vinny's**. But there is John Rider, a fifteen-year veteran of the D.C. street food scene who's famous for a few things: zipping through his perpetual block-long lunch line with the flair of a carnival barker, talking newbies into the mango-habanero "Goose sauce" he now bottles and sells, trusting customers to make their own change from a box stuffed with ones and quarters, and (this one's most important) being the first D.C. sidewalk cart with the gumption to go through the red tape to get city approval to sell something other than hot dogs or packaged foods. John started vending in the mid-1990s with a coffee cart on the George Washington campus, but in 2000 he got the green light from the city to start selling burritos (hence the Pedro) and pasta (that would be Vinny). He chalks it up to "going through a bunch of stuff with the city and knowing how to write up standard operating procedures," but essentially he was able to secure a vegetarian-only vending permit that lets him prepare food other than hot dogs on his cart, as long as there's no meat involved. Fine by him—the line is long enough as it is. ◉

DC Central Kitchen is all about second chances. Among other services, the nonprofit offers a program that provides culinary training for the formerly home-less and/or the recently incarcer-ated, which has put hundreds of cooks into D.C.'s restaurants. In hopes of turning a few of them into business owners as well, Central Kitchen launched a food cart in 2008, giving participants a taste of the owner-operator life that's infinitely more acces-sible than opening a full-scale restaurant. A year later, Stir Food Group came on board, rebranding the cart as **Zola on the Go** (7th and F Sts. NW) and bringing in the menu of chef Bryan Moscatello, winner of a *Food & Wine* Best New Chef nod in 2003 for his work at the restaurant group's flagship, Zola. Now instead of the usual lineup of hot dogs and half-smokes, employees get experience pre-paring items like lamb meatball sliders with grilled romaine, pepper slaw, and goat cheese aioli, plus they get the crowd that loves them. ◉

Butter Chicken Sâuçá Serves 8

MARINATED CHICKEN
1/4 cup finely minced garlic
1/2 teaspoon kosher salt
3/4 cup plain yogurt
1 1/4 teaspoons chili powder
1 1/4 teaspoons garam masala
2 teaspoons olive oil
1 1/2 pounds boneless, skinless chicken thighs, cut into 1-inch chunks

SAUCE BASE
4 1/2 teaspoons olive oil
1 1/2 teaspoons tomato paste
2 cinnamon sticks
1/2 teaspoon ground cardamom
1 bay leaf
2 or 3 Thai green chiles
1 tablespoon minced fresh ginger
1/4 cup water

1 (14-ounce) can diced tomatoes
1/4 teaspoon chili powder
1/4 teaspoon garam masala
1/4 cup very finely chopped salted cashews
1 teaspoon ground fennel seed

SÂUÇÁ
1 1/2 cups uncooked basmati rice
1 1/2 teaspoons olive oil
1/4 cup unsalted butter
1/4 cup heavy cream
1 1/2 teaspoons honey
1/2 teaspoon kosher salt
1/4 teaspoon freshly squeezed lime juice
1/4 cup chopped fresh cilantro, plus more for garnish
8 pieces flatbread (preferably Kronos), paratha, or roti
1/2 cup chopped salted, roasted cashews

To make the marinated chicken, combine the garlic, salt, yogurt, chili powder, garam masala, and olive oil and stir to combine. Pour over the chicken and seal in a large resealable bag. Let marinate in the refrigerator overnight.

To make the sauce base, heat a large, heavy saucepan over medium heat. Add the olive oil, tomato paste, cinnamon sticks, cardamom, bay leaf, Thai chiles, and ginger and cook for 2 to 3 minutes. Add the water to the pan and deglaze, scraping the pan to remove any bits stuck on the bottom. Add the tomatoes, chili powder, garam masala, cashews, and fennel seed to the pan. Lower the heat, cover, and simmer for 30 minutes. Remove the cinnamon sticks and bay leaves from the sauce, transfer the sauce to a blender, and purée. Set aside and keep warm.

To make the Sâuçá, prepare the rice according to the package instructions. Meanwhile, heat the olive oil in a nonstick skillet over medium-high heat until just smoking. Drain the marinade from the chicken and transfer the chicken to the skillet, searing on all sides until browned all over but not cooked through.

Add the reserved sauce base to the pan with the chicken and bring to a simmer for 1 minute. Add the butter, cream, honey, salt, and lime juice and simmer on low for 5 to 6 minutes. Bring the sauce to a boil, remove from the heat, and fold in the cilantro.

Spoon about 1/2 cup of the rice onto your favorite flatbread, top it with the chicken mixture, and garnish with the chopped cashews and cilantro. Roll the flat-bread around the filling, and enjoy. Repeat to make 7 more sandwiches.

Fresh Local

KEEP UP WITH IT: www.freshlocaltruck.com

Plenty of people toss around the dream of escaping to a quaint small town for their own little piece of Mayberry. But Michelle Louzaway actually did it. She had a Northwestern law degree but wasn't using it. She was living in Fargo, North Dakota, but wasn't feeling it. She found a book on small towns, picked one, and moved to it. As it turned out, Portsmouth, New Hampshire, was exactly what she was looking for. "I didn't want to live the rest of my life shuffling my kids around in a car, never walking anywhere, living in a place where the food is all white: white flour, white sugar," Michelle says.

So she packed up her family and moved to New Hampshire, settling in Newington, a town of fewer than a thousand people next to Portsmouth, where she got to work planting a garden, acquiring chickens for eggs, and, eventually, splitting from her husband. She worked her way through the classic *Mastering the Art of French Cooking* long before *Julie and Julia*, and even took a cooking school vacation to Julia Child's former French château. In 2003 she bought a restaurant in downtown Portsmouth and, like many unprepared restaurateurs, she quickly learned she needed help. "My general contractor said, 'I have a guy who can do odd jobs,' so he brought this kid in. He was always smiling, but I thought, 'Why is this fifteen-year-old boy smiling at me?'" Michelle says. "My contractor said, 'You might want to talk to him. He's actually the head chef at one of the most successful comfort food restaurants in Portsmouth, Lindbergh's Crossing.'"

Michelle's "fifteen-year-old handyman" was Josh Lanahan, a twenty-nine-year-old CIA grad with a passion for small towns, cooking local, and, it turned out, Michelle. A decade his senior, Michelle channeled her inner cougar and jumped in headfirst. The couple ran the restaurant for two years before itching to do something different. Over a bottle of Patrón one night, they decided to buy a fish taco truck for sale in Portsmouth, applying the "fresh" and "local" mantra that governed their lives to this mobile kitchen. In weeks Michelle was setting up the truck for business, while Josh went to work concocting a menu of falafel using herbs and onions from the couple's garden, burgers made from grass-fed cows raised just up the road, and breakfast sandwiches of his own eggs, sausage from a local legend nicknamed "Popper," and Lebanese-style pita from a nearby bakery. Wrapped and grilled to order, these took on the name "Purritos," and they exploded in popularity when Fresh Local launched in summer 2007.

In fact, everything was a hit. So much so that the couple added a brick-and-mortar location to their plate. They kept the truck, too, and it's become a fixture at the Prescott Park Arts Festival, a summer venue for music and plays on the banks of the Piscataqua River. But to operate the truck year-round, Michelle and Josh are looking into buying a 1940s gas station off the highway where they would park Fresh Local, construct a seating area, secure a liquor license, and create a destination out of an old, dusty lot. That's one way to keep your town in the types of books that inspire life-changing decisions.

Josh's Smooth & Smoky Mac & Cheese Serves 4 to 6

1 pound elbow macaroni or corkscrew pasta

1½ teaspoons olive oil

1 small onion, diced

2 cloves garlic, minced

½ teaspoon red pepper flakes

2 cups half-and-half

¼ pound smoked Gouda cheese, shredded

¼ pound American cheese, shredded

¼ pound Cabot Cheddar cheese, shredded

Salt and freshly ground black pepper

Cooked bacon, chopped, for garnish
  (optional)

Basil, cut into thin ribbons, for garnish
  (optional)

Fresh tomatoes, diced, for garnish (optional)

Bring a large pot of salted water to a boil, add the pasta, and cook until just a tad mushy (as opposed to al dente). Drain, reserving the pasta water, and transfer the pasta to a large serving dish.

Heat the olive oil over medium heat in a saucepan. Add the onion and garlic and sauté until the onion is translucent, about 4 minutes. Add the red pepper flakes and half-and-half and bring to a gentle boil. Add the cheeses, stirring until they're thoroughly melted. Transfer the mixture to a blender and carefully purée. Pour the cheese mixture over the pasta and stir to blend. If the pasta and cheese mixture seems too dry, add a little of the reserved pasta water. Season to taste with salt and pepper. Top with the bacon, basil, and tomatoes, and serve.

INDEX